CHURCH VERSUS STATE IN SOUTH AFRICA

In a tea room during a break in the Schlebusch trials in Pretoria: (*from left to right*) Theo Kotze, Peter Randall, Roelf Meyer, Beyers Naudé.

Church versus State in South Africa

The Case of the Christian Institute

PETER WALSHE

19 83

C. HURST & COMPANY, LONDON
ORBIS BOOKS, MARYKNOLL, NEW YORK 10545

Published in the United Kingdom by
C. Hurst & Co. (Publishers) Ltd.,
38 King Street, London WC2E 8JT
and in the United States of America by
Orbis Books, Maryknoll, New York 10545
© 1983 by Peter Walshe

ISBNs
(*Hurst*) 0-905838-81-5
(*Orbis*) 0-88344-097-0

Library of Congress Cataloging in Publication Data

Walshe, Peter 1934—
  Church versus state in South Africa.

  Includes bibliographical references.
    1. Church and race relations—South Africa.
2. South Africa—Race relations.   3. Christian
Institute of Southern Africa.   I. Title.
DT763.W335   1983   261.8'348'00968   82-14533
ISBN 0-88344-097-0

Printed in Great Britain

To the women and men of the Christian Institute who understood Paul's words: 'You must want love more than anything else; but still hope for the spiritual gifts as well, especially prophecy' (I Corinthians, 14.1-2)

ACKNOWLEDGMENTS

In writing a work such as this, I have come to rely on the efforts of a wide range of individuals. The footnotes offer some indication of my debts in this regard. At a more personal level, I have enjoyed the friendship of many who have helped me to gain a deeper understanding of the struggle for justice in South Africa. While it would be imprudent to name all of these, I must acknowledge the vital assistance of Theo and Helen Kotze. Without their encouragement and help this book would not have been written. Moreover, their example of fortitude and good humour has been an inspiration to me and to many others in South Africa, Europe and North America. I also wish to make specific mention of my colleague the Rev. Tjaard Hommes, Professor of Theology at the University of Notre Dame. Over the last few years, as we co-taught a course entitled 'Hope and the Human Condition', I gained a great deal from his scholarship and wisdom. My thanks must also go to Professor Kenneth Kirkwood of St. Antony's College, Oxford, as well as to the Rev. Elliot Kendall and the Rev. Brian Duckworth of the British Council of Churches who helped in a number of practical ways. I am grateful too for the monotype which appears on the cover, the work of Douglas Kinsey, Professor of Art at the University of Notre Dame.

This research could not have been undertaken without the support of the University of Notre Dame (including the Zahn Travel Fund) and a Maryknoll Walsh-Price Fellowship. I acknowledge this generous assistance with appreciation. In addition my thanks go to the Master and Fellows of St Edmund House, Cambridge, for their hospitality during part of a sabbatical year. My deepest debt, however, is to my fascinating and irascible wife Ann, who threatened to leave me if I wrote another book — but didn't. The typing of the manuscript was completed with great efficiency by Hilary Beeching. Although I have received help from these many sources, of course the work, together with any errors it contains, is my responsibility.

What is now substantially the Preface was first published as part of an article 'Mission in a Repressive Society: The Christian Institute of Southern Africa' (*International Bulletin of Missionary Research*, 5, 4, October 1981). Much of Chapter 1 first appeared as '*Inside South Africa: Exploitation, Dissent and Repression*' (*Cross Currents*, 28, 4, Winter 1978–9). I wish to acknowledge permission to use these articles.

University of Notre Dame,   PETER WALSHE
Indiana, 1982

CONTENTS

PREFACE

By the mid-twentieth century, the white-controlled churches of South Africa had been very largely absorbed into the country's cultural and legal patterns of racial discrimination. Although there were exceptions to this passivity, it was only after a decade of sporadic black[1] passive resistance, which culminated in the massacre at Sharpville in 1960,[2] that a major and sustained church-state confrontation developed. This confrontation occurred in the aftermath of the Cottesloe Consultation (1960) and escalated after the formation of the Christian Institute in 1963 under its Director, the Rev. Beyers Naudé. With the founding of the Institute, a vigorous prophetic witness entered the life of the churches. It aroused the hostility of the state and the white Dutch Reformed Churches (DRC); it discomforted the multi-racial denominations.

At first the Institute attempted to wean Afrikanerdom from what Naudé saw as its idolatrous commitment to a dominant, privileged and separate future; but increasingly its energies during the 1960s were spent on expanding ecumenical and interracial commitments. The Institute encouraged its members to associate in Bible study groups designed to explore the social implications of the Gospel; it worked with the South African Council of Churches for improved co-operation among the multi-racial churches; and Naudé maintained a special interest in the black DRCs — the *Sendingkerk* (Coloured), the *Kerk van Afrika* (African), and the small, recently formed Indian Reformed Church. The Institute also established a volatile relationship with the fragmented world of the black independent churches, helping to pull approximately forty of these into an African Independent Churches' Association. In addition the Institute took what it saw as a major initiative in sponsoring a training programme for independent church ministers. By the late 1960s, when Naudé and his staff collaborated with the South African Council of Churches to produce 'A Message to the People of South Africa', the Institute (with its journal *Pro Veritate*) had become the seminal Christian organisation in the country.

In spite of these initiatives, the actual state of the Institute in the late 1960s was not too encouraging. Far from riding the crest of a wave, it was struggling to overcome a sense of anticlimax and even failure. The DRCs had extruded it; membership had stagnated, and Africans continued to show the same reservations toward the Institute that they had shown to any white-dominated organisation. It had been hoped that the multi-racial churches would respond quickly to the Institute's challenge, but here too there were very few signs in the white parishes of a supportive Christian witness. Individual clerics and lay persons might join, often because of deep frustrations with their own denominations. But apart from periodic public pronouncements at the level of principle, there was little emanating from the church hierarchies to encourage Naudé and his colleagues.

While the situation in the late 1960s and early 1970s was bleak, it was not without hope. The Institute was gathering increasing support from abroad, particularly from the Netherlands. Most important of all, the Reformed Ecumenical Synod, meeting in Luntern, Netherlands, in 1968, once again condemned racial discrimination and supported the Institute's stance, thereby sharply increasing the gap between the worldwide Reformed churches and the DRCs in South Africa. As the Study Project on Christianity in Apartheid Society (SPROCAS) got underway, the Institute's understanding of structural injustices was deepened, which increased its receptivity to black critiques of white-dominated churches and apartheid. Simultaneously the World Council of Church's decision to support the welfare activities of the Southern African liberation movements, the spread of civil war in the region, and the resurgence of African nationalism in the form of the black consciousness movement produced a new historical context. In short, the Institute was faced with the need for a new praxis.

If the Institute was to remain open to the liberation of the poor and oppressed in this new context, that is, open to the unforseeable conse-quences of its Biblical commitments, it had to grow in its under-standing of mission. To confront the established powers with a demand that they reform themselves was one thing; to work for the giving of power to the powerless, as the Institute now began to do, was another. As the 1970s progressed the Institute's understanding of the Scriptures moved into sharper and sharper contrast with the civil religion of the DRCs and the dualistic Christianity that was rife among whites in the multiracial churches. This dualism placed the Kingdom of God outside history. It focused solely on personal salvation, saw mission as the numerical extension of formal church membership — in its crudest form a head-count — and emphasised charity to the neglect of justice. This socially conservative religion did not offer any Christian hope for political and social transformation.

By 1973 the Institute was moving into a period of closer contact with black organisations as it tried to prepare for a situation 'where more and more blacks will take the lead — not only in the Christian Institute but in society as a whole.'[3] As the spectre of civil war approached, the Institute continued its efforts to find a non-violent third way; but it now realised that in a situation of increasing black–white polarisation it had to take the option of the poor more directly and with much greater vigour. This meant curtailing its ineffectual efforts to generate reform from within the white establishments of church and state, and committing itself instead to supporting black initiatives for justice and a black vision of the future. In the years that followed, from 1973 until it was banned in October 1977, the Christian Institute formulated a strategy designed to encourage black consciousness and to prepare whites for a future in which blacks would exercise predominant political power. This strategy included conscientious objection.

It was through this involvement with the black consciousness movement that the Institute deepened its understanding of Christian mission still further, learning not only from its attempt to identify with the poor but from the evolution of black theology. Stimulated in part by the writings of black theologians in the United States, and increasingly aware of liberation theology in Latin America and of political theology in Europe, young black thinkers began to articulate an indigenous theology growing out of the South African predicament itself. This black theology meshed with much of the Christian Institute's own evolving liberation theology. Both sources of inspiration were presented as the basis for a potential revival of Christian witness within phlegmatic churches; both theologies envisaged the renewal of society through a concern for the poor and hence the promotion of black hopes; both agreed that blacks (the poor) were about to appropriate the Scriptures with unpredictable consequences for salvation history.

During these last years of its existence, as black pressures for change increased and eventually erupted in the SOWETO student protests of 25 June 1976 (with an initial death toll of 176), the Christian Institute pursued two further initiatives that contributed to its being banned in 1977. In addition to condemning the ruthless state violence, Naudé and his staff further alienated the Afrikaner church establishment by extending their contacts with the black DRCs. At the same time the Institute refined its analysis of structural injustice, probing behind the country's institutional racism and becoming increasingly aware of the dimension of capitalist exploitation.

There are several ways of interpreting this evolution of the Christian Institute's prophetic and dialectical understanding of Christian mission. At one level, the Institute functioned as part of a matrix of personal contacts that facilitated the dissemination of ideas — a vital network when African political organisations had been repressed. In addition, an important part of the Institute's role was to redefine Christian commitment, which it did by rejecting both the civil religion of Afrikanerdom and cultic aspects of the white-dominated multi-racial churches. This helped the Institute free itself from the stultifying grip of capitalist culture, which in turn permitted it to interact with South Africa's strain of black theology. The result was an indigenous liberation theology with its primary impulse in the struggle for identity and justice taking place in the black community.

If the Christian Institute very largely failed in its efforts to transform the understanding of mission in white hierarchies and white parishes, and so failed to alter the politics of established white interests, its leading personalities can nevertheless be seen as a progressive group of thinkers. Working from a Biblical theology, they came to identify with the poor and oppressed and in so doing eventually recognised the elements of class conflict as well as racism in the South African situation. All this meant that the Institute's leadership came to see the exploited classes — meaning essentially the vast majority of the country's black population — as the potential source of energy that might, with increased political consciousness, eventually move society towards more egalitarian structures. It would be true to say that the Institute remained deeply suspicious of Communism, yet its understanding of mission and its political analysis pointed it in the direction of democratic socialism. The evolution of the Institute, therefore, provides yet another important reminder of the common ground that can be shared by democratic socialism and a prophetic Christianity when the latter has been galvanised by the praxis of a liberation struggle.

Finally, the Institute's activities can be viewed as an example of the historical phenomenon of recurring hope. Time and again over the centuries, individuals, groups, and even classes have expressed a vision of greater equality. John C. Bennett has called this the discernment of 'the radical imperative'.[4] Sometimes such hope has focused on a redistribution of economic resources; at other times the concern has been for more democratic forms of government; often the vision has embraced both economics and politics. There are innumerable examples, some of which (but by no means all) were inspired by Biblical values. They range — to mention but a few — from the Hebrew prophets condemning new stratifications in Israel to Athenian democracy, peasant revolts in fourteenth-century Europe, and the Levellers and Diggers in the period of the English civil war. Further modern, if obvious, examples are the American, French and Russian revolutions as well as the reaction of African, Asian and Latin American peoples against colonialism and economic imperialism.

Such eruptions of hope are often associated with a drive to transform the basis of legitimate government. Occasionally, like the French Revolution of 1789, they succeed. With this in mind, it may not be fanciful to see the Christian Institute and the wider global phenomenon of liberation theology as an important ingredient of a late twentieth-century worldwide thrust toward more egalitarian social structures, the establishment of which could renew the basis of legitimate government. This complex and still largely frustrated movement, of which radical Christians are but a part, offers an alternative to the widespread erosion of civic virtue and legitimate government as privilege allies itself with tyranny in many countries around the world.

NOTES

1. The term 'black' refers to African, Coloured (mixed descent) and Indian South Africans. The term 'Coloured' is no longer acceptable to the political activists of that community.

2. Hundreds of Africans were wounded and sixty-nine killed when the police panicked and opened fire on passive resisters.

3. Christian Institute of Southern Africa, '*Director's Report for the Period* August 1, 1972 to July 31, 1973' (Johannesburg, 1973), p. 3.

4. J.C. Bennett, *The Radical Imperative* (Philadelphia, Pa., 1975).

ABBREVIATIONS

AICA	African Independent Churches' Association
ANC	African National Congress
BCP	Black Community Programmes
BPC	Black Peoples' Convention
DRC	Dutch Reformed Church
IDAMASA	Independent African Ministers' Association
MDALI	Music, Drama, Arts and Literary Institute
NGK	*Nederduitse Gereformeerde Kerk*
NUSAS	National Union of South African Students
PAC	Pan Africanist Congress
SACC	South African Council of Churches
SAIRR	South African Institute of Race Relations
SASM	South African Students' Movement
SASO	South African Students' Organisation
SCA	Student Christian Association
SOWETO	South Western Townships (of Johannesburg)
SPROCAS	Study Project on Christianity in Apartheid Society
TECON	Theatre Council of Natal
UCM	University Christian Movement
WCP	White Community Programmes
WAAIC	Womens Association of African Independent Churches
WCC	World Council of Churches

Part I
APARTHEID AND THE FORMATION OF THE CHRISTIAN INSTITUTE

1
THE COMING OF THE APARTHEID STATE

White contact with Southern Africa goes back a long time. Portuguese traders and explorers were fumbling their way around the West African bulge in the mid-fifteenth century, seeking African allies against the Islamic empires of North Africa and reaching for a sea route to the East Indies. In 1487 Bartolomeu Dias entered the Indian Ocean and Portuguese activity was extended from the coast of Angola to that of Mozambique. Almost two centuries later, in 1652, the Dutch East India Company established a victualing station *en route* to the Indies. It was from these peripheral and tentative beginnings that the white presence expanded into the interior during the nineteenth century. Eventually, after considerable turmoil, the traditional African clans and kingdoms, with their communal organisations and hallowed patterns of consultative democracy, were subdued.

The core-state of the modern Southern African complex is the Republic of South Africa with 28 million inhabitants, an industrialized economy and a resolute white power-structure under the leadership of Afrikaner nationalism. Approximately 60 percent of the 4.5 million whites, today's Afrikaners, trace their heritage back to the Dutch settlers of the seventeenth century who were supplemented by German and Huguenot immigrants. These early settlers were brought under foreign rule when the Cape was taken over by Britain during the Napoleonic wars and English-speaking colonists added a new complexity to the scene.

Gradually, but with increasing determination as the scramble for Africa became more intense, and after diamonds (1860s) and then gold (1880s) were discovered in the hinterland, Britain extended its authority over white and black alike. This hegemony required a series of treaties as well as wars against African resistance, the most widely known being the crushing of the Zulu empire. It also required the trau-

1

matic and prolonged Boer War (1899–1901) to subdue the Afrikaner republics which had grown up in the interior after the Dutch exodus or 'great trek' from British rule at the Cape.

In seeking to end the Boer War and heal the breach between whites, Britain laid the foundations of white privilege and bequeathed a racist parliamentary system to South Africa within which the Afrikaner majority was eventually able to assert its control. Indeed, having won the war, Britain in 1910 offered independence to South Africa, the model of political evolution being that of the Dominions — Canada, Australia and New Zealand. In this way power was handed to white South Africans and the indigeneous inhabitants became second-class citizens without the civil rights of their white rulers.

The Afrikaner National Party entrenched racial discrimination and has ruled South Africa along apartheid lines since its electoral victory of 1948. That victory was the culmination of a long defensive struggle against British influence and the *swart gevaar* (black danger). In the struggle against the British, the humiliation of defeat in the Boer War gave way to political manoeuvring within an all-white parliament. As Afrikaners were approximately 60 per cent of the white population, electoral arithmetic suggested that they could capture the state if Afrikaner nationalism were consolidated. The twentieth century has witnessed that consolidation, at first around the white Dutch Reformed Churches (DRC) and a language movement which produced Afrikaans dictionaries and grammars and a body of literature. One result was that in 1925 Afrikaans replaced Dutch and so joined English as an official language. In addition, an Afrikaner National Party had been formed in 1913 and a secret society of DRC ministers, teachers and farmers, the *Broederbond* (Brotherhood), took shape in 1918, dedicating itself to the cultural and economic regeneration of the *volk*. The *Broederbond* also accepted a moral imperative to maintain the Afrikaner nation at all costs. It was determined to establish Afrikaner political power over the new industrial order, and developed a civil religion which placed Afrikanerdom and apartheid in the vanguard of God's plan for Southern Africa. The intensity of this struggle and its religious overtones can be seen in an address by Dr D.F. Malan, leader of the National Party. Speaking in 1938 at the battle site of Blood River, one hundred years after an Afrikaner victory against the Zulu, he honoured the *trekkers* (the wandering vanguard of the nation) who 'received their task from God's hand' and became 'a new people'. Their task had been completed, but a second *trek* (wandering) was now underway — the culturally dangerous process of urbanisation:

In that new Blood River [the city], black and white meet together in much closer contact and a much more binding struggle than when one hundred years ago the circle of white tented wagons protected the *laager* [defensive encampment], and muzzle-loader clashed with *assegaai* [spear]. Today black and white jostle together in the same labour market.

To meet this situation unity had to be established. Only then would 'the future of Afrikanerdom . . . be assured and white civilisation . . . saved'.[1]

By the 1930s, as a significant minority of Afrikaners began to flirt with Nazism,[2] separate Afrikaner student and welfare organisations were being established. To these organisations were added the corporations of *volk* capitalism which set out to challenge the English-speaking economic ascendency — Afrikaner banks, insurance companies, factories and eventually mining houses. The *Broederbond* simultaneously orchestrated a drive to repress what was seen as the threat of class divisions by establishing separate Afrikaner trade unions. In this way the socio-economic foundations were being carefully laid down for a disciplined white Afrikaner nationalism.[3] A well-organised National Party and the electoral victory of 1948 then brought the state under Afrikaner control, ushering in the era of apartheid.

The original and idealised version of apartheid, a pipe-dream of separate but equal opportunities, envisioned the territorial, economic, cultural and political separation of South Africa's ethnic groups. The long-established economic integration of the races was to be reversed so as to protect the Afrikaner nation from dependence on black labour and the inevitable political challenge that would follow. Africans were to be returned to the 13 per cent of the country allocated to them, their reserves or Bantustans. Whites would retain control of 87 per cent of the land, including the metropolitan areas of Johannesburg, Durban, Cape Town, Port Elizabeth, Bloemfontein, East London and the country's lesser industrial centres. However, any possibility of implementing this version of apartheid had long since been destroyed by the integrating effects of rapid economic growth.

Following the discovery of diamonds and gold in the late nineteenth century, South Africa experienced an industrial revolution which by the First World War had drawn all population groups inescapably into a common economic order. Erstwhile African and Afrikaner farmers now rubbed shoulders with English-speaking whites, Coloureds and Asians in the mines, factories, transport system, commerce and construction industry of the white-owned economy. By the 1950s, two thirds of the African population were living outside the reserves in the 87 per cent of the country preserved for white privilege. Trying to envisage a practical alternative to this deepening interdependence of the races, the government's pro-apartheid Tomlinson Commission[4] reluctantly came to the conclusion in 1955 that, given the demographic situation and the labour requirements of the white-owned economy, the best that could be hoped for was a 1:1 ratio of blacks to whites in the 'white' areas by AD 2000. Moreover, this would require massive expenditures to facilitate industrial development in the reserves. Without such a policy, the ratio would be 4:1 and only 20 per cent of Africans would be living in the reserves.

Rather than implement a programme which would have sharply raised the level of taxation on whites and checked the rate of growth in established industrial areas, the Afrikaner government rejected the major recommendations of its own Commission. Only 17 per cent of the minimum suggested level of expenditure was undertaken, and by the early 1960s apartheid had lapsed into a soil conservation programme for the deteriorating pastures of the already overpopulated reserves.[5] To this was added a modest programme of industrial decentralisation termed 'Border Area Development', in essence a range of fiscal incentives to encourage white investment, not in the reserves but in white-controlled towns within 30 miles of their borders. Even this bastardised version of separate development has had little success. Today, after more than thirty years in control, the Afrikaner National Party administers a system of white power in which racial discrimination is superimposed on a society bound ever more closely into a common economic order. During the 1970s approximately 200,000 additional Africans have been coming into the job market *every* year, whereas during the twenty years from 1960 to 1980 less than 300,000 decentralised jobs in the border areas and reserves have been created. In short, the reserves are chronically overcrowded and incapable of absorbing their own population increase. Apartheid has therefore become a system whereby African labour continues to be bureaucratically controlled and exploited for the growth of the white-owned economy.

Although strongly entrenched, the apartheid regime has not been without its constitutional opposition — white political parties unable to check the majority power of the Afrikaner National Party within a British-type system where parliament is supreme. There has also been a long-established extra-constitutional black opposition, in particular that of African nationalism.

The central organisation of African protest has been the African National Congress which was formed in 1912 in the aftermath of Union. Seeking to divert white South Africa from the path of segregation, Congress continually challenged the racist principles that lay behind the stream of discriminating legislation. For almost half a century its methods were those of moral protest, resolutions and polite deputations. Then, after a series of humiliating reversals which culminated in the victory of the Afrikaner National Party in 1948 and the yet more rigid discrimination of apartheid, Congress turned to passive resistance. In essence the judgment had been made that black South Africans would themselves have to bear responsibility for the future. Moral appeals had fallen on deaf ears and organised mass pressure would have to prise concessions from the closed fist of white power. However, once confrontation was embarked on, the African nationalist movement was systematically harassed and its organisations were formally banned in 1960.

NOTES

1. T.D. Moodie, *The Rise of Afrikanerdom: Power, Apartheid and the Afrikaner Civil Religion* (London, Berkeley, 1975), pp. 198–200.

2. W.H. Vatcher, *White Laager: the Rise of Afrikaner Nationalism* (New York, 1965), ch. 5, 'The Impact of Nazism'.

3. R. de Villiers, 'Afrikaner Nationalism', in M. Wilson and L. Thompson (eds.), *The Oxford History of South Africa*, vol. II, 1870–1966 (London, 1977), provides a useful survey of these processes.

4. *The Commission for the Socio-Economic Development of the Bantu Areas within the Union of South Africa* (Pretoria, 1955).

5. The South African Institute for Race Relations, *The Economic Development of the Reserves: the Extent to which the Tomlinson Commissions Recommendations are being Implemented* (Johannesburg, 1959). A.P. Walshe, 'The Changing Content of Apartheid', *The Review of Politics*, 25, 3, July 1963, pp. 343–61.

2

A SENSE OF CRISIS: SHARPVILLE AND THE COTTESLOE CONSULTATION, 1960

For the first sixty years of the twentieth century, the white-controlled churches of South Africa were very largely absorbed into the country's economic, cultural and legal patterns of racial discrimination. Although a great many black and a handful of outspoken white Christians struggled doggedly if ineffectually to arouse the conscience of the ecclesiastical, corporate and government establishments, the churches drifted with the economic and political currents of South African history. In doing so they failed in their prophetic responsibilities. Governments were rarely embarrassed by occasional and usually mild protests from official church leaders; dominated by powerful economic interests and a racist electorate, they systematically tightened up the legal apparatus of discrimination as black labourers were inexorably drawn into the mines, white-controlled agriculture and an industrial revolution.

The white Dutch Reformed Churches, having identified themselves with the rise of Afrikaner nationalism, nurtured and legitimised the attempts to transform segregation into a policy of separate development or apartheid.[1] In the years following the electoral victory of the Afrikaner National Party in 1948, their rare and heavily muted criticisms accepted the parameters of government policies. The English-speaking white-controlled churches, although less directly involved in politics, adopted a complaining but essentially passive mode of relating to the established culture of white power, economic privilege and the disruption of human fellowship which was an integral part of apartheid. Nevertheless there were a few important exceptions to this passivity after apartheid was launched in 1948 and as black political protests intensified during the 1940s and 1950s. These involved church authorities and individual clergymen. When the Bantu Education Act was passed in 1953, the Anglicans and Roman Catholics refused to accept its provisions, the former closing their schools and the latter picking up financial responsibility for maintaining them independently of the state. Four years later the English-speaking churches objected strenuously to the 'Church Clause' in a bill designed to give the Minister of the Interior power to bar Africans from attending churches in white areas. In this case the Anglican Archbishop of Cape Town, the cautious Geoffrey Clayton, was goaded into leading the opposition. As a result, a modified version of the bill was passed into law and sufficient pressure was mounted to dissuade the government from using its new powers.[2] Other examples of incipient activism included the protests of two Anglican clerics, the Rev. Michael Scott and the Rev. Trevor Huddleston. Scott's anti–apartheid stance and his strong support at the United Nations for the people of South West Africa led to his being declared a 'prohibited immigrant' in 1950.[3] In Huddleston's case, his sympathy for the passive resisters of the Defiance Campaign and his persistent protests against the Bantu Education Act, the Resettlement Bill and the destruction of Sophiatown, led in 1956 to his being recalled by his superiors to England.[4]

Even within the DRC the beginnings of what were to become serious tensions emerged as the apartheid government proved incapable of evolving a policy which could give any substantial meaning to 'separate development'. In 1955 Professor B.B. Keet of the *Nederduitse Gereformeerde Kerk* (NGK) seminary at Stellenbosch dismissed the biblical defence of apartheid in his book *Whither South Africa?* 'Our colour prejudice', he wrote, 'is probably the greatest factor in producing non-white agitators and revolutionaries.' The fruits of apartheid were 'even greater estrangement and hostility'. In attempting to defend apartheid on scriptural grounds, the DRC stood alone and in error — the major error being the 'false assumption that diversity is synonymous with separation', a separation 'at variance with God's ordinances'.[5] As with Keet, the realisation was growing, at least among a few DRC ministers, that the application of apartheid was intensifying injustice — not least in the vicious destruction of African family life. The migratory labour system was being deliberately maintained; Africans were legally speaking 'visitors' in the white areas where they were treated as mere labour units, to be tolerated there insofar as they served white interests. Aroused too by the confrontation developing between Afrikaner and African nationalism as the decade of the 1950s drew to a close, eleven DRC theologians published a book entitled *Delayed Action* — another attack on racial discrimination from within the citadel of Afrikanerdom. One of the contributors was Professor A.S. Geyser who held the chair of New Testament Theology at Pretoria and was later to be a major figure in the formation of the Christian Institute. Writing on the nature of Christian community as a call to surmount all social divisions, he condemned state policies which interfered with such fellowship; he also attacked the maintenance of racial discrimination within the segregated Dutch Reformed Churches as in conflict with the Scriptures.[6]

The Afrikaner church and political establishments reacted sharply. Newspaper columns were filled with angry retorts as apartheid was vigorously defended: it was vicious myth-making to suggest that the DRC judged 'non-whites' to be the descendants of Ham and so hewers of wood and drawers of water. Apartheid, it was argued, did not imply black inferiority; a policy of separation 'could be defended from the Christian point of view and was the only realistic solution to the race problem.'[7] As the NGK put it in 1958 when it endorsed a statement of the General Assembly of Reformed Churches meeting in Potchefstroom: 'No single race may deem itself superior to other races. [. . .] This neither denies nor ignores the fact of the multiplicity of nations, but in that multiplicity the unquestioned equality of all races and peoples must be recognised according to the Scriptures.'[8] These were important clarifications; but they did not attack the principle of apartheid, nor did they call for any radical change in the position of the dispossessed and exploited majority.

Because the Christianity of whites in South Africa had been so heavily conditioned by the culture of Afrikaner nationalism, race and class privilege, and because whites had so much to lose in terms of state, economic and church power, further prophetic judgements quickly stirred up increasingly visceral antagonisms. A major example of this was the condemnation of apartheid and criticism of the DRC made in 1958 by the somewhat acerbic Anglican Archbishop of Cape Town, Joost de Blank. While the ensuing exchange was complicated by the long-standing and mutual suspicion between the Anglican Church of the Province of South Africa and the DRC, the Archbishop's judgements and the responses they elicited were but precursors of the bitter confrontations that followed after the Sharpville massacre of 1960 and the formation of the Christian Institute in 1963.

While lecturing in the United States, the Archbishop argued that all churches, including his Anglican communion, had failed to form South African society along lines compatable with the Gospels. They had failed to renew society in that 'personal religion had become divorced from political responsibility,' spiritual behaviour from cosmic redemption, conventional attitudes from creative obedience to God, and domestic developments in the country from global commit-ments.[9] Rather than being challenged by the churches to build wider human community, whites had been left to maintain their belief that the country was a white paradise over which they were entitled to main-tain control.[10] De Blank went on to attack the practice of apartheid and singled out the Dutch Reformed Churches for special comment. They were to be honoured for their missionary and educational efforts; but unlike the other churches which opposed apartheid, they supported it. Moreover in their attempts to justify apartheid on scriptural grounds, they were producing a misguided interpretation of Calvinism which was out of step with Calvinist churches around the globe.[11] Later, on British television (during a programme that was interfered with by jamming from a private transmitter), the Archbishop argued that in the long run apartheid would be a suicidal policy for whites.[12]

Back in South Africa there was very little support for the Archbishop among whites and he polarised his own church. A restrained but typical reaction from within the white English-speaking community was the editorial of the *Cape Times*. Ignoring the enthusiastic response of black opinion to the Archbishop's criticisms, the paper saw a 'very real danger' of self-righteousness and argued that such attacks would never convert the DRC.[13] Afrikaner churchmen, editors and politicians were outraged by de Blank whom they saw as a newly-appointed foreigner meddling in South African affairs before foreign audiences. The NGK and its sister-churches withdrew from an ecumenical conference planned for December 1958, which was then cancelled. *Die Kerkbode*, the official mouthpiece of the NGK, saw the Archbishop's stance as sheer propaganda against South Africa, delivered abroad on a visit to solicit funds for church schools and for the defence of those in the Treason Trial. Moreover, it pointed out that the Anglican Church was administered by twelve white, foreign-born bishops, and that two-thirds of its clergy were white whereas two-thirds of its communicants were black — a century and a half had not produced much multiracialism.[14] Dr T.E. Dönges, Minister of the Interior, welcomed the surge of South African loyalty that had resulted as churchmen of many denominations, including Anglicans, had spoken out against the Archbishop's attack.[15] The Rev. C.B. Brink, a former Moderator of the NGK, reminded the Archbishop that the Federal Council of the NGK[16] had made it clear in 1957 that 'all men are created in the image of God . . . and all men are of equal worth.' This was not in conflict with his church's acceptance of apartheid as the 'only practical policy in the present circumstances'. It was not, he argued, a policy designed for inferior populations. However, he went on:

The church does have due regard to the responsibility of the state and its own responsibility toward 12,000,000 non-Europeans to whom our democratic system of government must seem one great riddle, as the vast majority of them do not know their right hand from their left when it comes to parliamentary democracy. It is neither their fault nor their shame, but it is a fact to be taken into account by any person who wishes to start public agitation.[17]

Later, in the House of Assembly, the Minister of External Affairs, Eric Louw, attacked de Blank as a 'bigoted cleric' who had vilified the DRC.[18]

Two years later these issues erupted again after police opened fire on African passive resisters at Sharpville. On 21 March 1960 bullets were indiscriminately sprayed into an anti-pass law demonstration, killing sixty-nine Africans, the majority of whom were women. Most of the dead were shot in the back and at least 186 people were wounded. The government's response to its own use of state violence was to declare an emergency and to ban the African National Congress (ANC) and the Pan Africanist Congress (PAC). In de Blank's view South Africa faced the gravest crisis in its history as Africans were not only rejecting white oppression; they were also turning away from a Christianity that was all too clearly associated with the injustices of apartheid. All churches stood condemned and Anglicans, he confessed, were or should be 'deeply penitent' for their failures. But as a church, and with all other churches except the DRC, they condemned the policies which led to the crisis. Unless the DRC now publicly repudiated 'the doctrine and practice of compulsory segregation', the Archbishop argued, the spread of the Christian faith would be seriously endangered.[19]

It was because of these fears that de Blank appealed to the World Council of Churches (WCC) to initiate a consultation with South African churches in the hope of establishing a more united and determined Christian witness to justice. In his letter to Dr Visser 't Hooft, General Secretary of the WCC, the Archbishop went so far as to argue that 'the future of Christianity in this country demands our complete disassociation from the Dutch Reformed attitude. . . . Either they must be expelled or we shall be compelled to withdraw.'[20] After an exploratory visit to South Africa by the Associate General Secretary, Dr Robert Bilheimer, the WCC went ahead with plans for an urgent consultation. In doing so it declined the Archbishop's advice on expelling the Dutch Reformed Churches, hoping instead to encourage increased understanding and reconciliation.

Although the DRC were themselves in some anguish about the turbulent political scene, they were again outraged by foreign and domestic criticism — not least that of the Archbishop. Their overall reaction was well expressed in a statement issued by nine leading members of the NGK. They were unable to 'condone the continuous besmirching of our country, people and church.' The 'unqualified support and encouragement given to one particular section of the population' would 'surrender civilisation and Christianity (as represented by both white and non-white) to the subversive activities of unscrupulous and irresponsible elements'. The West was trying to outbid the East in 'hysterical efforts' to gain 'the favour of the non-whites of Africa'. The NGK had made it clear that the 'policy of independent distinctive development' could be justified provided it was carried out 'without offending human dignity'. Therefore Christians and 'other responsible non-whites' should spurn the 'false promises of agitators . . . trying to create chaos and confusion. . . . In spite of real or supposed grievances the church [could] never condone any attempt to create disorder and lawlessness in the community.'[21]

With opinions continuing to polarise over what the church could or could not condone, the WCC's offer to sponsor a consultation was accepted by eight South African churches: the Bantu Presbyterian Church; the Presbyterian Church; the Church of the Province of South Africa; the Congregational Union; the Methodist Church; the NGK, Transvaal (including two black ministers from the *Sendingkerk*); the NGK, Cape; and the *Nederduitsch Hervormde Kerk*.[22] In December 1960 ten delegates from each of these churches gathered at Cottesloe, a residence hall of the University of the Witwatersrand on the outskirts of Johannesburg. With six representatives from the WCC including its General-Secretary W.A. Visser 't Hooft, there were eighty-six participants plus an observer: the Rev. Arthur Blaxall, Secretary of the Christian Council of South Africa.[23] Seventeen representatives, or one-fifth of the Consultation, were black — six from the Bantu Presbyterian Church. They included the recently appointed Anglican Assistant Bishop of St. Johns (Transkei), the Rt Rev. A.H. Zulu; Professor Z.K. Matthews, Emeritus of Fort Hare, the country's pre-eminent black academic, a veteran statesman, member of the ANC and Treason Trialist; the Rev. E.E. Mahabane, General Missionary Secretary of the Methodist Church and a Vice-President of the Christian Council. Among the white clergy were the outspoken Archbishop of Cape Town; the Rev. A.M. Meiring, Moderator of the General Synod of the NGK, Transvaal; the Rev. C.F. Beyers Naudé, Assessor of that Synod; and the Rev. A.J.G. Oosthuizen, Chairman of the *Hervormde Kerk* Synod. There were also thirteen academic theologians from the Afrikaans universities at Stellenbosch, Potchestroom and Pretoria. The small number of white lay persons included three well known Anglicans: the writer and leader of the Liberal Party, Alan Paton; the eminent anthropologist, Professor Monica Wilson of Cape Town University (the sole woman representative); and Edgar Brookes, Professor of History at the University of Natal. Although the Consultation was ecumenical and multi-racial, it was essentially a white affair — at its core, a group of anguished white clerics setting out to listen to each other and to pay polite attention to the small minority of their black colleagues.

Those who gathered at Cottesloe from 7 to 14 December 1960 envisaged themselves as embarking on a vitally important if unpredicatable and probably tempestuous discussion of race relations and public policies. They were not to be stage-managed and there was no commitment to a communiqué or *pronunciamento*. Their essential task was to clarify Christian responsibilities amid the mounting unrest. If at all possible, they also hoped to begin the process of healing the sharp political and theological divisions that had emerged between denominations and now within particular churches. Sharpville and the repression of black protest movements suggested that South Africa was entering an era of moral and political turmoil in which a violent reassertion of white privilege and Afrikaner power would lead eventually to countervailing violence. The task of the churches was to deepen their own and society's understanding of justice and so head off this prospect. Their task was to offer the hope of an alternative future.

All the churches had prepared working papers on five themes: the factual situation; race relations and church understanding of the Gospel; contemporary history from a Christian standpoint; the meaning of the current emergency situation in South Africa; and the witness of the church with regard to justice, mission and co-operation. As the papers were discussed, fundamental differences re-emerged. It also became clear that the DRC contributions would be of seminal importance if the conference was to exercise any influence on government policy.

The DRC representatives accepted the principle that each racial group should maintain 'its own separate destined path to the future. . . . each must therefore make its own *trek*'.[24] From this viewpoint differentiation was not to be confused with the negative term and practice of discrimination. On the other hand, white and black representatives of the English-speaking churches generally were opposed to this acceptance of apartheid principles, opting instead for a multi-racial future within one shared state as 'one team in which our different races are yoked together for that united pull that gives strength to one many-peopled nation'.[25]

The overwhelming majority of white representatives tended to agree that Christian trusteeship — a more felicitous term, some suggested, might be Christian responsibility — remained an important concept in that the ward ought to be prepared for maturity. Blacks representatives were very uneasy with this approach, particularly when it was associated with the refusal of whites to listen to black political leaders: 'Bantu and Coloured people. . . . resented being told who their leaders must be.' In the diplomatic, understated tone of the Consultation Report, it became apparent that 'Bantu men of standing' did not consider 'tribal authorities as the only effective instruments of consultation.'[26] Black representatives rejected the argument that the current emergency was the result of agitators; unsatisfactory social conditions were at the root of the unrest. In addition, 'Bantu members asserted that we are all South Africans together, but laws are made by one group only to apply to all.' The Bantu were generally law-abiding, but 'they did not feel bound by laws which they have no hand in making'[27] — a point the ANC leader, Nelson Mandela, was to make with passion and eloquence during his trial for treason in 1964.[28]

In the discussion on church and mission, two broad views emerged.

One simply proclaimed the right of the church to preach the gospel to all people — an approach, found within the English-speaking denominations, which centred on individual salvation and the afterlife. The other view provided an important example of a broad if highly abstract agreement between the DRC representatives and many of the English-speaking participants. This view was expressed in an amended version of a Methodist working paper. In the past, it was argued, Mission signified the sending of agents from long-established Christian communities to distant lands where they transmitted an amalgam of Christianity and their own culture. Missions had been 'foreign' and converts 'uncivilised' or 'backward peoples'. Now, with the rise of the younger churches in Africa and elsewhere, with the rise of Communism and materialism in Europe and America, the frontiers of mission were to be found in every land wherever 'Christ is denied in personal unbelief, in public action, or in national policy'. Mission therefore involved a life of fellowship and service: the church was to 'make known the Lordship of Christ in every realm of national, social and personal life'.[29]

If there was an element of agreement at the level of principle, the practical implications in terms of public policy soon turned out to be highly contentious. When subsequently the white Dutch Reformed Churches interpreted this broad view of mission in terms of support for 'separate destined paths to the future' and segregated 'daughter churches', they were increasingly isolated. Over the next two decades, other church hierarchies, the South African Council of Churches (successor to the Christian Council) and the WCC became progressively more outspoken critics of apartheid. After its formation in 1963, the Christian Institute was to be intimately associated with this radicalisation and a seminal influence in articulating an understanding of mission that evolved a radical critique of the existing social order, a view which led inexorably to confrontation with the DRC and the South African state.

But, at least for the moment, it appeared as if the Cottesloe Consultation might head off such an outcome. While the expected disagreements had indeed been exposed and explored, a sense of mutual respect and even of fellowship began to permeate the gathering as the week of consultation drew to a close. All were united in 'rejecting unjust discrimination' and, to the surprise of many representatives, an attempt to draft a statement proved successful in spite of the 'widely divergent convictions. . . . on the basic issues of apartheid'. The Cottesloe Statement recognized that one group rejected apartheid in principle as 'contrary to the Christian calling and unworkable in practice'. The other contingent was convinced 'that a policy of differentiation can be defended from the Christian point of view'.[30]

In the event, the final communiqué which momentarily bridged this chasm contained two crucial passages which were to lead to a bitter aftermath of inter-church and political recriminations, the withdrawal of the Dutch Reformed Churches from the WCC and the formation of the Christian Institute under the leadership of the Rev. Beyers Naudé. From the pro-apartheid viewpoint, the contentious passages could be interpreted as accepting separate development where that could be justly carried out. Understood in this way, the full equity of peoples meant full equality within a modified system of apartheid — separate where possible and different but equal. However the passages could also be interpreted as breaking with the essentials of apartheid in asserting the right of permanently urbanised blacks to enjoy full social, political and economic liberties in what had been the areas of exclusive white power and privilege.

Part II, paragraph 1, of the Cottesloe Statement read as follows:

We recognise that all racial groups who permanently inhabit *our country* are a part of our total population, and we regard them as indigenous. Members of all these groups have an equal right to make their contribution towards the enrichment of the life of their country and to share in the ensuing responsibilities, rewards and privileges.[31]

The term 'our country' was to prove problematic, particularly as the Prime Minister, Dr Verwoerd, envisaged the eventual political independence of the reserves or Bantustans. In contrast to Verwoerd's view, the paragraph implied a united South Africa with at least some common participation in the central political institutions of what had previously been an all-white state.

In its original form, the second crucial passage of the Cottesloe Statement, Part II, paragraph 15, read:

It is our conviction that the right to own land wherever he is domiciled and to participate in the government of his country, is part of the dignity of the adult man, and for this reason a policy which permanently denies to the economically integrated non-White people the right of collaboration in the government of the country of which they are citizens cannot be justified.[32]

The NGK (Cape) representatives had suggested the phrase 'economically integrated non-white people', but the two words 'economically integrated' were deleted from the final communiqué. The effect was to make the commitment less definite. If Africans were to become citizens of the Bantustans and migratory labourers in 'white' South Africa, they would not necessarily have to participate in the political institutions which controlled 87 per cent of the country. To clarify their position, the NGK (Cape and Transvaal) representatives issued a separate statement. As the preamble to the Cottesloe Statement had put it, 'a policy of differentiation can be defended from the Christian point of view', and in their judgement differentiation provided 'the only realistic solution to the problems of race relations and [was] therefore in the best interest of the various population groups.' They did not consider paragraph 15 incompatible with this and had voted for the resolution:

provided it be clearly understood that participation in the government of the country refers in the case of the white areas to the Bantu who are domiciled in the declared White areas in the sense that they have no other home-land.[33]

The distinction between the deleted phrase 'economically integrated' Africans and the new terminology 'domiciled in the declared white areas' was a subtle one. For the NGK representatives the distinction was nevertheless vital in what had become an intricate argument. Millions of recently urbanised Africans, and even labourers regularly dependent for employment on white farms or industry in the cities, might be judged 'economically integrated', an approach which would destroy the main thrust of apartheid — its 'separate futures'. However, 'domiciled' implied a smaller group, an African minority that could be safely diagnosed by the government as non-migratory or permanently resident in the 'white' areas. With this approach, it was argued, a new flexibility would have entered the apartheid system and its obsessive racism could be expunged. The maintenance of an all-white Afrikaner nation by means of an all-white state would no longer be an absolute. At the same time, the small African minority that might be accepted under this formula would not undermine Afrikaner control over the Afrikaner future. The scriptural principle of the 'unity of the human race' might thus be recognised existentially in the South African predicament of an industrial revolution and rapid urbanisation. An inflexible and objectionable racism would have been dismantled, but the rich 'diversity and pluriformity' of God's creation would not be threatened.[34] As the *DRC Monthly Newsletter* put it in an analysis of the NGK representatives' stand at Cottesloe: 'If complete territorial separation was impossible, then full rights, including political rights, could not be indefinitely withheld from those Bantu living in White areas.'[35]

The NGK representatives at Cottesloe, black and white, had conceeded that the state should recognise the reality of a minority of Africans living permanently in the urban areas, Africans who would not owe allegiance to any future Bantustan government. Prompted by the exploratory working documents of their own Afrikaner academics, the intense discussion of biblical principles, the sense of crisis following the Sharpville shootings and the ecumenical as well as international fellowship nurtured at Cottesloe, they had taken an initiative which, had it been accepted by the DRC synods, might have moved Afrikanerdom away from its racist policies of apartheid and uncompromising white control.

This major adaptation of apartheid by the NGK delegation fell far short of the commitments of black representatives and many of their white colleagues in the English-speaking churches. For different reasons it was also unacceptable to the intransigent representatives of the *Nederduitsch Hervormde Kerk* who judged the NGK delegation to have made dangerous and imprudent concessions. In a separate statement, the *Hervormde Kerk* delegation re-asserted their 'conviction that separate development [was] the only just solution to our racial problems'; they rejected 'integration in any form' and recorded their 'gratefulness to the government for all the positive steps it [had] taken to solve the problems.'[36] It was this dogmatic stance which proved to be more closely in line with the thinking of Afrikaner political leaders and the NGK synods. Although the NGK representatives at Cottesloe pushed for some serious re-thinking in the apartheid camp, they were to be humiliated and their stance rejected by their own church and by Afrikanerdom at large.

While African domicile in 'white' South Africa was the central political issue, there were other passages in the Cottesloe Statement which called the churches to 'a fearless witness within society' and to reject nationalism as an absolute value. These too inflamed large segments of Afrikaner opinion. The Consultation had seen 'no objection in principle to the direct representation of Coloured people in Parliament'; no one who believed in Jesus Christ should 'be excluded from any church on the grounds of his colour or race'; there was special need for more effective consultation between the government and 'leaders accepted by the non-white people'. Mixed marriages could not be prohibited on scriptural grounds — although their advisability might be questioned. Migratory labour was condemned for its destruction of African family life; the right to a fair trial was reasserted; and state interference with either Christian fellowship or the right to preach the gospel was rejected.[37]

Achieving more than its sponsors had dared to hope for, Cottesloe established the fragile beginnings of a consensus on fundamentals which might have bridged the gap between the South African churches. Archbishop Joost de Blank was deeply moved and issued a statement commending 'the courtesy, understanding and patience' of the NGK representatives. He remained convinced that 'discriminatory segregation gravely jeopardises the future of the Christian faith in South Africa'; but he apologised for at times having 'spoken heatedly and, through ignorance . . . [having] cast doubt on the sincerity of those' who did not accept the wisdom of his public actions. In helping to nurture this flicker of hope for a more just future, the NGK delegates had shown the 'fullest fellowship'.[38] At least Cottesloe had shaken up some church leaders and stirred their thinking. Many came away from the Consultation with an understanding that Christian mission was a more complex phenomenon than it had appeared to be in earlier decades, and that there was a major responsibility to test the structures of society against the Gospels — that is, publicly to address the issues of justice and not simply the demands of charity. There were differences over public policy and for many white churchmen only an inchoate understanding of the implications of justice; but the majority of Afrikaans- and English-speaking participants agreed that, to a very large extent, the spread of Christianity depended on the churches being prepared to face these issues.

At the level of principle, these were considerable .achievements which appeared to have opened up the churches to new social responsibilities and unpredictable futures. Unfortunately, it must also be said that the proceedings of the Consultation revealed that the large majority of white representatives were still heavily conditioned by the culture of white paternalism. Whites were firmly in control of church affairs and the negative term 'non-white' was still used for Africans, Coloureds and Indians. Although African political organisations had long rejected the term Bantu on account of its co-option into apartheid terminology, it too was still a regular part of the vocabulary of white churchmen. Rather than working to give power to the black Christian leadership that had already emerged within the churches and in African politics, there were many white delegates who thought in terms of 'cultivating Christian leadership for the Bantu.' What is even more remarkable is that they requested the 'government to co-operate with the churches in developing such leadership',[39] and this at a time when wholesale repression was being mounted against black political movements.

There were yet more subtle examples of this paternalism which was embedded in the white, Western cast of mind and which sustained an extraordinary level of naivety and ignorance of African political attitudes. The report of one discussion group referred to those 'who have a greater cultural, religious, economic or technical development' and their 'duty towards the less developed'. The 'less advanced' had to be educated 'to full maturity'.[40] At no point in the records of the Consultation was there any recognition that, in contrast with the communal values of African cultures, the rapid change and social disintegration engendered by South African capitalism might not be 'development'. Had the white representatives been listening more closely to the underprivileged, to the protests of and alternative futures envisaged by blacks, Cottesloe would have had to confront the church and government establishments with a much more radical set of challenges than it did. There would have been talk of 'one man one vote', of predominant political power for Africans, a major redistribution of land and the nationalisation of the mines.[41] In the event, the Consultation reflected the insularity of white-led churches formed by a smug white culture that was complacent in its Western world-view. The Cottesloe Statement's political and economic challenge to the authorities might have had profound long-run effects, but it was not in itself a revolutionary document. Rather it was a carefully, even cautiously worded plea for prudent adaptations of a white power structure in the direction demanded by Gospel values.

In contrast with increasingly harsh repression by the state, Cottesloe aroused new hopes among African leaders. As Visser't Hooft put it, 'non-white Christians who had begun to feel hopeless about the role of the churches' were encouraged by the sense of being part of a world community 'gathered by the same Lord, whose task is to make the transcendent power of Christ tangible in deeds of justice and fellowship'.[42] Cottesloe offered the prospect of long-run fundamental changes, as it appeared to be the start to what might become sustained political pressure from the churches. Professor Z.K. Matthews regularly challenged white attitudes when he attended the Consultation, and Dr Robert Bilheimer of the WCC met several other Treason Trialists during his exploratory visit to South Africa in April 1960. African leaders were beginning to get a wider hearing from international Christian and humanitarian organisations and their messages were often profound. This was certainly the case when Albert Lutuli, the banned leader of the ANC and himself a Treason Trialist, offered his view of Christian mission and a generous assessment of Cottesloe in his Nobel Lecture at Oslo University on 11 December 1961:

The Church in South Africa — though belatedly, seems to be awakening to a broader mission of the Church, in its ministry among us. It is beginning to take seriously the words of its Founder who said 'I come that they might have life and have it more abundantly.' This is a call to the Church in South Africa to help in the all-around development of man in the present, and not only in the hereafter. In this regard the people of South Africa, especially those who claim to be Christians, would be well advised to take heed of the Conference decisions of the World Council of Churches held at Cottesloe, Johannesburg, in 1960, which gave a clear lead on the mission of the Church in our day. It left no room for doubt about the relevancy of the Christian message in the present issues that confront mankind.[43]

But the opportunity, Lutuli continued, would have to be taken and the message given some practical effect. Writing shortly after Sharpville and the banning of the ANC in 1960, Lutuli pointed out that the churches had 'simply submitted to the secular state for too long'; some had even supported apartheid. It was 'not too late for white Christians to look at the Gospels and redefine their allegiance'. But, he went on, 'I warn those who care for Christianity, who care to go to *all* the world and preach the Gospel. In South Africa the opportunity is .three hundred years old. It will not last forever. The time is running out.'[44]

Lutuli was not all that unusual in offering such insights as a Christian and as a statesman — it was rather that he received more attention than other African leaders whose talents and wisdom had been tragically squandered in South Africa for decades and even centuries.[45] In the aftermath of Cottesloe, the Rev. Zaccheus Mahabane, Wesleyan minister and a predecessor of Lutuli as President General of the ANC, spoke out once more on themes that he had reiterated time and again since the 1920s. Moreover his unquenchable hope and sheer determination led him to call for another ecumenical conference as a follow-up to Cottesloe. His reasons included the overriding responsibility of human beings to work with God for the transformation of this world — there had to be '*saamwerking* [co-operation] between God and man'. In this 'marvellous upheaval, in this social, political, ideological revolution', the church had a vital part to play — Christians had to try and try again for a 'change of heart' in South Africa.[46]

There were others who did not feel a change of heart or a change in apartheid policies were necessary. Rather than a follow-up conference, the momentary consensus of Cottesloe was to be shattered.

NOTES

1. T.D. Moodie, *The Rise of Afrikaner Nationalism* (Berkeley, 1974). There were three white churches: the *Nederduitse Gereformeerde Kerk* and two smaller churches, the *Nederduitsch Hervormde Kerk* and the *Gereformeerde Kerk*.
2. A. Paton, *Apartheid and the Archbishop: the Life and Times of Geoffrey Clayton* (New York, 1973), pp. 283–8.
3. M.Scott, *A Time to Speak* (London, 1957).
4. T. Huddleston, *Naught for Your Comfort* (London, 1956).
5. B.B. Keet, *Suid Afrika. Waarheen?* (Stellenbosch, 1955), pp. 17, 19, 33.
6. A.S. Geyser, 'The First Gospel and the Unity of the Church as Witness to Christ', in A.S. Geyser (*et al.*), *Delayed Action* (Pretoria, 1960), pp. 23–4.
7. *Dutch Reformed Church Monthly Newsletter* (Johannesburg), June 1960, pp. 2–3.
8. *Ibid.*, p. 3.
9. *Cape Argus*, 9 June 1958.
10. *Cape Argus*, 10 June 1958.

11. *Ibid.*

12. *The Times* (London), 26 June 1958; *Cape Argus*, 7 July 1958.

13. *Cape Times*, 10 June 1958.

14. *Die Kerkbode*, 25 June 1958, pp. 1–3.

15. *Cape Argus*, 26 June 1958.

16. The Council, a consultative body, included the white, African (*Kerk van Afrika*) and Coloured (*Sendingkerk*) NGK churches.

17. 'Dutch Reformed Leader Replies to Archbishop', *South Africa* (Cape Town), July 1958.

18. *Cape Times*, 20 August 1958.

19. South African Institute of Race Relations, *Annual Survey of Race Relations, 1958–1960* (Johannesburg, 1961), pp. 94–5.

20. A.H. Lückhoff, 'Die Cottesloe-Kerkberaad' (unpublished Ph.D. thesis, University of the Witwatersrand, Johannesburg, 1975), p. 19, as quoted in J.W. de Gruchy, *The Church Struggle in South Africa* (Grand Rapids, 1979), p. 63.

21. 'Statement on the Riots in South Africa', *Statements on Race Relations* (Information Bureau of the DRC, Johannesburg, 1960), pp. 12–14.

22. Neither the NGK, Natal, nor the NGK, Orange Free State, attended as they were not members of the WCC. The African independent or separatist churches were likewise not members, and they too were not represented.

23. While each of the eight churches was a member of the WCC, the Christian Council was not formally associated with the world body. Three years later, the Rev. Blaxall was to be sentenced to twenty-eight months' imprisonment for assisting banned organisations. In fact he had organised a Dependents' Aid Fund for the families of Treason Trialists and political prisoners and was deported.

24. L.A. Hewson (ed.), *Cottesloe Consultation. The Report of the Consultation among South African Member Churches of the World Council of Churches, 7–14 December, 1960* (Johannesburg, 1961), p. 17. Hereafter, Hewson, *Cottesloe Consultation*.

25. *Ibid.*, pp. 17–18.

26. *Ibid.*, pp. 32, 46.

27. *Ibid.*, p. 56.

28. N. Mandela, *The Struggle Is My Life* (London, 1978), pp. 155–75.

29. Hewson, *Cottesloe Consultation*, p. 71.

30. *Ibid.*, p. 73.

31. *Ibid.*, p. 74. Author's italics.

32. *Ibid.*, p. 77.

33. *Ibid.*, p. 80.

34. *Ibid.*, p. 36.

35. 'Conference Causes Controversy', *DRC Monthly Newsletter*, March 1961, p. 3.

36. Hewson, *Cottesloe Consultation*, p. 79.

37. *Ibid.*, pp. 74–7.

38. *Ibid.*, p. 81.

39. *Ibid.*, p. 46.

40. *Ibid.*, p. 38.

41. For the evolution of African nationalism in South Africa in the decades following the formation of the African National Congress in 1912, see Peter Walshe, *The Rise of African Nationalism in South Africa* (London and Berkeley, 1971); Gail Gerhart, *Black Power in South Africa* (London, 1978).

42. W.A. Visser't Hooft, *Memoirs* (London, 1973), p. 287.

43. A. Lutuli, *The Road to Freedom is via the Cross* (London, c. 1965), p. 15.

44. A. Lutuli, *Let My People Go* (London, 1962), p. 119.

45. P. Walshe, *The Rise of African Nationalism*, pp. 7, 158-62, 339-48.

46. G.M. Carter and S.W. Johns (eds.), *The Good Fight: Selected Speeches of Rev. Z.R. Mahabane* (Evanston, Illinois, c. 1965), pp. 99-100, being the 'Presidential Address delivered at the Annual Conference of the Inter-Denominational African Ministers Federation, August 9, 1961'.

3

THE FORMATION OF THE CHRISTIAN INSTITUTE: THE AFTERMATH OF THE COTTESLOE CONSULTATION

The Dutch Reformed Churches played a pivotal role in the courteous if at times wrenching debates of the Cottesloe Consultation. Their leading churchmen and academic theologians were listened to with rapt attention; their working papers were the focus of prolonged discussions. The Consultation's final Statement had been produced with the full co-operation and, at times, leadership of the NGK representatives as the element of understanding (not necessarily of agreement) increased on both sides of the apartheid divide. Clearly, the statement had not been foisted on any one group even if some recommendations appeared likely to initiate a process of national soul-searching among Afrikaners. In general, blacks seemed to approve of Cottesloe; the white English-speaking parishes were unlikely to take their church leaders too seriously; but for Afrikaners, whose sense of nationhood had been so closely identified with the DRC, the situation was more problematic. Their broad political consensus on current apartheid policies and some of their most cherished formulas for the future had been challenged by respected Christian spokesmen from within their own *volk*. A major debate and perhaps a national catharsis had to take place.

In fact the NGK delegates walked from the conference hall into a maelstrom of political and ecclesiastical condemnation — a response orchestrated by the *Broederbond* in an attempt to curtail discussion by discrediting the ecumenism and multiracialism of Cottesloe. The opening attack was led by Prime Minister Verwoerd in a New Year radio message rejecting political multiracialism of any kind: it was without moral foundations as well as being a threat to the heritage and independence of the white nation. The NGK representatives, he argued, had acted imprudently as individuals and the true 'voice of the churches [had] still to be heard' through their synods. There was no world organisation, be it the United Nations or the WCC, that 'could make any permanent impression on our South African thinking . . . and our decisions on how to act with justice.'[1] The *Nederduitsch Hervormde Kerk*, having already rejected the Cottesloe Statement, quickly withdrew from the WCC. The NGK (OFS and Natal), not being members of the WCC and so not present at Cottesloe, called on their larger sister-churches, the NGK (Cape and

Transvaal), to resign from the world body.[2] A storm of anti-Cottesloe protests erupted from NGK parishes while Afrikaans newspapers attacked the WCC for its alleged Communist influences, its links with the Roman Catholic Church, its humanism and its liberal tendencies. Afrikaner academics, politicians and churchmen, including Dr A.P. Treurnicht who was the most powerful Transvaal influence in the *Broederbond* and the Rev. J.D. Vorster, Actuary of the NGK (Cape) and brother of the Minister of Justice, held an anti-Cottesloe symposium entitled *Grense* (Boundaries). Their theme was the Tower of Babel — the folly of attempts to unify mankind. As Dr H.B. Thom, Rector of Stellenbosch University, put it in his forward to the proceedings, their purpose was to offer 'a pure image of the Afrikaners of South Africa'.[3] Simultaneously the debate on apartheid strategies which surfaced in the South African Bureau of Racial Affairs (SABRA) was cut off as the *Broederbond* successfully manoeuvred to replace the few probing minds on the Bureau's executive. SABRA was to be an instrument of the Afrikaner National Party, not an independent Afrikaner 'think-tank', and so non-conformists like Professor N.J.J. Olivier of Stellenbosch were dropped.[4] An example of the crude closed ideological thinking that was reasserting its ascendency in high places was provided by the Administrator of the Transvaal, F.H. Odendaal, when he spoke at a Kruger Day celebration: Kruger had bequeathed an 'Afrikaans-Protestant-Calvinist way of life' which was the best of Western culture. The Afrikaner nation, Odendaal continued, stood by that way of life and rejected freedom, equality and brotherhood as neither Western nor Christian values. It was not that one race was better than the other; rather 'whiteness means for us the continuation of the Western way of life', a way 'to remain a Christian people'.[5]

By the time the NGK (Transvaal and Cape) Synods met, the atmosphere was hardly conducive to calm, reflective judgments. In spite of attempts by many of the Cottesloe participants to defend their stance, the Cottesloe Statement was rejected and both churches withdrew from the WCC. The clearest explanation came from an *ad hoc* Commission of the NGK (Cape), the majority report of which condemned the Cottesloe findings for three major reasons: they 'infringed on and undermined the policy of separate development'; they conflicted with the principle of differentiation insofar as they 'advocated political integration and . . . pleaded for social and church integration'; and they dealt with 'practical politics on which the church should not express itself unless some scriptural issue was involved.'[6] Following up their efforts with the *Grense* Symposium, the Rev. J.D. Vorster (who was soon to be elected Moderator of his church) and Dr Treurnicht (who was later to head the *Broederbond*) were prominent in influencing their Synods. As Vorster explained his stance on the eve of the Cape Synod: the Cottesloe resolutions were objectionable because they had 'rightly been seen by the English press and the English churches as [a] victory of their attitude'.[7] It was not surprising that when Dr Robert Bilheimer of the WCC returned to South Africa he was disheartened 'by the unwillingness of people in high places to engage in serious debate about Cottesloe'.[8]

One important result of this unilateral stand by the white NGK churches, the full consequences of which were not to emerge until the 1970s, was to set in motion a deterioration in their relations with the black 'daughter' or mission churches. At first this was more apparent with the *Sendingkerk* (Coloured). Leading members of the *Sendingkerk* had been well-disposed towards Cottesloe and Dr R.E. van der Ross, a prominent Coloured educationalist and Principal of the Battswood Training College, gave some indication of how they felt. He also offered a warning. The white Synods' negative decisions had left 'a sense of deep disappointment . . . of having been let down and of having been slapped in the face.' Cottesloe held out the hope of 'reinstating Christian values,' building Christian fellowship and broadening the understanding of nation from Dr. Verwoerd's narrow concept of 'the white people of South Africa.' Although this vision had been rejected by the white synods, the Coloured people would not leave the DRC. Nevertheless, they and their church would 'not be prepared for much longer to remain attached to a Mother Church which plainly placed them outside the communion of believers, outside the status of full members, and outside the status of full citizenship.'[9]

As the *Broederbond*, the National Party and the DRC synods turned against Cottesloe, the pressures on dissident churchmen grew intense. The first to take the brunt of what became a vendetta against those who continued to exercise their own judgment was the Rev. Albert Geyser of the *Nederduitsch Hervormde Kerk* — the church whose representatives immediately disavowed the Cottesloe Statement. Geyser had not been an official representative at Cottesloe, but he ruffled many feathers with his contribution to the contentious publication *Delayed Action*. Moreover, as a personable, robust and jovial character, he was potentially dangerous as someone who was capable of developing a substantial following. In the tense aftermath of Cottesloe and in step with its recommendations, he had the temerity to oppose Article III of the *Hervormde Kerk*'s law which placed a racial restriction on church membership. At the *Hervormde Kerk* General Assembly, which was held three months after Cottesloe, Geyser and Dr A. van Selms, both professors of the *Hervormde* Theological Faculty at Pretoria University, proposed that Article III be 'tested by the Word of God in the Scriptures'. The motion was heavily defeated. In addition the

Assembly went on to limit any renewed criticism of Article III to official church meetings at regional or national levels, so repressing any popular discussion at the parish level.[10] Geyser refused to accept this ruling and soon faced the fury of the *Broederbond* — that organisation where the political, religious and economic power of Afrikanerdom converged.

Events moved rapidly.[11] In September 1961 Geyser was called to account before the *Hervormde Kerk* Commission of the Assembly and given one week in which to resign his Professorship of New Testament Theology, a chair subsidised by the *Hervormde Kerk*. Simultaneously three students charged him with heresy and insubordination; he was also suspended from exercising his responsibilities as a minister of the *Kerk*. Geyser's trial dragged on from October 1961 to May 1962. Although the Commission found 'strong indications of guilt', he was acquitted on the charge of insubordination; however he was convicted of heresy and defrocked. This verdict led Professor van Selms to resign from the *Hervormde* Theological Faculty at Pretoria and he too was expelled from the ministry. These events put a severe strain on relations between the *Hervormde Kerk* in South Africa and the 'Mother Church' overseas. In the judgment of leading theologians in the Netherlands, the distressing Geyser affair had not been discussed or decided on Biblical grounds but had been a carefully planned political manoeuvre engineered by the *Broederbond*.[12]

Albert Geyser took the matter to the South African Supreme Court where his good standing was restored — at least at the legal level. The *Hervormde Kerk* decided it would be prudent to curtail the proceedings and settled out of court; whereupon the Commission's findings against Geyser were annulled, he was reinstated as a minister and the *Kerk* agreed to pay all legal costs.[13] However, in human terms the outcome was more complex. Geyser and his wife were both ostracised, physically threatened and generally put under the most intense social pressures — in part because Geyser continued his public dissent, becoming with the Rev. Beyers Naudé a leading personality in the formation of the Christian Institute of Southern Africa in August 1963.

Like Albert Geyser, Beyers Naudé, the founding spirit of the Christian Institute, was quintessentially an Afrikaner nurtured in a family that had been at the centre of the *volk*'s struggle for survival, not least against British imperialism.[14] Born in 1915 at Roodepoort on the Witwatersrand, he was named after General Christian Beyers with whom his father, Jozua Francis Naudé, had served as a young volunteer during the Boer War. Jozua, a teacher and a *predikant* (pastor), was chosen by the Boer troops to function as a chaplain. The young pastor and General Beyers became the closest of friends, so that after the General joined the abortive Afrikaner rebellion of 1914 and was drowned while fleeing from government troops, his name was taken for the infant Naudé born in the following year.[15] One of eight children, the young Beyers Naudé was raised in a politically and theologically conscious household in which public affairs were constantly and passionately discussed: the tragedy of military defeat in the Boer War, the poor white problem, the Rand Strike of 1922, Hertzog's victory in the general election of 1924 and the great depression. It would have been unthinkable to divorce the scriptures from the everyday struggle for justice, and in 1918 the Rev. Jozua Naudé became a founding member of the *Broederbond*. In 1921 the family moved to a new parish at Graaff-Reinet in the Cape where Beyers Naudé, aged six, was old enough to remember the intense emotion with which his father struggled to establish an Afrikaans-medium school in the town (possibly the first such school in the Cape) and to replace High Dutch with Afrikaans as the language of the NGK.

Having attended the new Afrikaans-medium *Hoer Volksskool* (People's High School), and having been one of five members of the matriculating class who warned the headmaster that several of the school's teaching methods and regulations were oppressive, Naudé went on to Stellenbosch University for a B.A. (1935) and M.A. in theology (1937). During these years he was prominent in student affairs, *inter alia* chairman of the debating society and a founder of the student monthly *Pro Libertate*.[16] He then followed in his father's footsteps and entered the NGK ministry in December 1939 as an assistant pastor in a farming community at Wellington in the Western Cape. It was at this time that he too joined the *Broederbond*, 'so I could serve my people better . . . because I saw it as a way to obtain a position of influence in the church and within the Afrikaner community.'[17] After further parish experience in the Karoo and then the Transvaal (Pretoria-South), Naudé became a leading figure in establishing a NGK youth organisation, was elected as its first chairman and filled a politically sensitive position as student chaplain at the University of Pretoria from 1949 to 1954. It was in these years that he broadened his view of South African and church affairs by travelling overseas, spending six months observing Christian youth organisations in Britain, the United States, the Netherlands, Sweden, West Germany, Switzerland, France and Italy.

Starting in these post-war years, Naudé began a prolonged process of re-examining his theological and political preconceptions. His contacts with students encouraged this as did his move to Potchefstroom, a farming and university town where in 1955 he accepted a call to serve the NGK congregation. The South African scene was also changing with some rapidity. Afrikaner nationalism had triumphed in the general election of 1948, and the coming to power of the National

Party meant that the theory and application of apartheid had to be worked out in some detail. While Naudé was at Potchefstroom, the publication of Professor Ben Marais' *Colour Crisis and the West* forced him to focus on these issues and to undertake a critical reassessment of the scriptures as well as of the NGK's teachings on ecumenism and race relations. By the 1950s the colonies of tropical Africa were moving towards political independence, and in 1952 the African National Congress and its allied organisations launched the Defiance Campaign — on the tercentenary of Jan van Riebeeck's landing at the Cape.

As his father had struggled with the aid of the scriptures to understand the predicament of the Afrikaner people in the aftermath of the Boer War, so Naudé struggled to understand his South Africa of the mid-twentieth century. In this effort he was challenged, stimulated and consoled by the ecumenical fellowship he encountered in the informal discussion groups or *predikante broederkring* (ministers' fraternals) which he helped to form during the 1950s. At the same time a wider range of ecumenical contacts was opening up through a series of inter-church conferences sponsored by the DRC; these were a response to the country's increasing race tensions and took as their themes 'God's Kingdom in Multi-Racial South Africa' (1954) and 'The Task of the Church in Areas of Rapid Social Change' (1959). However, Naudé was most profoundly disturbed and challenged by personalities he met at the international gathering of the Reformed Church Synod which gathered at Potchefstroom in 1957. In the long run the most influential of these contacts turned out to be leading figures in the Reformed Churches of the Netherlands, persons who in later years were to offer increasingly vital support to Naudé's Christian Institute.

Although he was not an official South African representative in 1957, but an observer, Naudé attended the Synod's open meetings and mixed with the delegates as he tried to get his bearings in what he saw as four problem areas: the unity as well as the diversity of the human race; the unity and diversity of the church on earth; the church's social responsibilities in history; and the urgent necessity that the church offer a path of reconciliation in situations of serious social tension. By the late 1950s, having wrestled with these issues while his own understanding and experience of Christian fellowship was being extended beyond the confines of denomination, race and nation, it had become clear to Naudé that the Dutch Reformed Churches in South Africa had corrupted their message. In his judgment all the country's churches had failed in their responsibility to reconcile and heal in that they failed to work courageously for justice; but the DRC were peculiarly crippled. By making the divisions between peoples their decisive, primary focus, and so reducing the unity of humankind to a subsidiary concern, the Afrikaner churches had locked themselves into a tradition that 'was contrary to the insight of the Bible.'[18] In coming to this private judgment, Naudé was about to move into confrontation with the Afrikaner religious and political establishment and to turn on to a collision course with the *Broederbond*. He had come to see that the 'central message of the Gospel', the central task of the Christian, was 'to act in the name of God as reconciler between those who live in tension, in hatred and bitterness one against each other'. For the moment, however, he was 'afraid to proclaim the full implication of this message, because I realised something of what it would entail for my position and my future.'[19]

In 1958, as race relations continued to deteriorate, Naudé was appointed Acting Moderator of the NGK (Transvaal), a position that brought him into close contact with the younger missionary *predikants* working in African and Coloured communities. Having been somewhat cerebral in his approach to blacks, he was now shocked to discover the full extent of their poverty and the way in which the divisive policies of apartheid were thwarting the growth of Christian fellowship. Apartheid, he recognised, had become a serious obstacle to Christian mission and the source of increasing bitterness; yet the vast majority of whites were 'not aware of the feelings, the experiences, the pain and the tension in the hearts and lives of our Black communities'.[20]

By 1960, the year of Sharpville, Naudé had taken up a new parish assignment in the wealthy Afrikaner suburb of Aasvoelkop, Johannesburg. It was to take him at least another decade to understand the full complexity and viciousness of racial discrimination as it interacted with class exploitation, but his contacts with the black NGK 'Daughter Churches' meant that he was at least beginning to live between two worlds. This led to yet another fraternal group — this time a small multi-racial fellowship which included members of these black churches. Consequently, when the Sharpville tragedy occurred, he was able to sense something of the deep shudder of revulsion that ran through black communities. For Naudé, a broadly-based consultation became an urgent necessity, a desperately needed ecumenical and multi-racial gathering to avert further tragedies. Without such an initiative, what loomed ahead was escalating race violence as an irrelevant and deformed 'Christianity' destroyed the church's mission.

Naudé attended Cottesloe as a NGK (Transvaal) representative after having served on the Planning and Executive Committee which established guidelines for the Consultation. In fulfilling these responsibilities he worked in the closest co-operation with Visser 't Hooft, Bilheimer and Clark Fry of the WCC. Both before and during the Consultation, Naudé played a pivotal role and was profoundly influenced by the fellowship he experienced behind the scenes and in the formal discussion sessions. At the time, he was Assessor of the NGK General Synod and a member of the inner circle of the *Broederbond*; he was also a leading contender for the position of Moderator of the NGK General Synod. In fact he was at the heart of Afrikanerdom. Nevertheless, when Naudé's hopes for a more ecumenical future and a reassessment of apartheid policies were shattered by the Dutch Reformed Churches' rejection of the Cottesloe Statement and their withdrawal from the WCC, he had no alternative but to exercise a prophetic judgment in what was to be a loving, anguished and increasingly fierce confrontation with his DRC community. As the synods handed down their negative decisions, the Afrikaner establishments of church and state quickly repaired the circle of their exclusive *laager* and repressed the murmurs of dissent within. In a fearful and graceless effort, they set about shoring up their political power and reasserting the authority of church hierarchies that were deeply and uncritically enmeshed in the ideology of Afrikaner nationalism — apartheid.

In an attempt to focus the ecumenical debate on the implications of Biblical witness in church and society, and hoping to keep the dialogue alive within the DRC, in May 1962 Beyers Naudé, Albert Geyser, Fred van Wyk of the South African Institute of Race Relations, the Rev. Ben Engelbrecht, Bruckner de Villiers and other like-minded souls launched a new monthly journal called *Pro Veritate*. Although its approach was anything but shrill, *Pro Veritate* was immediately attacked in the Afrikaner press as a 'propagandist newspaper' which 'strikes at the heart of the [Dutch Reformed] Church'.[21] With Naudé as editor, this 'Christian Journal for Southern Africa' had an ecumenical, multi-racial editorial board and drew subscriptions from a wide range of denominations. At its inception, the journal's promoters hoped to have the support of approximately 400 DRC ministers: the broad, unco-ordinated mass of dissenting theologians who had been drawn into the pre-1960 debates and were part of the post-Cottesloe ferment. But under the pressure of the synods' decisions, this number plummeted to no more than eighty DRC clergy who were prepared to maintain discreet contact with Naudé and his colleagues through *Pro Veritate*. The ecumenism of the 1950s was being checked, open discussion within the Afrikaner community was being suffocated, and churchmen were coming to heel. By the time the *Pro Veritate* initiative was followed by the formation of the Christian Institute in 1963, the number of DRC clergy prepared formally and publicly to support Naudé had dwindled still further to less than a dozen.

The final stage in this all but complete evaporation of support from ministers of the DRC was triggered by Naudé's break with the *Broederbond*. Up to this point there had been attempts to draw him back into the bosom of the community, back into working constructively within the establishment. Naudé remained deeply committed to the processes of dialogue with his own people, but the break was to be complete. Since Naudé had sworn himself in 1939 to unflinching loyalty in what he assumed at the time to be the identical tasks of serving God and the Afrikaner nation, his resignation from the *Broederbond* in March 1963 was a traumatic event.[22] For Naudé, resignation turned his world upside-down; for the *Broederbond* it was an act of treachery, striking at the very heart of Afrikanerdom.

News of the resignation was leaked to the Afrikaner press and presented as a national scandal. The initial vindictive anger aroused by Naudé's 'betrayal' soon increased to hatred when it was learnt that he had also provided secret *Broederbond* documents to Albert Geyser for his defence in the heresy trial. This break with the *Broederbond*'s commitment to total secrecy was seen as a breach of trust even more damning than his resignation, an act verging on treason for which he has never been forgiven. Naudé was publicly to apologise to the *Broederbond* on several occasions for the intense grief he had caused, but he was effectively drummed out of the *volk* and extruded as an agent of alien ideas and unpredictable loyalties.

Naudé's resignation followed two painful years of wrestling with his conscience. Ultimately the decision rested on two grounds. Careful reflection on the scriptures amid the tumultuous aftermath of Cottesloe convinced him that his past acceptance of the *Broederbond*'s principle of secrecy conflicted with the Bible's call to openness in all one's dealings.[23] He was also appalled by the fact that the *Broederbond*, intimately meshed with the DRC hierarchy, was manipulating the church and destroying its freedom to act as an independent Christian institution. In his assessment the position had been reached where there was 'no possibility of working for change from within since [the *Broederbond*] were determined to take away even the freedom of conscience'.[24]

When the Christian Institute was formed in August 1963, Naudé, who was now Moderator of the Southern Transvaal Synod of the NGK, was offered the position of Director. As a result, he was plunged into yet another crisis by a Church he correctly judged to have entered into 'a fear-ridden process of isolation'.[25] Having gone through what was normally a routine procedure of seeking permission to take up an outside appointment while maintaining his status as a minister, Naudé was brusquely told by the Examining Commission of the Transvaal Synod to choose between his NGK ministry and the post as Director.[26] The issue came to a head in September when Naudé accepted the Directorship of the Institute, appealed to the Transvaal Synod asking it to over-ride its Examining Commission, and was again denied the prospect of remaining a minister. He had therefore to preach his last sermon to the Aasvoelkop congregation, an occasion when he tried to share both his distress and his vision. Naudé was also honest enough to speak of his resentment over unreasonable and unjust decisions which he prayed would be revoked.

Arguing from his text — Acts 5.29: 'We must obey God rather than men' — Naudé made it clear that he was not withdrawing from the NGK but seeking to serve it in a wider ecumenical context. The issue was not a choice between the DRC and the Christian Institute, but the much deeper problem of 'a choice between religious conviction and submission to ecclesiastical authority. By obeying the latter unconditionally I would save face but lose my soul.'[27] Developing this theme, Naudé took the congregation back to the confrontation Peter and the apostles faced with an earlier ecclesiastical authority, the Sanhedrin. In ignoring the latter's order not to teach in the name of Jesus Christ, the apostles had clearly been disobedient, for as Peter said: 'If God asks anything all other things must give way.' Ultimately, anyone who took a comparable stand could bring no other defence than that of conscience,

'that inner assurance of faith which God gives to all who after much agonising are willing to stand in complete dependence before God, completely willing to be convinced by God concerning the obedience he expects from us'.[28]

In taking their stance in the name of Jesus, Naudé argued that the apostles had offered conversion and forgiveness to their people.

As the sermon developed, some alarming parallels became clear for a congregation which was part of an Afrikaner community that had often thought of itself as a modernday Israel. The apostles' message to the Sanhedrin, Naudé continued, was simple and direct:

'Christ is willing to begin anew with the people of Israel, the door is still open, his mercy is still there [verses 30–2]. And they, what do they make of the offer? The council's reaction is immediate and sharp [verse 33]. The words cut to the heart, but in a directly opposite way from what happened among the crowds at Pentecost arousing animosity and wrath, resistance and resentment.'[29]

The analogy, Naudé suggested, was not presumptuous: the Afrikaner nation faced a comparable challenge at Cottesloe, yet the response of the synods was in effect to place a ban on all comment which conflicted with church policy or with the established DRC view of the past. The 'God-given right and freedom of the minister and layman to witness prophetically and true to Reformation principles to the truth of God's word' had been so drastically restricted that 'the minister of the Gospel is no longer in principle given the freedom to express his deepest Christian convictions and to express them at such a place and time as

God reveals to him through his Word and Spirit.' It was time to speak out against the crippling fear — a 'sign of unbelief' — that made people cling to the political kingdom of Afrikanerdom rather than work for the kingdom of God on earth. When 'we as the NGK' fear to take up our ecumenical responsibilities and refuse to face the issues of racism and injustice, 'then we fail our people, then we commit treason against our people.' If the NGK did not take up this 'obedience demanded by God' then, Naudé warned, it would suffer 'endless loss and sorrow' — not least in 'irrevocably alienating the hearts of our daughter Churches' and losing contact with 'the Churches of Africa'.[30]

This valedictory sermon was a moving occasion for a divided congregation, many of whose members had been profoundly disturbed by having to form their own judgment on their pastor's public stand. Naudé, they learnt, had made up his mind; he would stick with *Pro Veritate* and help to launch the Christian Institute. They also heard a last and almost desperate cry from the pulpit: 'O my Church, I call this morning in all sincerity from my soul — awake before it is too late. Stand up and give the hand of Christian brotherhood to all who sincerely stretch out the hand to you. There is still time, but the time is short, very short.'[31]

In accepting the directorship of the new Institute, Naudé not only lost his position as a minister, but he was also in a vindictive act deprived of his standing as an elder. When a member of another congregation objected to his election as an elder at Aasvoelkop, both the local and regional church councils over-ruled the objection; but when an appeal was made to the Transvaal Synod, a commission was set up and Naudé was judged without due process. The strong NGK tradition of a hearing on disciplinary matters was dispensed with, so that no charge or explanation for denying the status of elder was ever given.

The Christian Institute to which Naudé now devoted himself was 'an attempt to bring together Christians of all denominations into Christian fellowship to work for greater justice for all citizens of our land'; it was to 'give a more visible expression to the biblical truth of the unity of all Christians, all believers'.[32] Clearly the hope was to salvage something of the ecumenism of Cottesloe by drawing together individuals from different ethnic backgrounds and denominations who were prepared 'to be used by God to give practical expression to a growing desire for fellowship and understanding between Christians of our country'.[33] From a foundation of Bible study and prayer there were to be discussions, analysis and then service. Christians were to be 'equipped for a life of doing',[34] a life committed to reconciliation and to witnessing more clearly to 'the Kingdom of God in South Africa'.[35] However, it was not at all clear how this would translate into practice;

certainly the policies of the Institute evolved in unexpected ways during the fourteen tumultuous years before it was banned in 1977. But, for the moment, the approach was cautious. The intention was to offer library and information services, to organise conferences and to publish on issues such as migratory labour and home and family life. The key theme was unity and reconciliation without any well-defined idea of how these goals might be achieved in the face of a resolute apartheid state. The Institute, Naudé wrote,

'was launched in faith and lives by faith. Faith in the purpose of God to unite all its people in a renewed fellowship of love and service; faith in the healing power of Jesus Christ and His Gospel which is able to overcome the barriers of history, culture, tradition, language and race; faith in the Holy Spirit who remains the active agent of the Father's purpose and the Son's power and now seeks to bring about the reconciliation of all men everywhere.'[36]

The founding members of the Institute numbered 280 persons.[37] They were predominately white clergy from the English-speaking denominations and a seminal, small group of white DRC ministers and laity who gathered around Beyers Naudé — in particular Albert Geyser, Ben Englebrecht who took over as editor of *Pro Veritate*, and Fred van Wyk whose administrative experience at the South African Institute of Race Relations proved invaluable. In addition, a small number of Africans and Coloureds joined in what was essentially a white initiative. In witnessing to ecumenical fellowship, the Institute set out to work as closely as possible with the Christian Council of South Africa, the Protestant ecumenical body for inter-church co-operation. It also opened its doors to Roman Catholics and initially attracted approximately twenty socially-conscious clergy and laity from that denomination. In addition, and in spite of the severe setbacks they had already encountered, Naudé and his DRC colleagues still hoped that by working through the Institute they would be able to draw the DRC back into a renewed round of ecumenical dialogue.

The response of the DRC continued to be intensely hostile to any initiative associated with the Cottesloe experience, and particularly where Naudé and Geyser were involved. Although there were other issues that were to make co-operation virtually impossible, for example the acceptance of Roman Catholic membership in the Institute, the central bone of contention remained the call to Christian fellowship which conflicted with the DRC insistence on separate racial churches. Dr J.D. Vorster, who as we have seen was a staunch member of the *Broederbond* who had now risen to be Actuary of the NGK General Synod, made the point in his shrill way: segregated congregations dated back to the seventeenth century and the liberalistic move to blur racial boundaries in the churches was an evil which had as its name 'integration, world citizenship, equality and the return to Babel'. Moreover, liberalism was 'nothing but communism'.[38] In reality, of course, the issues were much wider than church affairs. Individuals like Vorster, and the Dutch Reformed Churches as institutions, were deeply involved in politics, neurotically defensive when the Afrikaner political and economic élites were criticised, and determined to destroy the fledgling Institute which they saw as a threat to the whole system of apartheid. The editor of *Die Kerkbode*, Dr A.P. Treurnicht, was typical of the resulting campaign to head off any serious criticism of government policies. Setting out to discredit the Christian Institute as a dangerous political organisation masquerading as a band of dedicated Christians, he warned the *volk* and Afrikaner students at every opportunity that the Institute's 'first message [was] not Christian but political'.[39]

Leading African spokesmen suggest that the country's black Christians were not impressed with these arguments and that their deepest concerns were not far removed from those of the Christian Institute. In contrast with the fearful, tradition-bound and parochial defence of segregated churches, the Rev. Zaccheus Mahabane saw the world 'moving toward a certain climax' in which the Christian commitment was to spread the good news of Jesus and establish widening circles of fellowship. This building of human community, he suggested, required some understanding of the increasingly complex and rapid movement of history. Preaching in 1963 at the opening of John Wesley College, a component of the Federal Theological Seminary at Alice in the Eastern Cape, he went on to link his prophetic stance with the search for freedom by individuals and among nations, a search which paradoxically resulted from the increasing interdependence of peoples. Speaking at the age of eighty-two, he took his audience of church dignitaries and young black seminarians through the turmoil of recent history, including the industrial revolution in South Africa, and then returned to his theme of increasing human interdependence. This interdependence, he continued, posed a special ecumenical challenge to Christians. In his judgment, the ecumenical movement was at the cutting edge of Christ's purpose in history; it could bring about the 'fulfilment of the Divine Ideal expressed in Christ's prayer: 'That they be ONE, even as thou, Father, art in Me, and I in thee, that they may be one in us, that the world may believe that thou hast sent me.'[40]

Naudé would have agreed with Mahabane. Similarly he would have had an immediate empathy with Albert Lutuli's hopes and fears — even if Lutuli's political vision would have stretched Naudé's imagination in 1963 to the point of discomfort. Interviewed in 1963 after being acquitted in the Treason Trial, and after eleven years of being banned and confined to the Lower Tugela area of Natal, Lutuli was asked what he sought for South Africa. Discussions with Prime Minister Verwoerd, he replied, and the full involvement of the African National Congress and its leadership in the future of South Africa. 'I would also wish', he continued,

'that the Christian churches in South Africa be more courageous and more forthright in speaking out against oppression and in developing African clergymen. I have no fear that Africans will become Communists. They will not do so. I do fear that black Africans will forsake Christianity. But of these, most of all, I would wish for talk, honest discussions between black leaders and white leaders of South Africa.'[41]

Naudé and the Christian Institute had a long way to go before coming to a full realisation of the centrality of the black viewpoint for the future of Christianity and of justice in South Africa. Nevertheless, something new had been started in the Institute. A prophetic Christian voice was being heard and simultaneously there emerged the prospect of a prophetic ecumenical movement.

NOTES

1. *DRC Newsletter*, March 1961, pp. 1–2.
2. *Ibid.*; *Cape Argus*, 4 November 1961.
3. *Grense. A Symposium Concerning Racial and Other Attitudes* (Stellenbosch, 1961), p. 1.
4. *Cape Argus*, 28 September 1961.
5. *Cape Times*, 11 October 1961.
6. *Ibid.*, 8 November 1961,
7. *Cape Times*, 28 September 1961.
8. *Ibid.*.
9. R.E. van der Ross, 'Cape D.R. Synod and Cottesloe', *Cape Times*, 2 November 1961.
10. K. Carstens, *Church and Race in South Africa*, pp. 12–13.
11. The account which follows relies essentially on K. Carstens, *Church and Race in South Africa*, pp. 10–14, which makes use of unpublished documents of the *Hervormde Kerk* Commission of the General Assembly, 28 February 1962.
12. *Cape Times*, 12 October 1961.
13. K. Carstens, *op. cit.*, p. 13.
14. Naudé's biographical details essentially are drawn from C.F. Beyers' Naudé, 'Curriculum Vitae', in *Fragmenten en citaten uit toespraken interviews en artikelen van Beyers Naudé* (de Vrije Universiteit Utrecht, 1972), pp. 34–6; International Commission of Jurists, *The Trial of Beyers Naudé* (London, 1975), pp. 54ff; and G.M. Bryan, *Naudé: Prophet to South Africa* (Atlanta, Ga., 1978), pp. 9ff. The latter has to be used with care as it has many inaccuracies.
15. The normal procedure would have been for the male child to take his mother's maiden or family name in addition to his father's name.

16. As Naudé was later to point out, this was 'not Pro Veritate!' (*Fragmenten en citaten*, p. 35).

17. *Ibid.*.

18. International Commission of Jurists, *The Trial of Beyers Naudé* (London, 1975), ρ. 59.

19. *Ibid.*, p. 60.

20. Ibid., p. 61.

21. K. Carstens, *Church and Race in South Africa* (United Nations Unit on Apartheid, 1971), p. 34.

22. International Commission of Jurists, *The Trial of Beyers Naudé*, pp. 77, 94; *Cape Argus*, 17 July 1972, Naudé's reflections on the 1963 situation.

23. John 1.5, 9, 14; Matthew 10.26-7.

24. John Sackur, 'Last Stand of the Christian Conscience in South Africa,' *Cape Times*, 27 February 1971; *Cape Argus*, 17 July 1972.

25. International Commission of Jurists, *The Trial of Beyers Naudé*, p. 73.

26. K. Carstens, *Church and Race in South Africa*, p. 35; A. Reeves, *State and Church in South Africa* p. 8.

27. International Commission of Jurists, *The Trial of Beyers Naudé*, p. 71. The full text of the sermon is reprinted.

28. *Ibid.*, pp. 69-70.

29. *Ibid.*, p. 70.

30. *Ibid.*, pp. 71-3.

31. *Ibid.*, pp. 76-7.

32. *Ibid.*, p. 55; C.F. Beyers Naudé, 'Curriculum Vitae', in *Fragmenten en citaten*, p. 36.

33. C.F.B. Naudé, 'The Christian Institute,' *Challenge* (Johannesburg), June 1965, p. 16.

34. *Ibid.*.

35. International Commission of Jurists, *The Trial of Beyers Naudé*, p. 55.

36. Naudé, 'The Christian Institute', *Challenge*, June 1965, p. 16.

37. *The Christian Institute of Southern Africa* (Johannesburg, *c.* 1971).

38. *Windhoek Advertizer* (Windhoek), 30 August 1965.

39. *The Friend* (Bloemfontein), 24 July 1965.

40. Mahabane, *The Good Fight*, p. 128.

41. W.R. Duggan, 'Three Men of Peace' (manuscript), p. 17.

Part II
THE EARLY YEARS: THE CHRISTIAN INSTITUTE, 1963–1968

4

STRESS WITHIN THE CHURCHES AND CONFRONTATION WITH THE DRC

Those who formed the Christian Institute in 1963 were not alone in their concerns. Leading clergymen in all the denominations were having to address political issues and judge the structures as well as the practices of apartheid. Even if the white parishes remained unruffled, it was becoming an uncomfortable predicament for those with official positions of responsibility. Many who should have had the courage to speak out boldly and to act publicly did not do so, yet Christianity in South Africa was moving into a creative period when the smugness of flaccid churches that had largely conformed to the culture of segregation was to be challenged.

Whereas Sharpville and Cottesloe produced turmoil in the DRC and led to the formation of the Christian Institute, ferment proceeded rather slowly in the multi-racial churches, the leaders of which already thought of themselves as anti-apartheid. Yet, with very few exceptions, white churchmen from these multi-racial churches had not supported the black political organisations in their passive resistance campaigns of the 1950s. Rather, the churches watched from the sidelines, offering verbal warnings of the dangers of injustice and disorder, while blacks struggled to purge society of its racism. This unwillingness to encourage black organisations, or to support their programmes of reform, persisted in spite of the public witness in the liberation struggle of such eminent black Christians as the Methodist Rev. Zacheus Mahabane, the Anglican Canon James Calata who served as General-Secretary of the African National Congress from 1936 to 1949,[1] and Albert Lutuli. While the DRC was attempting to legitimise apartheid and defend the repressive tactics of the state, none of the other churches spoke out forcefully and persistently against the banning of the African National Congress and the Pan Africanist Congress.

This situation was now changing; indeed 1960 can be seen as a watershed in the evolution of Christianity in South Africa. As the state of emergency was declared, as the apartheid government clamped down on radical dissent and African political organisations were crushed, the largely quiescent hierarchies of the multi-racial churches were forced to react more vigorously to the fact that the Gospel's call to create widening forms of human fellowship had encountered a massive roadblock in apartheid.

Although the Christian Institute disturbed the equanimity of the DRCs, and in so doing moved to the centre of an intensifying church-state confrontation, it must also be seen as contributing to this much wider intra-church ferment. Just as the Institute was to play a role in encouraging the independent judgement of the black Dutch Reformed Churches, so too it worked amid the often confused, always cautious multi-racial churches, informing them, encouraging their hesitant protests and helping them to focus on the major issues of injustice — not least their own ingrained patterns of racial discrimination.

The stress experienced within the multi-racial denominations as race relations deteriorated can be seen in the Church of the Province of South Africa. At the level of their teaching magisterium, the eleven Anglican bishops responded verbally and in general terms to apartheid, to the Defiance Campaign, the Sharpville shootings and the declaration of a state of emergency. 'The Gospel of Jesus Christ', they declared, was concerned with 'the whole of human life'. Therefore the Church had to 'openly and fearlessly condemn all that it believes to be evil and false in the social, political or economic life of any nation'. When this led to confrontation with the state, it was 'to God that our obedience must be given'.[2] At a more practical level there was action and protest by a few clergymen, but they were quickly judged by their white fellow-Christians to be contentious and even irresponsible individuals. One of these more courageous souls was Bishop Ambrose Reeves of Johannesburg who visited the wounded after Sharpville, so gathering affidavits to bolster his charge that the shootings were unprovoked and wanton. He then published his exposé *Shooting at Sharpville*. Reeves, who was then deported, had also been active during 1960 in establishing the Dependents' Conference which, under the aegis of the Christian Council, set out to provide financial assistance for the destitute families of an increasing number of political prisoners. When the Rev. Arthur Blaxall, a colleague of Reeves and recently retired as General Secretary of the Council, continued this effective support for political dependents and their families, many of whom had been members of the African National Congress before it was banned, he too was dealt with. Sentenced at the age of seventy-two to twenty-eight months' imprisonment under the Suppression of Communism Act, he was subsequently deported.[3]

Blaxall's experience is particularly interesting as an illustration of the tensions generated among whites when protests shifted from declarations of principles to action. He had been a moving spirit in a chapter of the Fellowship of Reconciliation, a small group of less than 200 Quaker-oriented pacifists committed to a 'peace witness'. Lutuli supported the Fellowship, but when he turned to the non-violent resistence of the Defiance Campaign in the early 1950s, the majority of the Fellowship refused to support him. Blaxall was among the few who continued to back Lutuli and, as a consequence, was attacked for 'taking political sides' rather than working for the reconciliation and conversion of the oppressor. Later, when Blaxall was prosecuted for assisting the victims of political oppression and convicted of thereby assisting members of the banned ANC, the Fellowship of Reconciliation formally disassociated itself from him.[4]

By 1963 when ill-health forced Archbishop Joost de Blank to retire from his see of Cape Town, he was well aware of the criticism from whites within his own communion that he had 'tried to go too far and too fast'. In his farewell message, however, he showed that he was certain that this was not so. Racial discrimination was a 'form of blasphemy'; to speak of separate development or territorial homelands was simply a camouflage, and it was 'a major tragedy that some who claim to be Christians still espouse gradualism and a step-by-step amelioration in inter-race relations'. Sin was sin and had to be 'repented of and forsaken completely here and now'.[5]

De Blank's unequivocal style had never endeared him to *Die Burger*, the nationalist Afrikaans newspaper in Cape Town; the paper did 'not lament his departure' and condemned 'his unpleasant, thundering, one-sided condemnations'.[6] There were white Anglicans who felt the same way, perhaps because the Archbishop had also tried to change the practice of his church. During his six years' tenure, the first black bishop was ordained who in turn ordained a white priest; de Blank's diocese established a lay Action Board to address issues of justice, and the multi-racial Bishop Gray Theological College was established at Zonnebloem.[7] These were important first steps, divisive as far as whites were concerned, overdue from the viewpoint of many blacks. Nevertheless, the Church was still overwhelmingly dominated by a white hierarchy and remained a paternalistic organisation within which it was very difficult to hear the voices of the majority — its black communicants.

Comparable tensions, ambiguities and elements of ingrained racism were present among Lutherans, Methodists and Presbyterians. It was not until 1963 that the Lutherans produced their first statement on race relations, a mildly critical and timid stand against the injustices of racial discrimination.[8] By contrast the Methodists were persistently outspoken in their condemnation of apartheid, and after Sharpville called for a National Convention 'representative of the leadership of all major racial groups'.[9] Prime Minister Verwoerd was not impressed. It was, he replied, an attempt 'to undermine the Government's policy and justice for the white man'. To gather all conflicting groups into one hall 'would be nothing but a breeding ground for communist conditioning'.[10] Unfortunately it was the same Methodist Church which failed rather miserably to live up to its own ideals. Although its membership was 80 per cent black, the Church, like the other multi-racial denominations, remained firmly under white control; its black ministers received well under half the minimum stipend set for whites and Methodist congregations remained essentially segregated.[11] In this unchanging context, the election in 1963 of the first black Methodist President, the Rev. S.M. Mokitimi, was a symbolic breakthrough but essentially a token gesture, for it was more than a decade before a black again held the highest office. The Rev. W. Illsley, a Past President, had been far in advance of the great majority of his white colleagues when, in the debate preceeding Mokitimi's election, he reminded them that Europeans would increasingly be 'called to serve and not to dominate, to learn as well as to teach, to receive as well as to give'.[12] It was to take the white Methodist establishment until the late 1970s, and the shock of confrontation with black ministers, black consciousness and black theology, before Illsley's insights would be taken seriously. In fact, it was not until 1976 that the first steps were taken to integrate the segregated Methodist circuits.[13]

White Presbyterian leaders were particularly resolute in resisting change within their own church structures, as they too exhibited the standard pattern of schizophrenia found in all the multi-racial churches. While they committed themselves in principle to eliminating racial discrimination, white Presbyterians did not witness in their own lives to non-racial Christian fellowship. When the General Council of the Presbyterian Alliance met in Frankfurt in 1964, approximately two-thirds of the South African delegates voted for a resolution calling members 'to witness to justice and equality in race relations by identifying with, and accepting responsibility alongside, those who suffer'. The Church was to undertake a serious study of the Scriptures and of politics 'to help its members face responsibly such hard problems as civil disobedience or violent action under the guidance of Jesus Christ'. Yet after the Frankfurt meeting, the official Presbyterian journal in South Africa moved in a different direction. Apartheid, it suggested, was not always blasphemy: 'Some people cannot live with others. Some national groups cannot live with others.' '*Baasskap*' had to be replaced by 'white leadership', but the issue was to avoid hardening white opinion, and the solution was partition.[15] Although the official voice of the Presbyterian Church was to overcome this ambivalence on the issues of apartheid and to condemn government policies, the only bold initiative was an inter-racial parish formed in East London in 1960. Starting out with twenty Africans, fifty Coloured and thirty-five whites, this solitary experiment struggled bravely against the barriers of the Group Areas Act and other crippling legislation until the parish disintegrated in 1970.[16]

The Roman Catholic Church was no exception to this syndrome of an impoverished, nominal Christianity enmeshed in the prevailing culture of racial discrimination. With very few exceptions, the largely expatriate hierarchy and clergy lacked a prophetic social vision and were incapable of applying the principles of the Church's pastoral letters. In 1957, 1960 and again in 1962, the Bishops condemned apartheid in clear, even ringing terms. Apartheid's basic principle was 'the preservation of what is called white civilisation', that is 'white supremacy, which means the enjoyment by white men only of full political, social, economic and cultural rights'. Under apartheid, the white man presented himself as 'the agent of God's will — determining the bounds of non-white development'. The Bishops trembled at 'the blasphemy of thus attributing to God the offences against charity and justice' that were 'apartheid's necessary accompaniment'.[17] South Africa was 'one community', a variety of peoples brought together by the Providence of God working in history. Within this community, the value and great dignity of each person had to be fully respected. In practice this meant ending the system of migratory labour, maintaining stable family life, initiating a colour-blind franchise and repealing statutes like the Mixed Marriages Act and the Group Areas Act which destroyed free association and the growth of human fellowship.[18]

Unfortunately the Roman Catholic Church had a staggeringly long way to go in living up to these ideals. Its seminaries were still segregated in 1963 and it was ten years before the hierarchy began to integrate them. The few African priests served African parishes and black seminarians were still being trained to be assistants to white 'missionary' clergy; when these seminarians were taught canon law, the section dealing with the rights and responsibilities of a parish priest was skipped.[19] Parish life remained segregated apart from the overlap of domestic servants living in white areas, and it is likely that the majority of white clergy were not fundamentally opposed to the principles of apartheid. A clear indication of this was that the South African-born Archbishop Denis Hurley of Durban, the moving spirit behind the pastoral letters condemning apartheid, came under severe criticism from his own white priests and white laity for taking his stand.[20]

So it was that by the early 1960s the churches had committed themselves to nurturing non-racial Christian fellowship, to extending the
bonds of human community, to the rapid dismantling of apartheid and
its colour-bars. At the level of their official pronouncements, they were
in favour of equal opportunity for all persons and had called for special
efforts to assist the poor. But these public declarations were too rare-
fied, too easy to make and soon unconvincing when they were not
followed by action. In the light of such good intentions, internal church
practices were becoming a scandal — if not to many whites, then to
black South Africans and to Christians throughout the world. If the
churches were ever to move beyond mere verbal condemnations of
apartheid to the point of confronting the state, perhaps with civil disobedience, they would first have to face up to their own internal
patterns of injustice.

The Christian Council (later renamed the South African Council of
Churches) was to become an increasingly important ecumenical centre
during the 1960s and 1970s where these issues of social and church justice were discussed. Functioning as a clearing-house for new ideas, the
Council's secretariat continued to hold dialogue with critical voices
from abroad — be they the World Council of Churches or the British
Council of Churches.[21] However, it was the Christian Institute that
became the most active and seminal influence among the South
African churches. It was the Christian Institute that became a
thoroughly disturbing prophetic voice: describing the full impact of
apartheid on blacks, condemning the structures of injustice, assailing
complacency, struggling to articulate an alternative vision for society
and trying to discern appropriate methods to bring something of that
vision into being. While the Institute was rejected and reviled by the
white Dutch Reformed Churches, its words and actions gradually
helped to focus some of the disparate energies of the multi-racial
churches. Being drawn from all denominations, Protestant and
Catholic, members of the Institute took new ideas and hopes back into
their own churches and many tried to activate their Christian
communities.

Working closely with the South African Council of Churches, the
Christian Institute came haltingly but with growing clarity to a profound understanding of Christian mission, an understanding formed
in the South African crucible but relevant to Christians everywhere.
From its foundation in 1963 until it was banned in 1977, the Institute,
despite its limitations, evolved into the ecumenical, non-racial cutting-
edge of Christian witness in South Africa — an inevitably flawed yet
persistent witness to the liberating power of the Scriptures for the poor
and oppressed as well as for the erstwhile oppressor.

As we have seen, the Institute came into existence in the aftermath of Sharpville, after the banning of African political organisations and after the Cottesloe Consultation between the South African churches and the World Council of Churches. It hoped to exercise a prophetic ministry and to work for justice and reconciliation, but there was a good deal of uncertainty as to how these responsibilities were to be fulfilled in an increasingly harsh political environment. State repression had created a vacuum in terms of black political leadership with the result that church organisations were beginning to function as a residual matrix for white and black opposition to apartheid. As the state undertook a massive mopping-up operation against the remaining pockets of black activists, as the newly-formed underground movement was smashed, and as further repressive legislation was passed by the white parliament in Cape Town, so the Christian Institute emerged as the vanguard organisation in an inchoate, essentially spontaneous movement of Christian dissent. Individual churchmen were banned or deported, attempts to nurture inter-racial Christian fellowship were attacked and the Institute was subjected to a vilification campaign launched by National Party politicians and the white Dutch Reformed Churches.

As these pressures intensified, the Institute discerned its most urgent task to be a renewed effort to wean Afrikanerdom from apartheid, from what Naudé saw as an idolotrous commitment to a dominant, privileged and supposedly separate future for the *volk*. Simultaneously the Institute worked for ecumenical co-operation between the multi-racial churches, among the black Dutch Reformed Churches and within the black independent church movement.

The banning of African leaders like Albert Lutuli, after their acquittal in 1961 at the end of the prolonged Treason Trial, had crippled black political resistance to apartheid. This was followed by further arrests and new patterns of harassment: the intimidation of witnesses, the first indications of torture in the prisons and a large increase in the number of police informers. This repression was particularly intense in Port Elizabeth and the Eastern Cape where the African National Congress had been most effective in the Defiance Campaigns of the 1950s. In this region alone, well over 1,000 Africans were arrested by security police in 1964/5, leaving approximately 4,000 women and children close to destitution.[22] The efficiency of this and other police operations was enhanced by the General Law Amendment Act of 1964 which permitted detainees to be held without trial and in solitary confinement for up to ninety days. In some cases individuals were released and immediately rearrested for a further ninety days. This inconvenience was overcome in 1965 through the Criminal Procedure Act which allowed detainees to be held without trial for 180 days. Two years later the Terrorism Act was passed permitting indefinite detention without trial of suspects and potential witnesses.

After the banning of African political organisations in 1960, the ANC underground organisation, *Umkonto we Sizwe* (Spear of the Nation), was formed and turned to sabotage, limiting itself for humanitarian reasons to attacks on property, particularly government installations. Although this was a precursor of the more violent struggle that lay ahead, *Umkonto*'s internal organisation had been destroyed by the mid-1960s after the arrest at Rivonia, near Johannesburg, in 1963 of the leading spirit Nelson Mandela and ten of his associates. In his speech from the dock before being sentenced to life imprisonment, Mandela pointed out that it was only after half a century of non-violent protests, and after all constitutional means of resistance had been destroyed, that Africans reluctantly turned to counter-violence as the last resort against a government that had lost any last residual element of legitimacy:

I have already mentioned that I was one of the persons who helped to form *Umkhonto*. I, and the others who started the organisation, did so for two reasons. Firstly, we believed that as a result of Government policy, violence by the African people had become inevitable, and that unless responsible leadership was given to canalise and control the feelings of our people, there would be outbreaks of terrorism which would produce an intensity of bitterness and hostility between the various races of this country which is not produced even by war. Secondly, we felt that without violence there would be no way open to the African people to succeed in their struggle against the principle of white supremacy. All lawful modes of expressing opposition to this principle had been closed by legislation, and we were placed in a position in which we had either to accept a permanent state of inferiority, or to defy the Government. We chose to defy the Government. We chose to defy the law. We first broke the law in a way which avoided any recourse to violence; when this form was legislated against, and when the Government resorted to a show of force to crush opposition to its policies, only then did we decide to answer violence with violence.

But the violence which we chose to adopt was not terrorism. We who formed *Umkhonto* were all members of the African National Congress, and had behind us the ANC tradition of non-violence and negotiation as a means of solving political disputes. We believe that South Africa belongs to all the people who live in it, and not to one group, be it black or white. We did not want an interracial war, and tried to avoid it to the last minute. If the Court is in doubt about this, it will be seen that the whole history of our organisation bears out what I have said.[23]

Mandela's arrest was followed in November 1965 by that of Bram Fischer, an eminent barrister who had been one of the defence team at the Treason Trial of 1956–61 and the Rivonia Trial of 1964. Fischer, a central personality in the Communist Party of South Africa, had finally gone underground early in 1965, having made the judgement that there were no longer any viable constitutional means of struggling against apartheid.

Like Beyers Naudé, Bram Fischer came from an eminent Afrikaner family and so he too was peculiarly threatening to the caretakers of Afrikanerdom. Born in 1908, his grandfather had been Abraham Fischer, State Secretary of the Orange Free State Republic and, after the Boer War, Prime Minister of the Colony. His father Percy Fischer had been Judge President of the Orange Free State. A South African Rhodes Scholar, Bram Fischer returned from Oxford in 1934, established himself as a barrister and married a niece of General Smuts. In the context of the great depression and hardening white racism, he joined the then legal Communist Party.

In 1964 Fischer with twelve other whites was charged with being a member of the illegal Communist Party (it had been banned in 1950) and was out on bail at the time he chose to go underground. Having arranged for the monetary equivalent of the bail to be repaid to his guarantors, he wrote a letter explaining his actions. At least some people, he hoped, would be forced as a result of his stand to think again and to abandon the apartheid policies they blindly supported. The black majority was fighting back against oppression with increasing hatred so that unless 'this whole intolerable system is changed radically and rapidly, disaster must follow and appalling bloodshed and civil strife become inevitable.' No longer, he continued, could he 'serve justice in the way I have attempted to do over the last thirty years'.[24] In Fischer's judgment the Verwoerd government, with its General Law Amendment Act and '90 day clause', had destroyed the rule of law, legalised torture and defined sabotage so widely as to include the painting of a slogan on a wall — a protest now punishable by death.[25]

In his speech from the dock, Fischer, like Naudé, offered hope, a vision of the future which in his case was grounded in a Marxist analysis of 'why one type of society must of necessity give way to a new and higher form'.[26] The urgent issue was to limit the element of violence in such a transition by changing the whole system 'radically and rapidly'. Naudé would have agreed with this call for fundamental change in the sense of eradicating racial discrimination; on the other hand, he would have been most uncomfortable with Fischer's emphasis on class conflict as the central process of history. By the mid-1970s, however, working from his Christian premises, Naudé too came to see the importance of linking radical economic changes with the elimination of racial discrimination. What Naudé was 'absolutely certain' of in 1965 was that a man of Fischer's integrity and DRC background would never have become a Communist had the church not refused to accept its call to work for social justice.[27]

The Christian Institute, the Christian Council and leaders of every multi-racial church were in agreement with Fischer on the point that the rule of law had been destroyed. As the Council put it, the '90 day clause' was a breach of the 'fundamental tenet of justice that there should be no imprisonment without trial'. Only the Dutch Reformed Churches refused to sign the combined church protest, throwing themselves once again behind an increasingly authoritarian state. In the NGK's judgement, the '90 day clause' was necessary: 'Today we are under the threat of a cold war that is being fanned by revolution and sabotage and which is a prelude to civil war and total war.' This justified 'unusual measures'.[28]

'Unusual measures' were now to be taken against individual Christians and church organisations with increasing frequency, all in the name of national security. A Defence and Aid Fund had been started to take over from the Treason Trial Fund, and with the new wave of arrests it stepped up its assistance to political prisoners and their families. It was banned in March 1966 with the accompaniment of intimidatory police raids on homes as well as offices.[29] Later in the year expatriate clergy were placed under a new constraint, being required to renew their residence permits annually.[30] Those who took a public stance were to be dealt with in the manner of the Anglican Bishop of Kimberley and Kuruman, Edward Crowther, who in 1967 was given fourteen days to leave the country and return to the United States. Crowther's offence was to have taken up the cause of the poor and destitute in his diocese, setting up an emergency relief fund and clashing with the authorities over the need for emergency food distribution in the Holpan and Mamuthla reserve north of Kimberley.[31] He also encouraged inter-racial fellowship, criticising white members of his church along with other white Christians for acquiescing in apartheid and so assenting in practice 'to the grotesque blasphemy of man's separation from his brother'.[32] Crowther was certainly not a left-wing, radical churchman in any economic sense, but these words and actions were enough to trigger state action. Indeed, his recipe for change was touchingly naive: 'a crash education programme offering equal opportunity for every individual to develop his talents fully'. This was to be the prelude to a 'moral revolution'.[33]

Within the next three years, state action was taken against forty clergy and church workers: South African citizens were refused passports and expatriates were deported or had their visas withdrawn.[34] Moreover, the Christian Institute was not spared a share of this intimidation, receiving its first overt attention from the security police in 1965 when its offices as well as Beyers Naudé's home and person were searched in what was supposed to be a raid for Communist and African National Congress documentation.[35]

As the Christian Institute tried to get its bearings and develop its tactics amid this increasing church harassment, it had to recognise that both the government and the white Dutch Reformed Churches were determined not to concede an inch on the issue of non-racial fellowship or the building of Christian community which would witness against the culture and structures of apartheid. Signs of the state's hyper-sensitivity on this issue were very clear. A conference of church leaders held by the Christian Council in Bloemfontein in 1965 'most humbly confessed part failures' to effect reconciliation in a racist society, and committed its participants 'to express effective fellowship' within their own churches. Being concerned to go beyond mere generalisations, the conference recognised that 'it is often both necessary and important that Christians of different races should be able to live under one roof and share a common board'.[36] Then it followed up this commitment by asking the Prime Minister to permit mixed residential gatherings at the Wilgespruit Conference Centre at Roodepoort.

Verwoerd's response was totally inflexible. 'Your churches', he wrote, 'should be able to fulfil their functions fully as other Protestant churches do, while observing the country's laws and customs as they exist.' His government would not 'change its political convictions to suit the different political outlook of opponents even if these are defended in terms of religion'.[37] The Minister of Bantu Administration and Development was even more direct. Christians were entitled to meet each other, but the request to live under one roof and share a common board was 'contrary to both accepted policy and custom'. It would not be entertained.[38] The following year the government reiterated its apartheid principles once again with a directive against multi-racial welfare organisations. In this instance it forced the Anglican Department of Community Services (Anglicare) to restructure itself by establishing an all-white controlling council and breaking up its administration into racially pure sub-agencies.[39]

The government, of course, was quite correct in pointing out that there was nothing new in its response to church pressures; it was simply applying a long-established approach to ordering the population, an approach which informed the Prohibition of Mixed Marriages Act, the Immorality Act and indeed all apartheid legislation. Yet the regime now took its divisive logic one step further with the Prohibition of Political Interference Act of 1968. This banned all inter-racial political organisations and led, *inter alia*, to the destruction of Alan Paton's non-racial Liberal Party. It also meant that multi-racial Christian organisations, although severely circumscribed in their ability to nurture Christian fellowship, were now the last organisations bridging the gaps between South Africa's racial groups. Both the Christian Institute and the Christian Council delivered strongly-worded if inevitably futile objections to this new attack on Christian fellowship. Without interaction, they argued, there was no hope of developing a 'common Christian mind' on vital matters of public policy. South African history had brought the races together and theology confirmed the importance of this reality — Christians had to work to increase communication between people, not cut it off as apartheid was doing with its false premises, its 'brutal and demonic logic'.[40]

It is difficult to imagine how many occasions for Christian fellowship have been cut off by the laws and culture of apartheid, how many opportunities to build human community have been destroyed. Church leaders might speak eloquently of the need for communication between the races, but the sheer brutality of white racism was seldom described in any detail. For this reason it is worth reading a report from the *Cape Times'* East London correspondent entitled '9 Barred at Funeral Service':[41]

Eight African men and a woman were barred by a Dutch Reformed Church minister from attending the funeral service yesterday of a white man because Africans are not generally admitted to the church.

The man buried was a 35-year-old Mr Dennis Hoft. The firm for which he worked closed their offices yesterday afternoon to enable staff members to attend the funeral.

Mr Hoft, who was described by his workmates as 'very popular with everybody', was particularly liked by the African staff.

The African workers each contributed 50c and bought a wreath inscribed 'God be with you till we meet again, Mr Hoft'.

The secretary of the company telephoned the pastor of the church, the Rev. S. D. van der Merwe, to find out if the Africans could attend the funeral service. He replied that this could not be allowed.

AT THE BACK

He was asked to allow the Africans to stand at the back of the church, and again said that this could not be allowed.

Asked if an exception could be made, as the Africans concerned had been particularly fond of Mr Hoft, Mr van der Merwe said he could not make an exception.

Telephoned by a reporter to verify the position, Mr van der Merwe, of the Nederduitse Gereformeerde Kerk in Settlers Way, Greenfields, said the admission of Africans to a funeral service in any NGK church depended on circumstances.

'I am not prepared to discuss this question with a newspaper,' he said.

As the hearse bearing the coffin entered the cemetery gates, the African staff members stood by the grave.

One of them, Mr Jonathan Sompali, who has worked for the firm for more than 20 years, said Mr Hoft was a friend of Africans.

'We feel it our duty to attend his funeral to pay our last respects to a man we will miss,' he said.

It was in this context of political repression, harassment of Christian dissenters and a growing awareness of how apartheid thwarted the growth of fellowship that the Christian Institute focused its criticism on the subservience of the Dutch Reformed Churches to the politics and ideology of apartheid. The result was a storm of abuse from the ecclesiastical and political establishments of Afrikanerdom and a pattern of increasing intimidation which never abated until the Institute was banned in 1977.

Just how sensitive the Afrikaner élites of church and state were to criticism, how easily unnerved, can be sensed by their over-reaction to two events. *Pro Veritate* had been printing extracts from the speeches of Martin Luther King, for example his address to the Washington Campaign, 'I have a Dream'.[42] When King received an honorary doctorate from the Free University of Amsterdam, the Cape Synod of the NGK felt obliged to pass a resolution condemning the award on account of Dr King's 'Communist sympathies and his furtherance of the Communist cause'.[43] In reality the fear was that Christians might be drawn into an anti-apartheid civil rights movement in South Africa. A comparable over-reaction, this time by the political wing of Afrikanerdom, occurred when a rare exception was made and a multiracial service was held in the Groote Kerk, Cape Town, to launch a revival campaign led by evangelist Eric Hutchings. 'Liberalism', *Die Transvaaler* thundered, 'is just as deadly a threat to the Afrikaner in the Church sphere as in the political sphere for it opposes any form of separation of the races. . . . Once the Church accepts the principle of multi-racialism it would be easy to introduce it in other spheres of life. This would seal the fate of the Afrikaner.'[44] It was this closed cast of mind that the Christian Institute attempted to transform.

Tension rose dramatically as the Institute set out to extend its contacts in the Arikaner community, circularising DRC clergy and promoting *Pro Veritate*. The result was a smear campaign launched by *Die Transvaaler* in September 1965 with a series of vituperative articles. It became commonplace for leading members of the DRC to use their pulpits to condemn the Christian Institute, reserving their most bitter comments for Beyers Naudé and his Afrikaner colleagues. The *volk* were warned again and again to oppose any blurring of racial divisions and the Institute's 'liberalistic' and 'Communistic' tendencies. Writing in *Die Burger* and being quoted extensively throughout the Afrikaner press, Dr. J.D. Vorster, Minister of the NGK Cape Town congregation of Tafelberg and Actuary of the Synod, claimed without any substantiation to have unmasked the Institute as a 'front-

organisation of the enemy of our policy'. The implications were clear:
the Institute was supposedly being manipulated by non-Christian
groups and duped for the purposes of an atheistic movement. Naudé
responded, as he had on several previous occasions, by offering to open
the Christian Institute to a full investigation by the DRC, an offer that
was not taken up.[45] At this time *Pro Veritate* was being sent to university
halls of residence and this elicited a sharp if inane cold war reaction
from the annual congress of the *Afrikaner Studente Bond*: the Institute was
in practice 'a tool in the hand of Communism' and had to be countered
by a vigorous reassertion of Afrikaner 'Christian national' principles.[46]
It was at this time too that Professor A.D. Pont, writing in *Die
Hervormer*, described the Institute, Naudé and Geyser as working to
overthrow the government and conspiring to do so with Communists
and the World Council of Churches. This was too much for Naudé and
Geyser who sued for libel and had the satisfaction of being awarded
R10,100 each plus costs — the highest damages to date for a libel
settlement in South African courts.[47]

   Using the pages of *Pro Veritate*, Naudé and his colleagues tried to
rebut the wild charges and to focus the debate once again on more substantial issues. As the Institute's Director, Naudé also travelled to
Britain and the Netherlands in 1965 alerting overseas churches to the
ruthless nature of the smear campaign and seeking their support, particularly that of the Reformed Churches in the Netherlands.[48] He was
much encouraged and upon his return took up the offensive. In
October Naudé, his assistant editor of *Pro Veritate*, Dr Ben Engelbrecht,
the Rev. J.D. Smith and Fred van Wyk sent an open letter — in fact a
twenty-page booklet — to 1,500 ministers of the NGK. While they
exposed the slanders of the smear campaign, their main thrust was to
call for open Christian dialogue. They also cautioned against the
increasingly powerful tendency among Afrikaners to make religion
subservient to politics: the political ideology of apartheid was replacing
the Word of God as the highest authority. Apartheid, they warned, had
deteriorated and become a 'demonised ideology which was silencing
the Christian conscience'. The constant harassing of the Institute and
the campaign of slander against its members, was 'this not hate against
Christ and his Gospel, manifesting itself from a passionate, religious
worshipping of the "gods" of nature (race, soil, blood, culture)?'[49]
The only way to judge the Christian Institute was against the Word of
God and the NGK Articles of Faith. This had not been done, so that
the Institute was being condemned without being heard, silenced
without the time-honoured Calvinist procedures of due process.[50]

   A few months later, when relationships showed no signs of improving, an editorial in *Pro Veritate* showed that the Institute had virtually
despaired of checking the 'hate campaign' unleashed against those

Christians who refused to substitute the idea of apartheid for the essentials of the Gospel. Apartheid was exercising a 'totalitarian claim'; it had become 'a national faith' and was being 'absolutised to such a degree that alternative policies were eliminated in principle.' Yet there was an alternative which was commendable in theory and practice — 'a political order in which justice is done to the brotherhood of all men and their essential equality before God and in which considerations of race and colour play no decisive role'. The 'Christ' dragged in to defend apartheid was in fact 'the anti-Christ, and the "congregation" . . . gathered around this anti-Gospel [was] the anti-Church.'[51]

The 'liberalistic', 'Communistic' Christian Institute with its renewed assertiveness was now perceived by the DRC hierarchies as a potentially serious threat to their authority. Consequently the quadrennial 1966 General Synod of the NGK, with but òne dissenting voice, condemned the Institute as representing false doctrine and prohibited all NGK members from joining it.[52] The deadlock was now complete. The last few serving NGK ministers who had joined the Christian Institute at its inception while remaining *predikants* in their congregations now resigned. Other Afrikaners also withdrew at this time, but a hardy group of 150 lay members of the NGK remained to defy the ban by simultaneously belonging to both *Kerk* and Institute.[53] The NGK had rebuffed every effort at dialogue and was now more ruthlessly intent on destroying Naudé's organisation. As a result the reassessment of the Institute's strategy had become an urgent necessity, for its capacity to attract new DRC members had received a crippling blow.

It was not that the Institute abandoned its concern for the Dutch Reformed Churches; in fact they remained a source of deep sorrow for Naudé and his colleagues. In their view the churches had been tempted by 'the patronage of the people and of political rulers' to betray their first love, Christ. To overcome this tragic situation and once again to work for the salvation of Afrikaners rather than for their servitude, the *Kerk* would 'have to allow itself to be crucified for the people by the people'.[54] There was no immediate prospect of this and the Institute now had to shake the dust from its sandals and face the possibility of crucifixion itself. It needed more hopeful ministries, other ways to bring the liberating message of the Gospel to South Africa. In opening itself to these new possibilities the Institute's understanding of the Christian mission was to deepen and evolve in unexpected and eventually radical ways.

NOTES

1. Canon Calata was banned in 1963, as much for his growing influence among black members of the DRC as for his continuing political ideals.

2. 'Statement of the Bishops of the Church of the Province of South Africa', *Cape Times*, 22 November 1963.

3. *The Times* (London), 18 October 1963; *Cape Times*, 26 October, 22 November 1963.

4. E. Regehr, *Perceptions of Apartheid* (Scottdale, Pa., 1979), pp. 267–8.

5. *Seek* (Cape Town), November 1963, pp. 1–3.

6. *Die Burger*, 2 October 1963.

7. *Good Hope* (Cape Town), February 1964, p. 5.

8. E. Regehr, *Perceptions of Apartheid*, p. 252.

9. Carstens, *Church and Race in South Africa*, p. 20.

10. *Ibid.*, p. 21.

11. *Ibid.*, pp. 17–19.

12. Rev. W. Illsley, 'Churches: Integrated or Divided?', *Cape Times* 3 June 1963.

13. E. Regehr, *Perceptions of Apartheid*, p. 258.

14. *Cape Times*, 14 August 1964.

15. *Cape Argus*, 25 March 1965.

16. E. Regehr, *Perceptions of Apartheid*, p. 162.

17. Southern African Catholic Bishops' Conference, *Pastoral Letters* (Pretoria, *c.* 1966), pp. 13–14, 'Statement on Apartheid 1957'.

18. *Ibid.*, pp. 27–9, 'Pastoral Letter, 1960.'

19. Author's *interview* with Fr O. McGrath, O.P., Rector of the African Seminary from 1957 to 1970, Mazini, Swaziland, 27 February 1973. Fr McGrath had become increasingly critical of the system and was one of the few potentially influential voices urging radical and immediate change within the Roman Catholic Church.

20. Author's *interviews* with Fr. O. McGrath, O.P., 27 February 1973; Archbishop D. Hurley, O.M.I., Durban 2 April 1965, and 15 February 1973.

21. For example, 'Statement Issued by the Christian Council of South Africa on the Report of the British Council of Churches on "The Future of South Africa" '. *The Christian Council Quarterly*, 73, Fourth Quarter 1964, pp. 3–6.

22. Christian Action, *The Purge of the Eastern Cape* (London, 1966), pp. 1, 16.

23. N. Mandela, *The Struggle Is My Life* (London, 1978), pp. 156–67, 'Mandela's statement from the dock in Pretoria Supreme Court, 20 April 1964, at the opening of the defence case'.

24. Christian Action, *Bram Fischer, Q.C.* (London, 1966), pp. 1–4.

25. *Ibid.*, p. 4.

26. Robert Birley, *The Foundations of Three Totalitarian Regimes* (London, 1975), p. 12.

27. *Pro Veritate*, 15 November 1965, pp. 12–13.

28. *Cape Times*, 26 May 1964.

29. *Cape Argus*, 18 March 1966; *Cape Times*, 19 March 1966.

30. *Sunday Times* (Johannesburg), 11 December 1966.

31. *Cape Times*, 14 October 1967.

32. Edward Crowther, 'The Churches' Task in South Africa', *The Christian Century*, July 1967, p. 934.

33. *Ibid.*, p. 935.

34. *Cape Argus*, 25 February 1971.

35. *Pro Veritate*, July 1965, p. 1.

36. *The Christian Council Quarterly*, Fourth Quarter, 1965, p. 2.

37. *Ibid.*, p. 7, 'Prime Minister to the Christian Council, August 20, 1965'.

38. *Ibid.*, p. 8, 'Minister of Bantu Administration and Development to the Christian Council, October 10, 1965'.

39. E. Regehr, *Perceptions of Apartheid*, p. 54.

40. *The Christian Council Quarterly*, Fourth Quarter, 1966, p. 7.

41. *Cape Times*, 29 March 1969.

42. *Pro Veritate*, 15 February 1965.

43. *Cape Times*, 9 November 1965.

44. *The Star* (Johannesburg), 29 October 1965.

45. *Die Burger*, 30 November 1965; *Pro Veritate*, December 1965, pp. 1–2.

46. *Pro Veritate*, August, 1965, p. 5; August 1966, p. 8.

47. Carstens, *Church and Race in South Africa*, p. 36; Reeves, *State and Church in South Africa*, p. 8.

48. *Pro Veritate*, 15 August 1965, p. 8.

49. *Sunday Times* (Johannesburg), 3 October 1965.

50. *Ibid.*

51. *Pro Veritate*, August 1966, pp. 5–6.

52. Carstens, *Church and Race in South Africa*, p. 36.

53. *Cape Argus*, 23 August 1969.

54. *Pro Veritate*, December 1966, p. 3.

5

THE SEARCH FOR NEW STRATEGIES: A MESSAGE TO THE PEOPLE OF SOUTH AFRICA AND CO-OPERATION WITH THE INDEPENDENT CHURCHES

In addition to causing a decisive break with the Christian Institute, the 1966 decision of the NGK Synod to anathematise Naudé and his colleagues led to a serious and eventually unbridgeable rift between the Calvinist churches of the Netherlands and their counterparts in South Africa. The former were coming to see the Institute as a sign of Christian hope and so were shocked by the blatant attempt to crush it. In the words of the General Synod in Holland it was now questionable 'whether the *Nederlandse Hervormde Kerk* [could] continue to recognize the *Nederduitse Gereformeerde Kerk* of South Africa as a church any longer.'[1]

Several appeals for co-operation between the Institute and the South African Dutch Reformed Churches were sent out from Holland, and a major effort was made to effect a reconciliation at the Lunteren Conference in 1968. Hope flickered for a moment as the NGK stalled, tried to repair its image and to that end belatedly set up a commission to investigate the Christian Institute's commitments in the light of Scripture.[2] In reality, however, the commission was a closed affair; neither Naudé nor any other representative of the Institute was called to give evidence, synods were denied the opportunity to discuss the matter, and the commission sat on its findings until 1974.[3]

Certainly the NGK was embarrassed by its confrontation with the Christian Institute and the consequent deterioration in its relationships with Reformed Churches overseas. Nevertheless it remained firmly in step with the National Party and simply reasserted its defence of apartheid. When Prime Minister Verwoerd, the pre-eminent strategist of 'separate development', was assassinated in 1966, the Moderator of the Cape Synod of the NGK, the Rev. J.S. Gericke, delivered the funeral oration, relying on the Book of Samuel, chapter 10. Verwoerd had led his small nation as a man of God, with courage and selflessness, never separating word, deed, principle and practice. Yet in seeking friendship, in sending envoys with messages of goodwill to other nations, he received the coarsest insults: 'Against him too did the nations combine in an unholy alliance.'[4] When the Minister of Justice, John Vorster, the architect of South Africa's security system and the person directly responsible for the brutal repression of African protests, took over from Verwoerd, the intimate interdependences of church and state were symbolised by one family. John Balthazar Vorster had become Prime Minister and his brother, the Rev. J.D. Vorster, was to be Moderator of the NGK. The new Prime Minister received telegrams of congratulation from all the executive committees of the NGK General Synod and from the provincial synods. In turn John Vorster placed himself in the service of the DRC. Broadcasting to the white nation, he recommitted himself to the service of God, who 'controls the ways of nations and of human beings'. South Africa faced a hostile world, but it would survive and flourish as 'a small nation believing in the values of Christianity and civilisation'.[5]

Such attempts to legitimise the state, indeed to sacralise it, were followed by a lengthy NGK report entitled 'Human Relations in South Africa' — in essence an elaborate restatement of support for the 'separate development' theories of apartheid. The report, its readers were told, had been drawn up 'in the light of Scripture', and started out from the 'diversity and pluriformity' of creation 'even before the Fall'. What followed had little to do with the understanding of Christian fellowship articulated by the Christian Institute and the multi-racial churches, namely fellowship as the ongoing building of human community that transcended the barriers of race. Rather the report argued that the diversity of people 'had developed further after the Fall', and that this 'implies a distinction in development and cultural maturity' so that 'the concept of Christian trusteeship becomes relevant.' This involved 'the calling of a Christian people to instruct in true neighbourly love the underdeveloped peoples', leading them through 'material rehabilitation and spiritual growth . . . [to] full cultural development'. The Church was not concerned with 'the soul of man only' but also with 'need and sin on the socio-economic plane'. Yet, while it must 'proclaim the justice of the Kingdom of God', the Church would not commit itself to any particular 'socio-economic programme or social doctrine'. In reality the report did just that in recommitting the NGK to the apartheid of Verwoerd and Vorster — in theory, the separate development of ethnic nations. For the 'diversity of such national groupings [was] in agreement with the revealed will of God'.[6]

When it came to the actual policies required to maintain this separation of peoples — for example, migrant labour and racially-defined churches — the report did not waver in its apartheid logic. (This was rooted in the theological premises of the DRC and ultimately served the paramount interests of the white 'trustee' nation.) The system of migrant labour would have to continue 'for the development of South African industries and as a result of the need of the Bantu homelands and the neighbouring African states for a market for their surplus labour'. Within these parameters the government should do 'everything in its power' to limit the extent of migrant labour 'by establishing border industries, encouraging capital-intensive industries in white areas, taking more stringent measures to control and discourage the influx of Bantu into white areas, and controlling all possible disadvantages which migratory labour may have for the personal and family life of the Bantu'.[7]

Having recognised that separate economic development and the territorial separation of Africans was a pipe-dream, Verwoerd had adopted a policy of 'border area development'. This was a belated and hopelessly inadequate effort to check the ever-growing economic interdependence of the races by decentralising some white-owned industry to the periphery of the reserves or Bantustans. The South African Information Service, the voice of government propaganda, could not have improved on the above NGK rationalisation of this revised version of 'separate development'.

As regards the separate 'daughter-churches', the NGK report explained that they would be encouraged to move through indigenisation towards independence so as to serve 'their own people'. The NGK would continue to be concerned about 'spiritual community', but there would be no 'forced exercise of community over all church, ethnic and denominational boundaries'. There was 'no so-called Biblical imperative' for this, and such an approach 'definitively [could] not be supported by the NGK'.[8]

Faced with such adamant resistance from within Afrikanerdom, the Christian Institute had to look elsewhere for support as it tried once again to articulate an alternative message for the people of South Africa. It needed new forms of leverage. Not only had the DRC hierarchy anathematised the Institute and drained it of DRC clergy, but with very few exceptions Afrikaner academics had been brought to heel and the earlier restiveness of some white missionaries in the black 'daughter-churches' had subsided. To ask whether in accepting apartheid the Dutch Reformed Churches had ceased to do the will of God was now seen as a traitorous act, traitorous to church and state. In this situation the Institute came to emphasise its ecumenical commitments by working with, informing and encouraging the Christian Council.

While redoubling the Institute's ecumenical efforts, Naudé was personally at pains to draw on his own tradition, on Calvin's vision of improved co-operation between the churches. Calvin, he pointed out, had expressed the hope that 'learned, serious men from the most important churches' should gather together to seek a common Christian mind on the great issues of the day and reconcile the churches 'so rent apart'. 'I personally would not regard it as too much trouble', Calvin wrote to the Archbishop of Canterbury in 1552, 'if it were necessary for me to cross ten seas to achieve this aim'.[9] The Reformed

Ecumenical Synod meeking in Lunteren in 1968, Naudé argued, had called for a comparable spirit; but the DRC had not responded. Still languishing under their peculiar interpretation of Abraham Kuyper's nineteenth-century theology of 'sovereignty in circles' of divinely ordained and distinct sub-groups in society, the DRC had produced a distorted neo-Calvinism, a cultural theory of separateness which was being used to justify 'our traditional racial attitudes and policies of the past'. This, Naudé continued, had been compounded by the temptation 'to identify the Afrikaner *volk* with the people of Israel as the elect people of God — a very human but very dangerous mistake'.[10] An alternative view, one calling the churches to greater unity and to effective social ministry that might begin to heal South Africa's divisions, was 'A Message to the People of South Africa'. This statement was issued in June 1968 by the South African Council of Churches. In Naudé's view it was 'a document Biblically as sound and prophetically as valid as any Calvinist confession could hope to be'.[11]

The Christian Institute had been working with the South African Council of Churches (SACC) on a series of initiatives which led to the Message. Being a smaller organisation and one with individual rather than institutional church membership, the Institute was more flexible and its leadership more progressive in exploring the social implications of the Gospels. As a result, its staff became a source of critical analysis for the SACC and exercised a major influence in raising the level of political consciousness among the leadership of the multi-racial churches. Gradually the Institute was able to move the discussion from an emerging consensus on principles to church practice; eventually it was also able to shift the focus of praxis, for at least some Christians, from charity to public policy and justice as the pre-requisite for reconciliation. This meant facing up to the country's racist and class structures and starting out on a prolonged process of working for alternatives within both the churches and the wider society. It is therefore worth taking a moment to explore the genesis of the Message so as to understand the theological foundations for a shift in Christian thinking that was to take place over the next decade, raise the consciousness of a minority of black and white Christians and transform their understanding of political power and Christian mission.

In 1961, after Cottesloe and having appointed the Rev. Basil Brown as its first full-time General Secretary, the Christian Council gradually established itself as an ecumenical clearing-house.[12] It arranged conferences, continued to help the families of detainees and started a Division of Inter-Church Aid. This latter contributed to a number of modest projects ranging from drought relief and rural community development to youth centres, the Ecumenical Lay

Training Centre at Edendale, Natal, the Wilgespruit Fellowship Centre and the rebuilding of small township churches for communities relocated under the Group Areas Act. By the mid-1960s, when Bishop Bill Burnett took over as Secretary, the Council was also sponsoring an annual National Week of Compassion with an appeal for funds and the distribution of tens of thousands of prayer leaflets.[13] After reconstituting itself in 1968 as the South African Council of Churches with twenty-seven member churches and associated organisations, including the Christian Institute and the newly-formed University Christian Movement, the Council began planning an Industrial Mission and an Ecumenical Research Institute to clarify 'mission strategy'.[14] As we have seen, in seeking to build Christian fellowship across racial lines, the Council also tried, but failed, to provide non-racial residential facilities at Wilgespruit.[15]

Like its member-churches, and indeed like the Christian Institute, the Council remained a white initiative, unconsciously patronising in its approach to blacks, radiating goodwill but still hopeful of engineering social change through moral appeals, education and the conversion of white South Africans. Nevertheless these predilections co-existed with a certain unease — a growing realisation that an unavoidable and traumatic confrontation was developing between the multi-racial churches and the apartheid state. Eventually, as the decade of the 1970s unfolded, this confrontation was to transform both the Christian Institute and the Council by bringing them into close co-operation with black leaders as a resurgence of black confidence led to mass protests. However, for the moment, with the black population heavily repressed and white paternalism still dominant in the churches, the public attacks on apartheid came from white liberal churchmen.

The first major pronouncement of the mid-1960s resulted from joint initiatives taken by the Christian Institute and the Council. Naudé, as Director of the Institute, and Burnett, as General Secretary of the Council, were among the South African delegates at the WCC 'Conference on Church and Society' held in Geneva in 1966. On their return, the Institute and Council sponsored regional conferences in Durban, Port Elizabeth and Cape Town to discuss the Geneva resolutions and to prepare for a 'National Consultation on Church and Society' in Johannesburg in February 1968. In this process, prominent laymen joined the leaders of the Institute and Council as consultants in what became a first, halting attempt to outline an alternative to apartheid, a comprehensive Christian social ethic.

Two things were immediately apparent. Once social issues became the focus, the gap between conservative and radical viewpoints cut across denominational boundaries which had been very largely formed by traditions of worship and ministry. The result was that denominational boundaries increasingly became irrelevant in the search for justice. In addition, it was soon obvious that a great deal more home-work would have to be done on history and current political economy if Christians were to move from general principles and criticism to well-informed proposals and action.

In the absence of a sustained programme of education, lacking a sensitive understanding of black viewpoints and without the creative goading of a confrontative black caucus, it was not surprising that the National Consultation remained white-oriented in its resolutions. The 'primary purpose' was still 'to create a deeper level of compassion in our society'. While this was an important goal at the level of abstract principle, it represented a naive view that showed more understanding of the virtue of charity than of the dialectical tensions associated with the pursuit of justice. Nevertheless the Consultation was emphatic enough when rejecting 'any idolatory of the nation and any loyalty that demands domination over other peoples or destroys the realised and potential unity of mankind'.[16] It noticed, as Naudé had done in the early 1960s, that the whole mission of the church in South Africa would be jeopardised 'by its tolerance of unjust laws and other features of the policy of separate development that increase racial discrimination'. In the past, it pointed out, church leaders who confronted the state received very little backing from the general run of church members — it meant white church members.

In reality, however, the Consultation was the voice of a past era when it went on to deny that apartheid was a threat to world peace and to argue that Christians could best participate in South African politics by using the 'presently existing structures'. Africans abhorred the structures of apartheid; yet without addressing this issue, without referring to the banning of the ANC and Pan Africanist Congress or explicitly recognising the heavily repressed state of black politics, the Consultation listed the structures that were to be changed from within: *inter alia*, political parties, parliament, municipal councils, the Chamber of Mines, ratepayers' associations and trade unions. Such reform would 'involve white persons in greater responsibility'. White Christians 'should also consider denying themselves, even if only for specific periods, all forms of entertainment and cultural activity so as to gain a more personal understanding of the many restrictions endured by many of their fellow-South Africans'.[17]

All this was well-meaning enough, but from any black perspective in 1968 it was hopelessly out of date. For half a century the ANC had tried every type of moral suasion before it was banned in 1960; consequently the white-centred views of the Consultation were seen by many black leaders as insulting. Within the next few years, blacks were to renew their own political drive for justice and simultaneously black

Christians began to confront the paternalistic white church hierarchies. A new generation of black students, theologians and churchmen were coming to see their problems as black subservience, white privilege, racism, the state's destruction of the rule of law, the class exploitation of capitalism and the build-up of apartheid's military and police power. The National Consultation on Church and Society spoke from the other side of the racial and class divide, as the voice of a troubled conscience among the comfortable, rich and powerful. From this viewpoint South Africa's 'gravest problem' was the 'apparent bankruptcy of compassion towards the under-privileged'.[18]

Within the next decade, the churches were to be challenged more directly to take a preferential option for the poor, challenged by a resurgent protest movement which gathered strength among the under-privileged themselves. Asserting their inherent dignity as persons, increasing numbers of the poor and oppressed set about their own liberation and so, in the course of the 1970s, created an historical situation which forced some church leaders to revise their understanding of mission. The church had to find new ways of being church. It was to the credit of the Christian Institute that its staff and members had the humility as well as the courage to open themselves up to these new influences and to listen more intently to the voices of black South Africans. Consequently the Institute was able to help in the articulation of a new hope and to a remarkable extent was able to co-operate with the new black leadership which emerged in politics and in the churches. Slowly purging itself of the tendency to patronise blacks, the Institute once again emerged at the cutting edge of a new socially aware and radical Christian consciousness that spread most rapidly in the black communities. After starting out with a special ministry towards the white Dutch Reformed Churches, the Institute painfully but consistently developed a greater empathy with the poor, exploited and oppressed, coming to see black pressures for church reform and the new currents within black politics as the basis for hope. While its new commitments heightened tensions within the multi-racial churches, the Institute's role remained seminal, its insights spreading to become part of a new understanding of mission which helped to release energies among blacks, including those within the black Dutch Reformed Churches.

However, for the moment, matters were still very much in white hands. A committee of eighteen coalesced as a result of the National Consultation on Church and Society. Working with the Theological Commission of the SACC, they set out to provide the first systematically formulated Biblical and theological statement on apartheid since Cottesloe and the Roman Catholic pastorals. There were three key writers: the Rev. John Davies (Anglican), Dr Ben Englebrecht (NGK) and the Rev. Calvin Cook (Methodist). Each was closely involved with the Christian Institute, Englebrecht as editor of *Pro Veritate*, Cook as Chairman of the Institute's Board of Management, Davies as an active member. All eighteen persons on the drafting committee agreed that 'in the eyes of its protagonists, apartheid had become a vehicle for grace among men'.[19] This had to be countered, and the result was 'A Message to the People of South Africa' in June 1968. Coming out just four months after the National Consultation on Church and Society, the Message was a stronger, clearer statement in fewer words. As the SACC presented the document, it was to be 'the basis for study and action'; the churches would have to undertake a major programme 'to work out the practical implications of this statement of faith'.[20] The outcome was to be the Study Project on Race in Apartheid Society (SPROCAS) — a further joint Christian Institute/SACC initiative which was launched in 1969 with the Institute's staff playing a central role.

The Message started from an ontological base in total contradiction to apartheid: the Gospel's 'good news that in Christ God had broken down the walls of division between God and man, and therefore also between man and man'. Christ was 'the truth who sets men free' from the pursuit of false securities. The crucifixion had been followed by the resurrection and the Gospel's message that it is God's 'purpose that shapes history', giving rise to 'the expectation of a new heaven and a new earth — the Kingdom of God'. In working for justice, Christians were being called to work for the coming of this Kingdom which was already incipient in history; they were called to work for 'the salvation of the world and of human existence in its entirety'.[21]

Becoming more specific, the Message argued that Christians were called to witness in their particular historical circumstances. In South Africa this meant amid the doctrine and policies of racial separation which were 'truly hostile to Christianity' — a 'false offer of salvation' being made in the name of Christianity, a 'false faith' offering peace and happiness through 'the preservation of racial identity'. The task of the church was to assist people to discriminate between what was being demanded of them by the state and what was demanded of them 'as disciples of Christ'. The first Christians, Jews and Gentiles 'discovered that God was creating a new community in which differences of race, nation, culture, language and tradition no longer had power to separate man from man.' The pursuit of racial identity denied the Gospel; it was in opposition to 'the Christian understanding of the nature of man and community', and in practice put an arbitrary limit on 'a person's ability to love one's neighbour as oneself'.[22]

The policy of separate development, the Message continued, was 'based on the domination of one group over all others'; it required 'the maintenance of white supremacy, thus it [was] rooted in and dependent on a policy of sin'. In fact the white 'South African way of life' had taken the place of Christ and 'become an idol'. The task of Christians was to witness to an alternative society so that people might 'see in the Church an inclusive fellowship' — an 'expression of God's reconciliation here and now'. As a result, every Christian in South Africa had to face the question: 'to whom, or to what are you truly giving your first loyalty, your primary commitment? Is it to a subsection of mankind, an ethnic group, a human tradition, a political idea, or to Christ?'[23]

There were mixed reactions to the Message. To some, even one or two who helped draft it, it was a flop, a damp squib.[24] It is true that as an essentially white initiative, an attempt to raise white consciousness, it put the issues clearly enough but had little effect on white society. On the other hand, 600 clergy signed the Message and with the exception of the Baptist Union it was endorsed by the member-churches of the SACC — even if some were less enthusiastic than others.[25] It must also be remembered that the Message led on to SPROCAS, a determined if still white-orchestrated effort to describe the South African situation in depth, analyse it and offer alternative policies to apartheid.

Clearly the Message reflected a cast of mind which stopped short of understanding the Gospel as a call for the under-privileged and poor to take their futures into their own hands. Certainly the full, and to whites startling, consequences of the theology being articulated had yet to be fully explored. Nevertheless the Message did delineate the social challenge to Christians at the basic level of Gospel insights, so disseminating more widely what had been the Christian Institute's position. In Naudé's terms it 'clearly and unequivocally refuted apartheid [from] a biblical standpoint'.[26] Whether it was a white initiative or not, the Message pointed in the direction of political and liberation theology, furthered the evolution of theology in South Africa and helped to raise political consciousness among a small minority of whites and many blacks who later were able to develop its insights much further during the turmoil of the 1970s. In pointing to the need for an analysis of the structural foundations of injustice, the Message helped to prepare the way for black theology which in turn contributed to the growth of the black consciousness movement. In other words, the liberating, open-ended nature of this clear statement was not to be circumscribed by an initially vague grasp of its full implications.

Quite understandably, Prime Minister Vorster was not pleased with the Message. Christian ministers, he warned, should 'preach the Gospel of Christ' and not turn their 'pulpits into political platforms', so doing the 'work of the Progressive Party, the United Party and the Liberal Party'.[27] The SACC responded by endorsing a resolution passed at Lunteren by the Reformed Ecumenical Synod, to which Vorster's NGK belonged, which encouraged 'the Church [to] speak courageously — and, where necessary, in criticism of the activities and policies of governments'.[28] This was followed by a statement issued by the Anglican Dean of Johannesburg, the Rev. Gonville ffrench-Beytagh, and an ecumenical group of Cape clergy which included the Rev. Theo Kotze, who was shortly to move from his Methodist parish at Sea Point to establish the Christian Institute's Cape Regional Office. They 'deplored the Prime Minister's attack' as it failed to recognise that Christ and his Gospel made disturbing claims on the political community. They also reminded Vorster that he never criticised his own DRC which frequently supported apartheid from the pulpit. In fact the Message needed to be reaffirmed as 'a warning and a protest'.[29]

Vorster bounced back with an attack on clergy whom he accused of trying to do what Martin Luther King had done in America: 'I want to say to them, cut it out, cut it out immediately, because the cloth you are wearing will not protect you if you try to do this in South Africa.'[30] This time twelve white churchmen responded with a lengthy open letter to the Prime Minister, the signatories including Bishop Burnett, General Secretary of the SACC, Beyers Naudé, Ben Engelbrecht, Albert Geyser and John Davies, all of the Christian Institute, and Archbishop Selby Taylor who had succeeded Joost de Blank in Cape Town. Addressing Vorster with 'great respect due to your high office', they agreed that it was not the churches' role to pursue party politics; yet 'the Church must bear its witness to the nature of the world and human life . . . [and] test the actions of the Government according to the criteria of God's Word.' When this was done, they continued, apartheid was seen to be 'in opposition to the obvious testimony of the Scriptures'; it 'fundamentally [denied] the divine act of salvation which was performed on Golgotha'. In these circumstances 'the highest service the Church' could offer was to urge the government 'in God's name to become converted from its ideology of apartheid'. If the Prime Minister was alarmed by the prospect of 'authoritarian Communism with its deceptive doctrine of salvation', then the 'Word of God' should be trusted, not apartheid. Moreover, should the state react with intimidation, it would not succeed, for the 'messengers of Christ' had been persecuted thoughout history and would not be silenced.[31]

In addition to working with the South African Council of Churches on the Message, the Christian Institute had taken several other initiatives, the most important of which was to establish close ties with some of the African independent churches. The separatist church movement comprised approximately 2,000 denominations of which 90 per cent were miniscule splinter groups; but taken as a whole these independent churches made up the largest and most rapidly expanding section of African Christians. This was causing considerable unease within the multi-racial or 'mission churches', where simply to anathematise this fissiparous movement was now seen by many to be both arrogant and simple-minded escapism. To fulminate against 'syncristic nativism' was obviously ineffective — 2.2 million Christians already belonged to independent churches by 1960, half of them in the industrial heartland of the Transvaal. Expressed as a proportion of the country's total African population, independent church membership had risen dramatically from 9.6 per cent in 1946 to 20.1 per cent in 1960. No such dramatic change occurred with the multi-racial churches. The Methodists declined marginally to 12 per cent; Anglicans and Roman Catholics (the latter increasing marginally) stood at approximately 7 per cent each; Lutherans and the black Dutch Reformed Churches (the latter increasing marginally) stood at 5 per cent each, Presbyterians and Congregationalists at 2 per cent each and Baptists at 1 per cent.[32] Given such statistics as well as the history of disunity and at times bitter competition between these 'mission churches', they were in no position to be too judgemental. The Cottesloe Consultation, in calling for ecumenical co-operation, therefore asked that 'attention be urgently given to a constructive Christian approach to the Separatist Sects'[33] — a sign of goodwill, yet one expressed in terminology which suggested that a good deal more humility would have to be shown by white churchmen before easy relationships could be established with African-controlled organisations.

Since the breakaway of the first separatist group in 1884 — Nehemiah Tile's Tembu Church which split off from the Wesleyans[34] — white churchmen, government commissions and academics have referred to a wide range of factors in trying to explain the formation of Ethiopian and Zionist churches.[35] Ethiopian congregations, it was argued, generally seceded as a result of racial tensions but usually retained much of the doctrine and liturgy of their parent churches. Some of the larger churches such as the Independent Presbyterian Church, the African Methodist Episcopal Church and Lutheran Bapedi Church struggled to sustain their own poorly-staffed training programmes and maintained religious practices which were well within the mainstream of Christianity. On the other hand, Zionist groups tended to be smaller and the followers of prophets who relied on their own charismatic appeal. These women and men emphasised the workings of the Holy Spirit and the gift of healing; they often adopted idiosyncratic liturgies and usually preached more syncretic doctrines than their Ethiopian counterparts. In addition to the argument that all splinter groups were in part reactions to white power and racial discrimination, it was suggested that tribalism, personal animus, desire for financial gain and ambition lay behind the breakaways. Commentators also saw the growth of the independent churches as a search for community as migrant labour and an industrial revolution undermined traditional orders and produced social distress. Viewed in this wider socio-economic context, autocratic white-dominated churches could be seen as exacerbating the decline in traditional values and practices when they simply transplanted foreign ecclesial structures and liturgies. As a result, it was argued, Africans often established independent churches in an attempt to be themselves, to live as Christians within their African heritage and to free themselves as far as possible from the unnecessary encumbrances of Western culture.

If these were some of the causes of fragmentation, the independent church leaders were often eccentric, their church organisations tended to become personal fiefs as ministers struggled to survive in a harsh economic environment, and the educational level of pastors and prophets remained extremely low. It was exceptional for a minister to have attended a year or two of high school; the great majority had only progressed to standards III or IV and some were illiterate. Many churches only had the vaguest sense of Scripture; all were theologically isolated, and not far below the surface there was often a deep bitterness towards the white-dominated 'mission churches'. To many in the independent churches, black ministers belonging to the multi-racial churches were simply 'the white missionaries' servants'. The 'white man's church [was] the black man's grave' as white Christians had 'failed to be the "light" which Christ says his disciples are'; they had 'failed to identify themselves with the African people and to share their problems, needs and frustrations'.[36] In any event, the independent church movement with its many, varied and unco-ordinated parts continued to drift apart from the multi-racial churches. As a result there was a twofold ecumenical challenge: to improve relations between independent churches and to establish contacts between them and the multi-racial churches.

When the Christian Institute was approached in 1964 by several independent church leaders with a request for help in improving the educational level of their ministers, this unexpected development was recognised by Beyers Naudé and his staff to be a major if problematic opportunity to begin a process which might gradually overcome past misunderstandings and bitterness. However, it was a delicate situation and any interaction with the independent churches required a great deal of sensitivity. Indeed the willingness of independent church leaders even to contemplate a relationship with the Christian Institute was probably due to it not being a church, not being a part of that painful history of white domination, but an ecumenical fellowship of individual Christians that would not threaten their independence. Should it agree to assist, the Institute realised that it would have to advise and act as a conduit for resources, but all the while exercising a rigorous self-restraint if it was to be reconciled with and serve this expanding section of the church.[37]

The result was an exploratory conference in January 1965 when a number of independent church ministers met on the Witwatersrand at Daveytown African Township, Benoni. Resolutions were passed asking the Christian Institute to help in establishing a theological training programme and offering to co-operate with the white-led churches in an effort to 'cut through all colour barriers'. A warning was also sounded that in any such effort the 'bigger churches should not regard us as inferior creatures in the vineyard of the Lord'.[38] Naudé and his colleagues, in particular the Rev. Danie van Zyl and the Rev. James Moulder, were to encounter much tension in their dealings with the independent churches; but at the level of principle they needed no such warning. In their view the independent churches arose 'as an unconscious protest against the spirit of racial superiority and paternalism of Western Christianity', while the conference revealed a 'maganimous attitude and [was a] sincere expression of Christian forgiveness'.[39]

A second conference in Queenstown followed in June 1965 at which an African Independent Churches' Association (AICA) was formed. Eighty churches paid their affiliation fees and another 150 were said to be showing a serious interest in this ecumenical effort. A co-ordinating committee to assist with a training programme was then formed with representatives from the Christian Institute, SACC, AICA and three other African organisations. The Interdenominational African Ministers' Association had been revived in the early 1960s to encourage the fellowship of African ministers in the multi-racial as well as independent churches. It was represented on the co-ordinating committee as was a rather fragile Apostolic and Zionist Assembly of South Africa, an organisation which developed alongside AICA as the latter was composed almost entirely of churches in the Ethiopian tradition. Lastly, the African Methodist Episcopal Church's Bishop Wright School of Religion at Evaton near Vereeniging was represented in the hope that, as a small independent seminary, it might be expanded so as to open its doors to members of any independent church. Such an initiative, it was argued, if allied to a correspondence course and AICA-sponsored literacy and refresher courses, would begin to transform the scriptural and theological training of independent church ministers throughout the country. Working with SACC and the co-ordinating committee, the Christian Institute undertook the responsibility of fund-raising, and successful approaches were made to overseas churches including the Reformed Churches of the Netherlands as well as the Bible Society and Theological Education Fund.[40]

In the event, a cautious start was made with the Rev. Danie van Zyl as the Christian Institute's adviser to AICA. A scholarship fund permitted ten individuals from independent churches to join the Bishop Wright School in 1967. Several Bible-study correspondence courses were already in existence and it was agreed that AICA should recommend the All Africa School of Theology at Witbank to its members — a course supported by the United Bible Society. Two refresher courses were held in 1966 under AICA auspices, the first on the theme 'The Life of our Lord Jesus Christ' being held in Soweto over eight days with forty-seven ministers enrolled. The second course drew seventy-five ministers to Durban and focused on 'The Church of our Lord Jesus Christ'.[41]

It was soon apparent that ministers' wives wished to have comparable assistance. Most of them were elderly, usually grandmothers who came from dire poverty and lacked any schooling. As a result the Christian Institute was asked to help at three levels. The women wanted literacy and basic Scriptural training as they were spiritual leaders in their own right and regularly undertook pastoral responsibilities; they also felt the need to improve their domestic skills through family budgeting, dietetics and hygiene. The outcome was that Naudé and van Zyl sponsored a gathering in 1967 at which the Women's Association of African Independent Churches (WAAIC) was formed. This was a sister-organisation to AICA but one with a mind of its own and a separate board of management.[42] In the following years van Zyl continued to advise AICA, Els te Siepe was invited to advise WAAIC, and several women's groups in the Netherlands 'adopted' WAAIC groups in South Africa. In the judgement of Els te Siepe, the women of the independent churches had 'given notice that they [were] no longer prepared to live in poverty and ignorance'.[43]

While these initial steps had been cautious, expectations in the Christian Institute ran high for the longer run. The potential for an independent church seminary, whether it be the Bishop Wright School or some new initiative, was 'so great' that it could 'within a few years become the largest in South Africa'. Moreover, offering the leaders of 2 million people a better understanding of the Gospels 'could become the most important contribution to missiological development in South Africa in the 20th century'.[44]

In practice these hopes were not to be realised. An important ecumenical initiative had been taken; a serious and ongoing dialogue was established and some new co-ordination occurred within the amorphous independent church movement. But in the years that followed, the Christian Institute found it increasingly difficult to maintain its close organisational ties with churches which remained hyper-sensitive to white involvement and particularly to any surveillance of funds. To complicate matters further, the leadership of the independent churches within AICA was riven by bitter inter-church rivalries, personality clashes and power plays which were triggered in part by the potential access to a new source of funds. A foretaste of these difficulties had occurred almost immediately after the formation of AICA when the Rev. Z.J. Malukazi, who assisted the Institute in making initial contacts, was not asked by the AICA board of management to become its full-time organiser. A good deal of personal animosity accompanied this decision and Malukazi broke away to form a rival group which he called 'The African Independent Churches Ecumenical Movement'.

Malukazi's venture soon disintegrated but the experience was an indication of what lay ahead. Given their own theological competence and administrative responsibilities for the use of funds, the Christian Institute's staff were always in an uncomfortable position when relating to the haphazard accounting procedures of AICA and the almost total lack of systematic theological training among its leadership. These and the other tensions already referred to led in the early 1970s to the Institute pulling back from its formal involvement with AICA, although it continued to work patiently for ecumenical understanding and to give *ad hoc* help. By 1974, however, AICA had virtually collapsed.[45]

With all these limitations, the initiative with the independent churches was nevertheless an important learning experience in the overall evolution of the Christian Institute. It pointed to the need to respect African initiatives, to work with African leaders, to help but to be prepared to do so to the point of white powerlessness. AICA's inter-action with the Institute was an invaluable process of consciousness-raising for a small group of whites who were slowly forced to recognise that the future of Christianity in South Africa depended more on the commitments of black Christians than on the white church establishments with their periodic, but largely futile, moral appeals to end racial discrimination. Simultaneously a realisation began very slowly to develop among the Institute's leadership that it would take black pressures and black leadership within the multi-racial churches and the DRC to purge these church structures of their racism, just as it would take the growing power of black political movements to end apartheid in the wider society. The Institute had in fact started a process of interaction with black organisations which was eventually to turn its world upside down and was to lead in the next decade of 'black consciousness' to a radical reassessment of Christian mission. For the moment however, the 'Message to the People of South Africa' laid a theological basis for these future commitments, and AICA drew the Institute more deeply into the black community.

NOTES

1. *Cape Times*, 5 November 1966; *Pro Veritate*, December 1966, p. 2.
2. *The Star* (Johannesburg), 27 October 1970; *Sunday Times* (Johannesburg), 25 October 1970.
3. *Infra*, p. 185.
4. *DRC Newsletter*, October 1966, pp. 3–4.
5. *Ibid.*, p. 2.
6. *DRC Newsletter*, November/December 1969, pp. 1–4, being a reprint of the 1966 report 'Human Relations in South Africa'.
7. *Ibid.*, p. 4.
8. *DRC Newsletter*, January/February 1970, pp. 2–3, being a continuation of 'Human Relations in South Africa'.
9. C.F. Beyers Naudé, 'What Calvin Really Stood For', *Sunday Times*, 2 May 1969.
10. *Ibid.* For a discussion of Kuyper's influence see, Moodie, *The Rise of Afrikanerdom*.
11. C.F. Beyers Naudé, 'What Calvin Really Stood For', *Sunday Times*, 2 May 1969.
12. The Roman Catholic Church did not join the Council and at this early stage there were no black independent church members. The Council therefore comprised the multi-racial Protestant and Anglican churches.
13. *Christian Council Quarterly*, 1965–8 editions.
14. These projects were made redundant by SPROCAS. *Infra.*, p. 102ff.
15. *Infra.*, p. 47.
16. *Christian Council Quarterly*, 86, First Quarter, 1968, p. 3.
17. *Ibid.*, pp. 3–4.
18. *Christian Council Quarterly*, 87, Second Quarter, 1968, p. 12.
19. Author's interview with the Rev. John Davies, London, 2 December 1972.
20. South African Council of Churches, *A Message to the People of South Africa* (Johannesburg, 1968), p. 7.
21. *Ibid.*, pp. 1–2.
22. *Ibid.*, pp. 2–3.
23. *Ibid.*, pp. 5–6.
24. Author's interviews with the Rev. P. Hinchliff, Oxford, 1 Dec. 1972; the Rev. R. van der Hart, O.P., Oxford, 2 Dec. 1972.
25. de Gruchy, *The Church Struggle in South Africa*, p. 120.
26. C.F. Beyers Naudé, 'Apartheid is in Stryd met God', *Ster*, 13 November 1970.
27. Carstens, *Church and Race in South Africa*, p. 39.
28. *Ibid.*
29. *Cape Times*, 25 September 1968.
30. *Die Vaderland*, 28 September 1968; Carstens, *op. cit.*, p. 39.
31. *Cape Times*, 28 October 1968.

32. J.E. Moulder, 'Background Information on the African Independent Churches with Special Reference to the Need for Theological Training' (Johannesburg, January 1965), pp. 5-6, Christian Institute typescript; D. van Zyl, 'Spies Out in the Cold: the Challenge of the African Independent Church Movement', *Pro Veritate*, May 1968, pp. 4-5.

33. *Cottesloe Consultation*, p. 72.

34. M. Wilson and L. Thompson (eds.), *The Oxford History of South Africa* (Oxford, 1971), vol. II, p. 82.

35. The distinction between Ethiopian and Zionist types was suggested by B.G.M. Sundkler in *Bantu Prophets in South Africa* (London 1961). See too *Report of the Native Churches Commission* (Pretoria, pp. 39-25); R.H.W. Shepherd, 'The Separatist Churches of South Africa', *South African Outlook*, March 1938.

36. Z.J. Malukazi, 'A Report on the African Independent Churches' (Cape Town, 1965) pp. 1-2, Christian Institute typescript.

37. J.E. Moulder, 'Memorandum on the Request of the African Independent Churches to the Christian Institute of South Africa to Assist them with obtaining Theological Training' (Johannesburg, 1965), p. 2, Christian Institute typescript.

38. 'The Independent African Churches Leaders' Conference, 17th-21st January, 1965', being a typescript page of resolutions.

39. Editorial: 'The Extended Hand', *Pro Veritate*, July 1965, p. 5.

40. D. van Zyl, 'Bantu Prophets or Christ's Evangels', *Pro Veritate*, October 1966, pp. 10-13; J.E. Moulder, 'Memorandum on the Request of the African Independent Churches', pp. 8-9.

41. D. van Zyl, 'Bantu Prophets', *Pro Veritate*, October 1966, p. 10.

42. *Pro Veritate*, October 1966, p. 11; February 1970, p. 13.

43. Els te Siepe, 'African Independent Church Women hit their Stride', *Pro Veritate*, February 1970, p. 13.

44. D. van Zyl, 'Bantu Prophets or Christ's Evangels', *Pro Veritate*, October 1966, p. 12. By 1972 AICA's membership had risen to over 400 churches.

45. For a detailed account of 'The Rise and Fall of AICA' see M. West, *Bishops and Prophets in a Black City* (Cape Town, 1975), Chapter 8, pp. 142-70.

6

A CAPACITY TO SURVIVE AND THE BEGINNING OF A NEW UNDERSTANDING OF MISSION

Having failed to free the Dutch Reformed Churches from their stultifying ties of mutual dependence with the *Broederbond* and the Afrikaner National Party, the Christian Institute had nevertheless maintained its prophetic stance against apartheid and turned its attention to the multi-racial churches. There it encountered a good deal of passivity and resilient patterns of internal racial discrimination. As the last chapter pointed out, this shift in focus culminated in 'A Message to the People of South Africa', a clear if for the moment largely ineffective call to Biblical values and to peace through justice. The South African Council of Churches, working with the Institute, could deliver the 'Message', but the churches themselves remained largely unmoved. As one contemporary observer put it, the Council was really 'a nervous system that had been dissected out of its body. It twitches to all manner of external and internal stimuli, but seldom moves the body into action.'[1] After these frustrated attempts to witness in the area of human life and community, had come the unexpected opportunity to work for reconciliation with the African independent churches. If this too turned out to be problematic, the Institute had at least been prepared to confront Afrikanerdom and challenge the churches, to innovate and to serve, even if in trying to live up to Gospel values it encountered hostility as well as indifference and ran the risk of failure.

Undergirding these efforts was the Institute's ecumenical organisation, an ongoing attempt to express within its own fellowship 'the unity of the Gospel of all Christians of all churches and colours'.[2] Most aspects of the Institute's life reflected the wide range of its membership, which drew individuals from the denominations represented at the SACC but also from Roman Catholicism and the African independent churches. Nonetheless, it was still an essentially white organisation with a formal membership fluctuating in the vicinity of 1,500–2,000 of whom approximately 10–15 per cent were black.[3] In the mid-1960s the twenty-member Board of Management was overwhelmingly white, and all full-time executive staff were still white. While the Institute's office-bearers and staff were busy cultivating a widening range of black contacts, its Bible study and fellowship discussion groups again were predominately white. Indeed these groups were frustrated by their inability to overcome black reservations about yet another white 'liberal' initiative; they also faced the systemic roadblocks to non-racial community which apartheid set up with its separate residential areas and pass system. As Dr Calvin Cook, Chairman of the Institute's Board of Management, put it: 'In spite of our belief that we whites were ready to learn and needed to know, we have not found an unending stream of black or Coloured teachers.'[4] The Institute looked forward to inter-racial rapprochement within its own ranks and those of the multi-racial churches, but unexpectedly most new contacts with blacks had been through the independent churches.

If the Institute had few successes and experienced frustration at several levels, *Pro Veritate* continued to function as a lively mouthpiece. It is true that its articles appeared in English or Afrikaans and not in Zulu, Xhosa or Sesotho; but the journal attracted some African contributors and under Naudé's editorship and then that of Ben Engelbrecht it provided consistently high-quality theological and polit-ical analysis. Its editorial committee of eight was thoroughly ecu-menical, it had three black members, and circulation increased rapidly overseas if more slowly at home. The editors were concerned to draw the South African churches into international debates — both Protestant and Roman Catholic — and the journal set out to expose readers to a wide range of denominational viewpoints and to different church traditions. But most important of all, *Pro Veritate* encouraged indigeneous theological reflection on the South African predicament and nurtured a social gospel to counter apartheid. By the late 1960s it was also beginning more systematically to explore the ethics of non-violent and violent resistance to injustice. A typical example of the journal's range and vigour was the June 1968 edition with an editorial on the World Council of Churches gathering at Uppsala (Sweden), a Roman Catholic priest writing on Vatican II, a tribute to Martin Luther King and an article on the Reformation as a mixed blessing — a rediscovery of the freedom of the children of God with an aftermath of disunity.

Thwarted in several of its early endeavours, yet looking for new opportunities, by 1968 the Institute was on the brink of two initiatives which were to be made possible in large measure by the growing finan-cial support it received from overseas. *Pro Veritate* had been subsidised by overseas grants, as was the training programme for AICA. In fact, a sharply increasing proportion of the Institute's budget was beginning to come from Protestant churches and individual supporters in America and Europe, particularly from the Reformed Churches of the Netherlands.[5] Such assistance, plus funds raised by the SACC, was to finance SPROCAS in 1969 as a follow-up to the 'Message'.[6] Overseas support also allowed the Institute to open its first regional office with Rev. Theo Kotze as Director in Cape Town.

Although Theo Kotze, a Methodist minister, joined the Institute a few months after its formation, it was several years before he met Beyers Naudé.[7] Once this happened, bonds of mutual respect and friendship were quickly established. The result was that in 1968 Naudé invited Kotze to leave his flourishing Sea Point parish in Cape Town, risk his future and establish the proposed Cape regional office. It was an important decision, for Naudé had chosen a large-hearted colleague who was to play a major role in the Institute's future. A free spirit, an innovative, humorous and at times pugnacious character who was passionately committed to ecumenical co-operation, Kotze's theological and political understanding was to evolve rapidly as Africans regained their political initiative during the 1970s. It was during this decade that black personalities came to exercise a profound influence within the Institute and helped to radicalise its white leaders including Kotze.

Like Naudé, Kotze came of Afrikaner stock. His father, a lawyer, had been gaoled for supporting the Afrikaner rebellion of 1914; but unlike other members of his family, Kotze senior had not been a devout member of the DRC and he remained critical of the aggrandising elements within Afrikanerdom. As his father would have nothing to do with organised religion, the young Theo was spared the burdens of churchgoing and Sunday School. Thoroughly conditioned by the racism of white society, he attended the University of the Witwatersrand as a student of architecture and then dropped out to take up a position as paymaster at Simmer and Jack, one of the Rand goldmines. A future of some mediocrity seemed assured as an administrator within a corporate structure that had no compunction about treating its African workers as mere labour units, there to serve white interests, to be harassed by police surveillance and to be packed off back to the reserves at the first sign of cantankerous behaviour.

All this was completely upset when in his early twenties Theo Kotze came under the beguiling influence of Helen Clegg, a Methodist choirgirl, the daughter of an English Methodist minister with a considerable reputation as a preacher. Perhaps it was a combination of the preacher and agape plus Helen and eros, for Kotze was converted to Christianity and through his future in-laws began to meet articulate black Methodists. One minister in particular had a major impact on the young man, the Rev. Seth Mokitini who in 1964 was to be the first African President of the Methodist Conference. By 1948 Kotze had entered a seminary and he was ordained in 1953. He then took up parish responsibilities amid the estates of the English-speaking sugar barons of the Natal Coast. There he developed some understanding of economic exploitation, of white greed and black poverty; he also maintained his friendships with black pastors and was sufficiently sensitised to the injustices of apartheid to experience the Sharpville shooting in 1960 as a major turning point in his life. From that time onwards Kotze's analysis focused with increasing clarity on the social implications of the Gospel, on the Christian call to a more egalitarian future and hence the need to scrap the whole edifice of apartheid.

After leaving Natal and accepting a new parish assignment at Sea Point, Kotze joined the Christian Institute in 1963. In the next few years he enjoyed a growing reputation as a pastor, expanding his congregation to the point where the local Adelphi Cinema had to be rented for major services of 1,000 to 2,000 people. A remarkably successful youth recreation and counselling centre was started, the parish published a high-quality newsheet, and in 1967 Kotze was awarded a Christian Fellowship Trust Scholarship to visit Britain and Europe where he made a range of important contacts.

But most important of all, in 1966 Kotze was appointed Methodist chaplain to the top-security prison on Robben Island where he conducted the liturgy for political prisoners — their favourite hymn was 'Fight the Good Fight'. There he was impressed by Nelson Mandela and formed a deep and lasting friendship with a fellow Methodist, Robert Sobukwe. Although his permit to function as chaplain was withdrawn after one year (according to the prison authorities he was 'not a suitable person to be a prison chaplain' as he did 'not know how to behave to prisoners'), Kotze's empathy with the black struggle for justice had been sharply increased through meeting individuals he came to see as 'great men of South African history.' In fact, one could say in retrospect that Kotze's life was transformed by his black Methodist colleagues, by black staff members who were to be recruited by the Christian Institute in the 1970s and by persons of the calibre of Mandela, Sobukwe and later Steve Biko. It was a process which resembled the transformation which the Christian Institute itself was to experience as it encountered the reality of the black consciousness movement of the 1970s.

A foretaste of what was to follow Kotze's appointment as Regional Director came in a widely-reported sermon he gave to the Sea Point congregation on Good Friday 1968, several months before he was asked by Naudé to accept the new position. Many whites in the congregation were disturbed; the sermon resulted in intimidatory visits by the security police, and the NGK journal *Kerkbode* described it as a blatant political use of the pulpit. In Kotze's mind there was 'no exclusive spiritual — or secular — area of life'; Christian values were meant to permeate the community, informing both private and public life. Had Jesus stuck to 'spiritual things' there would have been no crucifixion. Christians, like Jesus, had to 'challenge any authority, at whatever cost, that continues to deny the very basis of human existence. . . . the commandments — love God and love your neighbour.' In South Africa this meant 'Christians must fight with all their might and with the power of love (which is the hard way) the sheer wickedness of segregation, the blatant anti-Christian attitudes of intolerance and racial prejudice, the utter disregard of the ordinary human decencies.' Unfortunately fear was gripping the country, 'keeping the church silent and emasculating the Christian witness'; but it was Good Friday and an appropriate moment to realise that Christians must risk crucifixion by rejecting apartheid.[8]

Thus, by the end of 1968 the Institute was showing some signs of new life. AICA had difficulties but was functioning, SPROCAS was in the planning stage and the Cape Town office was being staffed. These were badly-needed indications of a potential capacity to adapt and survive, for the overall state of the Institute was still not encouraging. Far from riding the crest of a wave, Naudé and his colleagues were struggling to overcome several failures and a sense of anti-climax. As we have seen, the Institute had been extruded by the DRC; Africans continued to show the same reservations about the Institute which they showed to any white-dominated organisation; and there were no indications of a steadily expanding white membership. Yet the prophetic voice of the Institute was badly needed, for most denominations were still quiescent and where there was activity some of it was scandalous, as the following examples indicate.

Two cases of white intransigence illustrate the tensions which were reappearing within the Church of the Province of South Africa whose bishops and synods had on occasion spoken forcefully against apartheid. The children of a Coloured communicant, Mr J.S. Thomas, applied to three white Anglican schools in Cape Town. In each case they were turned away. This had been done, the Governors of St George's Grammar School explained, because

'the majority of members of council are of the opinion that, having regard to their responsibility as trustees for those supporting the School financially, and while having every sympathy for the application now before the Council, the custom and practice of the community, together with the trend of legislation, makes the immediate admission of these boys unacceptable and it is premature to try an experiment of this nature.[9]

Die Burger was much amused. Could not the Anglican Church recognise the difference between 'the holiness of its words, the sharpness of its admonitions to others and its deeds?' Support for apartheid, the paper asserted, was increasing among Anglican congregations where 'the conviction [was] growing that it is better to accept and apply separate development than to condemn separate development and apply it.'[10]

The strength of these reactionary views among white Anglicans was confirmed in 1967 when lay members of the Synod of the Diocese of Cape Town rejected three anti-apartheid motions calling for an end to all racial discrimination in the life of the church, condemning separate development as morally evil, and asking clergy to resign as civil marriage officers because as such they were bound by the Prohibition of Mixed Marriages Act.[11] Prime Minister Vorster was quick to 'convey [his] personal appreciation' to the Synod. Its decisions revealed 'how far we have progressed'; while 'probably not members of the National Party', lay members of the Church had 'judged in the interests of South Africa'.[12] Shocked by these events, Anglican leaders initiated a Human Relations and Reconciliation Programme in 1970 in an attempt to bring practice more into line with Biblical principles. The Programme was not an immediate success;[13] but when it was allied to the formation and growing effectiveness of black pressure-groups, the Church did make a serious effort during the 1970s to purge itself of racism. However, during the late 1960s the scene was not an encouraging one for the Christian Institute, the largest minority of whose members were anguished and protesting Anglicans.

While all white-controlled denominations faced comparable internal tensions and contradictions, the Roman Catholic Church offered a further very clear example of defensive white attitudes. The pastoral letters of its Bishops' Conference repeatedly condemned apartheid and all forms of racial discrimination, yet in 1964 Archbishop W.P. Whelan of Bloemfontein broke ranks and showed himself to be completely out of touch with black South Africans. Goaded by a number of forthright attacks launched by Archbishop Denis Hurley of Durban on the illusions of 'separate development', and by Hurley's insistence that the Bishops' Conference continue to speak out against apartheid, Whelan called a press conference. Presenting himself as Director of the Bishops' Board on Press, Radio and Cinema, he explained that he was not disturbed by events of the last few years 'because it is clear that the South African situation, in spite of its defects, is stable, secure and full of prospects for future development.' Asked if this optimisitic view meant abandoning apartheid, his answer was 'no — not necessarily'. In Whelan's judgement the principle of maintaining 'separate and distinct' national or racial identities was not against church teachings; it was only the actual South African practice that was abhorrent and should be modified. Gradual improvements should be made by working from within the system.[14]

Whelan was clearly a maverick because earlier pastorals had condemned apartheid as intrinsically evil. Nevertheless he muddied the waters and it is likely that the majority of white Roman Catholics heaved a sigh of relief when he spoke out. It is also true that while

Whelan was not supported by the Bishops' Conference, he had several like-minded, aged and expatriate colleagues in the hierarchy. Like the Anglicans and the other multi-racial churches, Roman Catholicism had a long way to go in South Africa before it began to purge its structures of ingrained paternalism which so easily underwent a mutation into racism. The Church was still heavily encumbered by a cast of mind inherited from a different age: as Bishop John Bokenfohr of Kimberley told an American audience, 'the South African native [was] similar to his counterpart in the United States, a peace-loving person who was happy when he had enough food and clothing.'[15]

Like the other white-controlled churches, Roman Catholicism was in dire straits with *de facto* segregation at all levels of church life, a situation which did not scandalise white Catholics. Whites maintained an exclusive parish world of their own. They were essentially ignorant of African society and established their priorities without reference to the needs of the church as a whole. Although still conditioned by an authoritarian ecclesiology and largely passive, African, Coloured and Indian Catholics were becoming resentful and black teenagers were increasingly cynical. In Johannesburg a hospital for whites staffed by expatriate nuns was to be rebuilt at a cost of R1.25 million. In Pretoria R800,000 was to be spent on a Catholic school for white boys — an amount approximating to the Church's annual budget for the black mission schools it had committed itself to maintain in the face of the Bantu Education Act. Fully immersed in the culture of apartheid, the Church's human resources were heavily skewed in favour of whites. In the Johannesburg diocese, where there were two black Catholics for every white, there were 279 nuns teaching in white schools and only thirty-nine in black schools. During 1967 the white Johannesburg suburb of Rosebank rebuilt its church for R87,000 and extended its school hall for R60,000. At the same time, on the other side of the city, Africans were circulating begging letters in an effort to finance an extension of their badly-overcrowded church in Orlando, a project which would have cost one-tenth of the above. The Rosebank Catholic schools enrolled 1,400 children; Orlando's turned away 500 every year and enrolled 1,000. Rosebank's white children were served by twenty-three religious and forty-five lay teachers, Orlando's children by two religious and eighteen lay teachers in classes double the size of their white fellow Christians. Black teachers' salaries in this Catholic school system were approximately one-fifth of those of their white colleagues.[16]

In the wake of Vatican II, Justice and Peace Commissions were set up throughout the country, and Archbishop Hurley did his best to bring them to life. It was time, he argued, 'to join the revolution. Not the revolution of violence, but the revolution of ideas and attitudes, the revolution of minds and hearts, the revolution that makes man our chief concern, and not any formula or policy or prejudice.' If such a revolution was undertaken, people would no longer allow themselves 'to be taken in by a label like separate development'.[17] Unfortunately it became clear as the 1970s progressed that with very few exceptions the Commissions were white-dominated and essentially tame discussion groups, quite incapable of witnessing effectively against apartheid and the intensifying repression required to maintain white power and economic privilege.

While the denominations were hardly vigorous in their support for the Christian Institute and only belatedly and clumsily starting to fight their internal battles — stirring with life, or, as some thought, twitching with death pangs — the Institute was also having to function in a context where the country's students were having difficulties. By the mid-1960s the Student Christian Association (SCA) showed signs of increasingly narrow elements in its leadership, individuals who were less ecumenical and more dogmatically evangelical.[18] The SCA also structured itself on ethnic lines with Afrikaner, English, Coloured and African sections.[19] Challenged in 1960 by the World Student Christian Federation to 'reject all forms of segregation and discrimination', and pressed by its black sections to establish 'full unity', the SCA prevaricated.[20] It then disaffiliated from the World Federation in 1964 when that body aligned itself 'with the growing number of Christians in South Africa who are openly opposing apartheid' and called for economic sanctions against the regime.[21] The next year the SCA disintegrated, each ethnic group going its own way.[22] It was in an attempt to reverse this process of fragmentation that the University Christian Movement was formed in 1967 — a seminal group which in its short life helped to nurture the seeds of black theology and the black consciousness movement. For the moment, however, the Christian Institute had a lonely struggle and could expect little support from either the multi-racial churches or from the student world.

Surveying this scene and the state of the Christian Institute after its first five years, Dr Calvin Cook, Chairman of the Board of Management, delivered a remarkably honest address to the Institute's 1968 Annual General Meeting. Exercising a prophetic judgement on the Institute itself, he noted its apparent inability to move Christianity in South Africa to new frontiers of commitment. There was a real danger, he suggested, that the Institute's influence would be 'like King Log: one big splash, then a few ripples, and finally a tranquil pond once more'. Despite the Institute, South Africa remained 'the most stable country in Africa: a financier's dream'. Rather than being the threat Professor Pont and others feared, the Institute was 'not even a paper tiger; it was a domestic tabby'. In Cook's judgement, and he was not alone in this, the Institute was in a very real crisis following an earlier 'shallow and false optimism'. The enemy was 'tougher, cleverer, meaner and more purposeful' than anticipated. 'The walls of apartheid have not collapsed despite repeated blasts from *Pro Veritate*.'[23]

As we have seen, the situation was troublesome but perhaps not quite so bleak. New initiatives were underway and at the very moment when Cook was administering his harsh purgative, the Institute was about to receive a major boost to its morale from the assembly of the Reformed Ecumenical Synod meeting at Lunteren in the Netherlands. The World Council of Churches had met a month earlier in July 1968 at Uppsala. There it condemned racism and moved a step closer to its commitment in the following year to become more directly involved in Southern Africa through its Programme to Combat Racism. This *inter alia* was to help fund education and humanitarian projects undertaken by the liberation movements, including the exiled African National Congress and Pan Africanist Congress. These WCC proceedings could be treated with derision by the Dutch Reformed Churches in South Africa; but the Reformed Ecumenical Synod, in which they still participated, was another matter.

The Lunteren resolutions were in essence a reassertion of the principles and guidelines laid down by the Cottesloe Consultation, save that the Reformed Synod did not mention South Africa specifically. Nevertheless it was explicit on the responsibility of Christians to criticise 'the activities and policies of governments'. The 'commandment of love in race relations' had to be applied 'to the affairs of civil government and the structures of society'. There was a special responsibility towards 'members of all races who suffer from poverty, under-development, and political oppression'. All member-churches were called on to renew their efforts to live by Biblical norms, 'to reject every form of racial discrimination. . . . and every attempt to maintain racial supremacy by military, economic, or any other means'. In more concrete terms, the Synod also rejected the more 'subtle forms of racial discrimination found in many countries today with respect to housing, employment, education, law enforcement, etc.'; it also condemned any state prohibition of racially mixed marriages and called for 'common worship, including Holy Communion, among Christians regardless of race'.[24]

The South African Dutch Reformed Churches were in an acutely embarrassing position. As a *Pro Veritate* editorial put it: 'The whole World Council of Churches can be dismissed as heretical and liberalistic and Communistic, but this trick cannot be repeated in the case of a body such as the Reformed Ecumenical Synod.' Yet to accept these resolutions, as the Christian Institute did with enthusiasm, would mean 'the end of apartheid as a sacrosanct system in South Africa'.

The ruling party had been utterly dependent upon the DRC and upon the NGK in particular 'for its ideology of apartheid, for its policy and power, for moral justification and majorities at the polls'.[25] To have accepted Lunteren would have ended this solidarity between church and state, a step the white Dutch Reformed Churches were as reluctant to take in 1968 as they were after Cottesloe in 1960. However this was no longer true of the *Sendingkerk*, the 'daughter-church' to which one third of the Coloured community belonged, a church that was slowly coming of age and beginning to show signs of concern over the questionable state of grace of its 'mother-church', the NGK. To the further discomfort of the NGK, the *Sendingkerk* endorsed the Lunteren resolutions and so gave public witness to the tensions building up between the black and white DRC.[26]

The device used to delay confrontation with the *Sendingkerk* and to postpone the formal isolation of the Afrikaner churches from their sister Reformed Churches around the globe was simple enough. When the Lunteren resolutions came before the NGK Synod of 1969 they were referred to a commission on race relations, the Landman Commission, which managed to delay its report until 1974. It then rejected racism but advanced a 'theology of differentiation'.[27] By this time relations with the black Dutch Reformed Churches had deteriorated further and tensions with the churches in the Netherlands were approaching breaking-point. When the break came, it was in part because of the latter's support for the WCC, an intolerable step for the white NGK in South Africa which in 1978 pronounced 'the close bonds which existed between us and the [Netherlands DRC] as severed'.[28]

In the years from 1968 to 1974, as the white DRC isolated itself, the Christian Institute was to draw ever closer to the Reformed Churches of the Netherlands, receiving from them spiritual and financial support. While this and other overseas financial support may have diverted the Institute from a more vigorous drive for local members, it made a major contribution to sustaining the initiatives that were to be taken in the context of a sharpening confrontation with the apartheid state. Strengthened in this way and being capable of sufficient humility and empathy, the Institute's leadership was able to respond effectively to the new black groups that were about to form in what became known as the black consciousness movement. In interacting both formally and informally with individuals, organisations and the restive black Dutch Reformed Churches, the Institute received an education on the nature of structural injustice as understood by the poor and the oppressed. This in turn helped to transform its understanding of the dynamics of social change and of Christian mission. As a result, the Institute gradually came to the recognition that Christian hope did not essentially reside in transforming the attitudes of those with power and influence. This might help; but the more fundamental process was the investing with power of those Christ came to serve: the despised and downtrodden, the economically exploited and politically repressed. In South Africa this meant that blacks, not whites, would hold the future in their hands, an understanding Beyers Naudé and his colleagues were slowly coming to.

While it was to take the decade of the 1970s to sharpen these issues, the early signs of a renewed anti-apartheid movement were discernable by the late 1960s. When, in the aftermath of the disintegration of the Students Christian Association, approximately seventy students gathered in Grahamstown in July 1967 to launch a University Christian Movement (UCM), they did so in consultation with representatives of the Methodist, Anglican, Congregational, Presbyterian and Roman Catholic churches. Their hope was to form a non-racial fellowship that would witness to an alternative social order for the country. The students were also supported by several Christian academics and university chaplains. These included Fr John Davies, Anglican chaplain of the University of the Witwatersrand, who played a major role in drafting 'A Message to the People of South Africa'; Dr Calvin Cook of that University's Department of Theology, who was also Chairman of the Christian Institute's Board of Management; Fr Colin Collins, Chaplain to the National Catholic Federation of Students, a past General Secretary of the South African Catholic Bishops Conference and a person with a wide range of contacts in the black colleges; Professor Danie Oosthuizen and the Rev. Basil Moore, both of Rhodes University. Moore, a Methodist, was to be the first President of UCM and Collins its first General Secretary.

In addition to forming a Christian fellowship, the intention of this essentially white initiative was to work with denominational student-groups in extending the Christian presence on all campuses through worship, innovative liturgies and service. Campus activities, it was hoped, would spill over into the wider society and raise consciousness on the Biblical call to service and justice. Recognising the deepening racial divisions, not least in the structures of education, and aware of the pattern of intensified political repression and vilification of protesting Christians, the inaugural gathering confessed its members' guilt in sustaining apartheid's injustices. The fledgling UCM then committed itself 'in humilty and obedience to God to bring about a more equitable and just society'.[29]

Within the next two years the UCM had thirty branches, having established its presence on all the white English-speaking campuses, at the Coloured University of the Western Cape, Natal University's African Medical School at Wentworth, the Indian College in Durban, the interdenominational Federal Theological College at Alice, St Peter's Roman Catholic Seminary for Africans at Hammenskraal, and at the Lutheran Seminary at Mapumulo. In spite of attempts by the college authorities to thwart its activities, UCM branches were also formed among African students at the tribal campuses. In addition, a vigorous branch was started at the University of Botswana, Lesotho and Swaziland, and a handful of Afrikaner students showed a flicker of interest at Potchefstroom and Stellenbosch.[30]

The movement had soon become unpopular in several quarters. Its relationships with the churches were jeopardised on account of unconventional liturgies and its increasingly radical interpretation of social justice. Simultaneously, however, it attracted increasing numbers of black students. These were the disillusioned and angry products of the ethnic colleges who, with all other avenues of protest blocked, were keen to widen their inter-black contacts as much as they were keen to make contacts with whites. UCM also gained this support as an alternative organisation to the National Union of South African Students (NUSAS) which, from a black point of view, continued to be dominated by assertive whites.[31]

By the second half of 1968 UCM had a majority of black students, and the black campuses were becoming increasingly restive. By the end of the year the Prime Minister was calling for tough disciplinary action and warning that UCM was under investigation; its members were being harassed by security police, the network of police informers on the campuses was being strengthened, and Basil Moore was denied a passport when, as UCM President, he wished to travel abroad. The first edition of UCM's publication *One for the Road* was banned. At Fort Hare the organisation was formally banned from the campus after students staged a sit-in and demonstrated in favour of a more democratic form of student representation. Police with dogs moved in and forcibly removed 200 students who were then suspended from their studies. All were later allowed to return save for twenty-one, most of whom had been participants at UCM's July 1968 annual conference.[32] It was at this conference that a caucus of sixty African, Coloured and Indian students formed the nucleus of what shortly was to become the South African Students Organisation (SASO).

The UCM was to evolve rapidly under the influence of its black caucus, the continuing leadership of Moore and Collins, and the charismatic presence of Steve Biko and Barney Pityana. As these white and black personalities fostered intense discussions on black theology, black consciousness, white consciousness and methods of political change, racial tensions within the Movement increased, white membership declined and the number of black recruits continued to rise. An initially hesitant white-led organisation, with a political predilection for a liberal alternative to aparthied, was being radicalised. While this was a disturbing phenomenon for the churches which had originally sponsored UCM, the more important development was the formal launching of SASO in December 1968. This 'think-tank' of black students quickly recognised that the future of South Africa would depend on black leadership and black political organisations.

The Christian Institute had struggled to survive for five years amid phlegmatic churches and in a heavily repressed political situation. That situation was now changing, at least in regard to black resistance to apartheid. With the advent of UCM, the coalescing of SASO and the incipient resurgence of African nationalism, Naudé and his colleagues were about to be faced with new demands. If in these changing circumstances the Institute was to remain open to the future, able to read the signs of the times and open to the unforeseeable consequences of its Biblical commitments, it would have to grow in its understanding of mission. To confront the established powers of church and state with the demand that they reform themselves was one thing; to work for power to be given to the powerless would be another. As Aelred Stubbs put it a decade later: 'The rise of the Black Consciousness Movement from 1968 was a miracle out of death, giving South Africa one last possibility of real political change with a minimum of violence.'[33] The Christian Institute came to understand this through the insights of a Biblically grounded faith, with the result that even before the committee hearings, seminars, statements and publications of SPROCAS were completed, the struggle for justice was to be continued in new ways.

The theological basis for this radicalisation of the Christian Institute, i.e. the foundations for the evolution of a South African theology of liberation, had been laid during the first five years of its existence. This can be seen not only in the Institute's public statements and in 'A Message to the People of South Africa', but in the writings of several theologians. Ben Engelbrecht as editor of *Pro Veritate* put it precisely if in rather stiff prose:

The task confronting Christianity in our country has shifted from a relatively uncomplicated, though difficult and demanding, work of christianisation among the heathen to the ordering of this heterogeneously composed unitary community and its arrangement on the foundations of justice, so that the country may be habitable and life livable for all, and life may here be lived in peace.[34]

Once such a shift in understanding had taken place, the Institute expected Christians to be drawn into the turmoil of politics, into a dialectical struggle with the privileged and powerful. This in turn required of Christians an informed judgement of social structures and a shrewd assessment of the consequences of public policies. As more and more Christians came to recognise oppression and exploitation, and judged social sin to be a denial of love for one's neighbours, the church in its future-directedness would be capable of fulfilling its responsibility to be 'that institution whose primary character is to indicate where un-love or separation between men is experienced'.[35] For the Institute this meant that the church's mission was God's purpose revealed in the Scriptures, an ongoing process to bring 'all men into unity with Himself and with one another', not to maintain any historically-dated separation of peoples. In other words, the church's mission was the fulfillment of God's love in history. In practice this meant encouraging a constant search for more humane social structures. While the institutional church should never become the agent of any political party and should never sacralize the *status quo*, it did mean assisting men and women to be more fully human, to live their lives to the full in justice, love, compassion, and celebration. In John Davies' words;

the scope of mission therefore extends to the overthrow of the forces of evil that separate man from his Creator and stultify him so that he is less than fully human. Mission embraces too the establishment of *shalom* — [that is] all aspects of human life in its full and God-given maturity: righteousness, trust, fellowship, peace, etc.[36]

Such an understanding of the Scriptures and of creation not only conflicted with the political theology of the Dutch Reformed Churches; it was also in stark contrast with the dualistic Christianity which was rife among whites in the multi-racial churches. This placed the kingdom of God outside history, focused solely on personal salvation, saw mission as a numerical extension of the church — in its crudest form a head-count — and offered no particular Christian hope for political and social transformations. Although it often claimed to be apolitical, in reality such dualism was invariably associated with political conservatism. The Rev. R.H.W. Shepherd offered a typical example of this cast of mind in a sermon from the pulpit of the Presbyterian Church in Alice: 'The salvation of mankind will come, not through political means, but by the prevalence, the increase, and the enriching of the Christian character.' Political and economic matters were not important, he continued; in any case South Africa was a land of stability. States to the north were in chaos and the thousands of migrant labourers entering the country every year was a 'reminder that South Africa offered Africans conditions that were far superior to those in the rest of Africa.'[37]

As we have seen, the Christian Institute's view was very different. For it, the church's mission involved a social and political struggle to bring humankind into harmony with God's plan. This meant working for reconciliation between peoples on the basis of an ever-deepening understanding of justice. It meant a willingness to serve one's sisters and brothers in the historical moment; it meant recognising that it is as neighbours that we are saved. As Professor J.J. Degenaar of Stellenbosch put it: 'Christianity demands of us not only that we should change ourselves but also that we should change the society in which we live. And since this is a continual change, we are involved in a perpetual revolution. And in this revolution the place of the Christian is always with the victim.'[38] With all the frustrations and failures of its first five years, the Christian Institute was beginning to understand this.

NOTES

1. Calvin Cook, 'Some Frustrations and Hopes of this Five Year Old', *Pro Veritate*, October 1968, p. 3.

2. International Commission of Jurists, *The Trial of Beyers Naudé*, p. 88.

3. Author's interview with the Rev. Theo and Helen Kotze, Notre Dame, Indiana, 14 January 1980; Christian Institute of Southern Africa, 'Budget for the Financial Year 1965/1966', mimeo.

4. *Pro Veritate*, October 1968, pp. 3–4.

5. International Commission of Jurists, *The Trial*, pp. 89–90.

6. *Infra*, p. 102ff.

7. The following biographical details are taken from C. Villa-Vicencio, 'Theo Kotze', *Pro Veritate*, November 1977, p. 173, and the author's interviews with Kotze, Notre Dame, Indiana 8 September 1979, 14–16 January 1980.

8. *Cape Times*, 13 April 1968.

9. *Cape Times*, 22 November 1965.

10. *Die Burger*, 8 July 1965. Four years later the leading Anglican high school in Cape Town, Bishops, refused to admit the son of a Coloured Anglican priest, in spite of pressure from the Archbishop.

11. *Cape Argus*, 16 October 1967.

12. *Cape Times*, 17 October 1967.

13. E. Regehr, *Perceptions of Apartheid*, p. 250.

14. *Cape Times*, 20 February 1964.

15. *Cape Times*, 17 June 1958.

16. International Movement of Catholic Students (Pax Romano), *Students in South Africa* (Fribourg, 1969), pp. 18–20; P. Goller, 'The Church in South Africa', *Pax Romano Journal*, 5, 1967; 'A Comparison of Parishes in South Africa', *Challenge* (Johannesburg), May/June 1967, pp. 7–8.

17. *Sunday Times*, 23 June 1968.

18. Calvin Cook, 'From Breakwater to Open Sea', *Pro Veritate*, September 1967, pp. 9–11.

19. Danie van Zyl, 'the S.C.A. — a Glance Around', *Pro Veritate*, February 1965, pp. 1–3.

20. W.H. Crane, 'The World Student Christian Federation and the S.C.A.', *Pro Veritate*, February 1965, p. 11.

21. 'The WSCF's Circular Letter to its Member Organizations, July 1964', *Pro Veritate*, February 1965, p. 15.

22. Calvin Cook, 'The S.C.A. in mid-1965', *Pro Veritate*, August 1965, p. 9.

23. Calvin Cook, 'Some Frustrations and Hopes of This Five Year Old', *Pro Veritate*, October 1968, pp. 3–6. Cook was Chairman of the Department of Divinity at the University of the Witwatersrand.

24. *DRC Newsletter*, September 1968, pp. 1–4; 'The Resolution of Lunteren on Race Relations', *Pro Veritate*, September 1968, p. 4.

25. *Pro Veritate*, September 1968, p. 1.

26. J.E. Plaatjes, 'Because of These Things', *Pro Veritate*, May 1968, pp. 11–12; I.J. Theron, 'Moeder en Dogter', *Pro Veritate*, July 1968, pp. 13–16.

27. International Commission of Jurists, *The Trial*, pp. 80–1; E. Regehr, *Perceptions of Apartheid*, p. 215; see too *infra.* p. 185.

28. E. Regehr, *op.cit.*, p. 221.

29. Stephen Withers, 'Christianity for Here and Now,' *Cape Times*, 4 November 1967; Calvin Cook, 'From Breakwater to Open Sea,' *Pro Veritate*, September 1967, pp. 9–11.

30. University Christian Movement, *Newsletter*, Second Semester, 1969, pp. 1–2.

31. Colin Collins, 'How it Really Happened', typescript, 1979, pp. 1–14.

32. International Movement of Catholic Students, *Students in South Africa*, pp. 16–17.

33. Aelred Stubbs, 'The Story of Nyameko Barney Pityana', *South African Outlook*, October 1979, pp. 152.

34. Editorial: 'Recklessness in the Good Fight', *Pro Veritate*, August 1968, p. 2.

35. John Davies, 'What is Politics?', *Pro Veritate*, January 1969, p. 15.

36. J.G. Davies, 'The Meaning of Mission', *Pro Veritate*, July 1966, p. 9.

37. *Daily Dispatch*, (East London), 31 May 1964.

38. J.J. Degenaar, 'With the Victim', *South African Outlook*, April 1973, p. 58, being an address entitled 'Religion and the Future of South Africa' given at St George's Cathedral, Cape Town.

Part III
THE SPROCAS YEARS: THE CHRISTIAN INSTITUTE, 1969–1975

7
INJUSTICE AND A CLIMATE OF INTIMIDATION

If the decade of the 1960s had been one of intensifying and at first sight successful supression of black dissent, the 1970s were characterised by political turmoil. The resurgence of African nationalism was at the centre of this unrest in the form of the black consciousness movement, a movement with which a new generation of Coloureds and Indians as well as Africans identified. While black consciousness drew its inspiration from several sources, at base it was a reaction to the constant experience of racial discrimination, humiliating powerlessness and gross economic inequality. This frustration was intensified by the level of police harassment, the absence of civil rights and, for Africans, complete vulnerability under apartheid's system of bureaucratically controlled migrant labour. In addition there were specific issues that aroused and focused black protests, the most inflammatory being inferior educational facilities for a burgeoning black population and stagnant wage levels in a time of inflation.

Clearly the harsh reality of apartheid offered no respite for the vast majority of blacks.[1] Their women, children, infirm and elderly were being 'endorsed out' as families were broken up and 'surplus' individuals dumped amid the destitution of the Bantustans.[2] Given population growth-rates for the black population in the vicinity of 3 per cent and the country's pursuit of capital-intensive technologies, unemployment was building up to over 20 per cent and was being administratively removed to these rural slums. While this cruel policy was pursued, the white-controlled economy nevertheless continued to become ever more dependent on black labour, with the number of Africans in the cities increasing from 6.8 million in 1960 to over 8 million in 1970. In attempting to control this labour force, the police were arresting an average of 1,730 persons a day for pass offences; overall, the black prison population was increasing by 15 per cent each year. Malnutrition was spreading in the Bantustans, where it was commonplace to find that one of every two children born alive had died by the age of five. In Port Elizabeth six out of every ten black children died before the age of five in contrast to one in fifty whites in the same age group; in Pretoria eight out of ten African school children suffered from serious malnutrition, and in Johannesburg seven out of ten Africans lived below the bread or 'poverty datum' line. Rather than narrowing, the wage-gap between African and white workers was increasing steadily. The educational scene was comparably grotesque. White children received their education free, whereas African parents paid fees for overcrowded and poorly equipped schools; for every white pupil the state spent R228 per year, for every African pupil R15.

The weight of legislation to deal with those who protested against these circumstances was already overwhelming and had destroyed the rule of law. By the beginning of the 1970s, an estimated 2,500 South Africans were gaoled or banned for political reasons, approximately 1,000 of them without trial.[3] Severe and prolonged interrogation of political prisoners was a routine procedure; police assault and torture were increasing. In the decade before 1972, at least twenty persons died while being held under security laws.[4] During the same period over fifty persons swore affidavits concerning torture they had suffered in detention: *inter alia*, extended solitary confinement, deprivation of sleep, assault, electric shock treatment applied to the genitals, forced standing on the edges of bricks, weight-lifting with pebble-filled shoes, and being hung upside down with hands handcuffed through their legs.[5] In attempting to control the renewed political protests of the 1970s, this repressive system was augmented still further, for example by the Riotous Assemblies (Amendment) Act of 1974. This statute gave sweeping powers to magistrates to ban gatherings, increased the penalties for attending banned meetings and gave the police still wider powers for dispersing them.

As leaders of the younger generation of blacks became more conscious of the systematic nature of this exploitation, they also recognised the failure of the multi-racial churches: the weakness of past Christian witness against injustice within church structures, and the churches' all too obvious unwillingness to confront the state on matters of public policy. There had been no serious efforts by the multi-racial churches to overcome the ethnic divisions of parish life, and their repeated declarations of principle were now seen by black activists to be pathetically ineffective. The result was that Africans were drifting away from the white-dominated churches, while in contrast the black independent churches were continuing to expand.[6] In fact the stage had probably been reached where, given the patterns of residential segregation and the intransigence of whites, the formation of Christian communities across colour lines would have required that whites leave their established parishes and join black Christian congregations, defying the law to do so. With the exception of a very small number of Christian radicals, nothing like this level of commitment existed among the white laity or the white clergy. Justice committees had been established in the multi-racial churches,[7] but as the Christian Institute came to recognise with the help of pressures from the black consciousness movement, blacks were not impressed by white-led groups intent on helping blacks. The message was becoming clear. White Christians would have to work *with* rather than *for* the poor and exploited if the church was to check the rapid polarisation taking place between the races and witness within its own communities to an alternative social order. It is true that the Christian Institute had been at the cutting edge of a deepening concern over these issues, but it was still not closely identified with blacks, with the poor and repressed.

While the black consciousness movement was in essence a reassertion of black dignity within a racist political economy — an attempt to re-establish black confidence amid systemic humiliation and deprivation — it was inspired in part by black theology. New generations of students were also discovering their peoples' past and recognising themselves as heirs to a long tradition of protest, a struggle against racism which dated back to traditional wars of resistance and more recently to the formation of the African National Congress in 1912. For a brief moment before being censored and then banned, a number of intensely political black theatre groups glorified this African history and so contributed to the new consciousness. The collapse of the Portuguese empire in Mozambique and Angola in 1974 after prolonged pressure from African guerrilla movements also helped, producing a surge of black confidence and more aggressive political attitudes. Sensing a new fluidity in the region as South Africa's buffer zone began to disintegrate, and aroused by a new leadership, young activists produced turmoil on the black campuses and later in the schools. Simultaneously labour unrest and a rash of strikes disturbed white complacency, raising the spectre of a resurgent African nationalism allied to politicised black trade unions.

The University of the North (Turfloop) erupted in 1972 following a graduation address by Onkgopotse Tiro, President of the Student Representative Council. Tiro had courteously but pointedly criticised the dominance of autocratic white administrators and faculty in what was supposed, even under the theory of apartheid, to be a black college. He went on to question the use of Afrikaans as a medium of instruction in certain courses and to condemn detention and banning without trial. It was all part, he argued, of an objectionable system of white privilege. Blacks who supported apartheid had become 'bolts of the same machine which is crushing us as a nation'. Becoming more provocative, he suggested that it was up to students to change all this by working for 'the liberation of our people' until 'all men shall be free to breathe the air of freedom'. When that day arrived, 'no man, no matter how many tanks he has, will reverse the course of events.'[8]

Tiro had taken full advantage of the occasion in addressing the gathering of African parents and his captive audience of embarrassed and angry white dignitaries. The authorities were not pleased; he was suspended, mass protests followed, the student body was expelled and all were required to apply for readmittance. When, on returning to the College, it was discovered that twenty-two students, including Tiro and the entire Student Representative Council, had been refused permission to continue their studies, 500 undergraduates walked off the campus, in effect closing Turfloop.[9] The unrest spread to other black colleges and to the white English-speaking universities. Although their demonstration had been banned at the last moment, 1,400 whites set off from the University of the Witwatersrand on a march to St. Mary's Cathedral in Johannesburg to protest in sympathy with Tiro and the students of Turfloop. Comparably large demonstrations occurred at St. George's Cathedral in Cape Town. In both cities the student gatherings were baton-charged by the police and broken up with brutality and some vindictiveness. In Cape Town, Theo Kotze, Regional Director of the Christian Institute, and the Dean of the Cathedral were among those arrested.

It was at this point that the rectors of the Afrikaans universities issued a statement defending segregated education and rejecting as 'totally unrealistic' the protesters' call for free compulsory education. In the rectors' judgement the student demonstrations were aimed at a 'radical revolution of the social and political order in our country' which they would 'oppose with all [their] might.'[10] The polarisation continued and by 1974, while the *Afrikaanse Studentbond* was being addressed by the Prime Minister and the head of the *Broederbond*, the white predominately English-speaking students of the National Union of South African Students were passing a resolution expressing 'solidarity with students and those who seek the freedom of all people in Mozambique, Guinea-Bissau and Angola'.[11] Later in the year SASO and other black consciousness organisations planned a rally to celebrate Frelimo's victory in Mozambique. Their gathering was banned and their leaders were detained under the Terrorism Act,[12] as from this point onwards the state moved with increasing ruthlessness against all forms of black protest.[13]

While student unrest was disrupting the black campuses, a series of strikes occurred in the country's second most important industrial complex — the Durban-Pinetown area of Natal. There were earlier signs of industrial unrest which were not associated with the black consciousness movement. During the middle 1960s an average of 2,000 Africans participated each year in a number of small-scale officially reported strikes and were prosecuted under the criminal code for their efforts.[14] After 1969 this number showed signs of increasing, and in 1971 13,000 Ovambo contract workers struck in Namibia, demanding improved working conditions plus increased wages, and bringing the mines to a standstill. In October the following year South Africa itself had a taste of the potential power of black labour when 2,000 stevedores disrupted the Durban docks. However, what followed in 1973 in the Durban-Pinetown area was on a different scale and moved the country into a new stage of social history, one in which whites were to be reminded much more forcibly that Africans were concerned not only about civil rights but also about the distribution of income.

Desperately low wages and the absence of negotiating machinery lay at the heart of the troubles; but by 1973 black consciousness was contributing to the ferment as well. In early January 1973 the entire workforce of 2,000 men at the Coronation Brick and Tile Co. struck, demanding an increase in their minimum wage from R8.97 to R20.00 per week. Tension had been rising for several weeks, with the Company taking a hard line and refusing to negotiate; management then went so far as to issue a notice threatening the ringleaders with severe punishment and claiming that talk of a strike was simply 'the work of Communist agitators'.[15] The notice, which was angrily rejected by the workers, triggered strike action which spread to several other firms in the area and threatened to ignite labour unrest throughout the country. By the end of January, the initial ripple of strikes in Natal turned into a wave when 6,000 Africans and Indians walked out of a large textile complex and 16,000 employees of the Durban Corporation closed down the city's essential services: rubbish quickly piled up, a backlog of corpses built up as graves went undug, and perishable food decayed in the city's markets. Given the potential threat to all South Africa's industrial centres, the government moved with caution. Nevertheless, sporadic violence broke out and Durban had to be patrolled by helicopters and paramilitary riot police in camouflage. They were armed with stenguns, FN rifles and for good measure their batons too. Wage settlements and the intervention of Kwa Zulu authorities temporarily calmed the situation; but the country had been offered a glimpse of black power, a glimpse of a very different future.[16]

While the black consciousness movement was gathering momentum, the campuses erupting and black workers coming out on strike, the Christian Institute had been exploring alternative futures in its Study Project on Christianity in an Apartheid Society (SPROCAS). Having collaborated on 'A Message to the People of South Africa', the Institute and the SACC continued to co-operate and so established the Project in 1969 as an elaborate, but imaginative, attempt to provide facts and analysis which might serve as the basis for informed critical judgements on public and church policies. SPROCAS was to 'challenge our South African society at every level of its existence'.[17] It was also a somewhat naively conceived venture in that it was hoped that when white South Africans were provided with more information on the injustices wrought by existing policies, and offered a range of alternative policies, they would be prompted to take a vigorous stand against apartheid. Of course nothing like this occurred. Rather the Institute had to struggle through SPROCAS I, SPROCAS II and a range of later initiatives in an effort not to be overtaken by events as blacks tried to take the future into their own hands and showed no inclination to wait any longer for some hoped-for response from whites.

Disturbed by the accumulating evidence of the SPROCAS surveys, and aware of the increasing polarisation and impending civil war being generated under apartheid, the Institute came to align itself more closely with the dispossessed and oppressed. It thereby kept itself in the vanguard of Christian protest. Other church groups also continued to oppose apartheid and an increasing number of individuals, in fulfilling their Christian ministries, found themselves in conflict with the state. Like members of the black consciousness movement, socially concerned Christians were to suffer increasing harassment: passports were withdrawn, individuals were banned and deported, as the level of intimidation increased for all groups showing any signs of potential influence in effectively opposing apartheid. The state also became increasingly vindictive in its hounding of dissenting Christians after the World Council of Churches decided in 1969, as part of its Programme to Combat Racism, to help fund the educational and humanitarian programmes of the Southern African liberation movements including the exiled ANC and PAC. Prime Minister Vorster threatened to take action against any churches that did not withdraw from the WCC; but although they disagreed with the contentious decision, the South African churches refused to be browbeaten into resignation. 'If such resistance leads to persecution and suffering,' Naudé argued, 'the church must joyfully take upon itself persecution and suffering.' The alternative was not only craven, but 'isolation from world moral concern'.[18]

The number of individuals being raided and searched by the security police, being denied visas or the renewal of visas, having their passports withdrawn, or being deported, detained or banned, soon became startling. From January 1968 to April 1972 at least ninety-two clergy and laymen were harassed in cases with strong political over-tones. Moreover, these numbers were increasing, with fifty cases occurring in the last twelve months. As Beyers Naudé pointed out in his Director's Report at the Annual General Meeting in September 1972, the Christian Institute received its share of this attention: 'Starting as early as February 1971, one staff member after another has — with almost monotonous regularity — experienced the expres-sion of government disapproval through deportation, banning and passport confiscation.' In addition the Institute had 'become the target of government action through the appointment of a Parliamentary Select Committee. . . recently converted into a Commission of Enquiry' — the Schlebusch Commission.[20] Fr. Colin Davidson, an Anglican member of the Johannesburg staff, had been deported. Fr. Mark Collier and Fr. Cosmas Desmond, both Roman Catholic members of staff, had their passports removed. Shortly thereafter Desmond, author of *Discarded People* which exposed the new rural slums being produced in the Bantustans as 'superfluous' Africans were 'endorsed out' of the urban areas, was banned. The Rev. Basil Moore, Methodist minister, founding President of the University Christian Movement and director of the theological correspondence course the Christian Institute developed for AICA, was banned. Fr Stephen Hayes and lay preacher David de Beer of the Anglican Diocese of Windhoek (both Christian Institute organisers) were deported from Namibia to South Africa and banned at the time their Bishop, Colin Winter, was exiled. Anne Hope, the Institute's Director of Group Work which included Bible study and literacy, had her passport removed as did Peter Randall, Director of SPROCAS, and Neville Curtis, Cape Regional Director of SPROCAS.[21] It was at this time too that Theo Kotze, Cape Regional Director of the Institute, Helen Kotze and their family faced vicious intimidation. As we have seen, Theo Kotze had taken on a high public profile having been arrested on the steps of St George's Cathedral while identifying with student protests in Cape Town. This was followed by a barrage of threatening telephone calls, petrol bomb scares and rifle shots at his house. On several occasions the hammer and sickle was painted on the Institute's office in Mowbray; at least two attempts were made to burn it down and St Thomas' Church, Rondebosch, was destroyed by arson the evening after the Institute held its regional annual general meeting there.[22]

These pressures continued as the 1970s progressed in what became a nerve-racking struggle to nurture and bolster members of the Institute in their Christian ministries, while keeping informers and the security police at arm's length. In addition to a host of passport and visa cases, members of the Institute refused to testify when sub-poena'd by the Schlebusch Commission and were prosecuted. Phones were tapped; homes and offices of the Institute and *Pro Veritate* were raided periodically. In 1973 Naudé, van Zyl and Randall were charged under the Suppression of Communism Act for allegedly publishing a document which quoted a banned person, and the first edition of the final SPROCAS report, *A Taste of Power*, was banned. With every passing year key personalities were neutralised, particularly where the Institute's activities overlapped with the black consciousness movement. In 1972 for example, Sabelo Ntwasa, the University Christian Movement's Travelling Secretary and Director of its Black Theology Programme, was banned. A year later Bennie Khoapa, Director of the Black Community Programmes which developed from the SPROCAS initiative, was also banned for five years. Khoapa had been editing the *Black Review*, an annual survey of black political and cultural activities which was a major project of the Black Community Programmes. The *Black Review* was also banned.[23]

So the list continued to grow with very different explanations of why all this was happening. To the Minister of the Interior, Theo Gerdener, there was 'a small but active group' of church leaders 'trying to bring about a massive onslaught on the government's policies, even if it would ultimately lead to violence'. Action, he told his National Party audience at Ladysmith, had to be taken against individuals — but 'genuine church-goers and the Government' should see to it that a church-state confrontation did not develop.[24] The *Southern Cross*, a Roman Catholic newspaper which was not given to courageous editorials, at least went to the heart of the matter on the increasing police intimidation and offered an alternative view. It was

becoming a situation of alarming proportions that Christian leaders . . . are being berated and interdicted simply because they are preaching the Gospel to the poor — a mandate they claim to receive from Christ. It does not matter a jot whether the victim is an Anglican, a Lutheran, a Catholic or whatever else. The fact is that the practice of Christian love is being stifled by a non-explaining, arrogant government.[25]

It is worth briefly exploring several cases of repression so as to obtain a better sense of the atmosphere within which the Christian Institute was now having to operate. Judging the church to be the last organisation capable of witnessing to reconciliation between the races, the Anglican Dean of Johannesburg, Gonville ffrench-Beytagh, had taken an active and public stand against what he saw as the violence of apartheid, which in turn was leading to an inevitable defensive counter-violence from the oppressed.[26] In addition to fostering racially integrated parish life at the Cathedral, he spoke out publicly on the issue of state violence against blacks, arguing that the defensive use of force by the oppressed might become legitimate, given the white electorate's refusal to change the basic structures of injustice. Ffrench-Beytagh also outraged the government by raising funds in South Africa and abroad for the Dependants' Conference, an Anglican-initiated organisation designed to aid the families of political detainees including the dependants of ANC and PAC political prisoners. In the process of raising this support, he visited Britain where he argued against further white emigration to South Africa and in favour of economic sanctions as a non-violent pressure for change.[27]

The state's response was to use a technique it pursued with increasing frequency. An informer, one Kenneth Jordaan, was placed in the Cathedral parish, a person who later became the key prosecution witness when the Dean was charged under the Suppression of Communism Act and with ten counts under the Terrorism Act. *Inter alia*, the Dean allegedly supported violent revolution in speeches to the SACC in 1969 and to the Black Sash in 1970, possessed ANC and Communist Party pamphlets, and channelled funds from Defence and Aid in London to members of banned organisations in South Africa. In pursuing this case the security police conducted at least twenty-five separate raids in what was becoming an orchestrated effort to intimidate politically-active Christian groups, and to portray Christian dissent as inevitably contributing to violent and Communist-inspired revolution. UCM, SACC and the Christian Institute were among the organisations searched. At first sentenced to five years imprisonment, the Dean was subsequently acquitted in April 1972 by the Appeal Court in Bloemfontein.[28]

Four further cases reveal the state's determination to stamp out any form of white Christian dissent, particularly where it was associated with black opposition to apartheid. The Rev. Basil Moore had been a central figure in launching UCM. Besides being a Methodist minister he was also a theology lecturer at Rhodes University, and had listened with care to the voices of the black caucus which emerged within UCM, a caucus which later formed the basis of SASO. He was therefore able to nurture the study of black theology, organising discussion groups and seminars which helped to focus an indigenous South African response to oppression which also took account of black theology as it had emerged in the United States. Clearly black consciousness had its own momentum as a broad movement within which black theology provided but one important strand of thought, a religious focus and Biblical terminology; moreover, it was indigeneous black theologians who were to thrash out the basic ideas and develop the concepts of black theology. Nevertheless, Moore was an important catalyst and, in the early stages of the discussion, a contributor of some importance, a radical Christian mind, someone who had come to see that both the church and South Africa's future depended on black initiatives — not pious appeals to the white establishment. In 1972, after three years of activity with UCM, and just as he was co-operating with the Christian Institute to produce a correspondence course for AICA, Basil Moore was banned. It was to be a painful period of confinement, one of continual threats and intimidation for Moore and his family which included having the pet kitten skinned and left on the front steps with a ribbon for adornment.

If Moore had been banned because of his activities with black students and the African independent churches, the Anglican Bishop of Damaraland, Colin Winter, was to be deported for his attempts to integrate the parish life of his diocese, for his identification with Namibia's struggle for independence and on account of his firm backing for the black hierarchy of the Evangelical Lutheran Church in their confrontation with the state. Matters were also brought to a head by Winter's support for the Ovambo miners and agricultural workers who struck in December 1971 over the contract system, its non-negotiable terms, its autocratic control of labour and its denial of a normal family life. No sooner had the Bishop spoken out in defence of the strikers and started to raise funds for their support, than his residence permit was withdrawn and he was forced out of the territory early in 1972.[29] It was at this time too that Fr Stephen Hayes and David De Beer were deported — key figures in the diocese who, with Winter, had been co-operating with the Christian Institute. In Beyers Naudé's words the deportations were a 'cruel blow' to the rapidly expanding work of the Institute in Namibia.[30] In Winter's judgement he and his colleagues had been deported for refusing to accept the ideology of apartheid and because they had 'chosen to act as the spokesman of those who are denied basic human rights and this the government will neither tolerate nor allow.'[31] This was indeed what had happened. But as with ffrench-Beytagh and Moore, Winter had come to the conclusion that 'manifestoes were out of date. Africans were sick of them.' Action was now required, and 'essentially in support of black initiatives'. Only in this way would the churches be able to take advantage of their opportunity to be 'the last meeting places where black and white might join in common pursuit of justice and reconciliation.' In addition, Winter came to the conclusion, although this was not publicly expressed before his deportation, that economic sanctions ought to be used to check apartheid. He also came to understand 'how a man can be driven to take up a gun', and respected such a decision, even if it was not his own way: 'my way is to shout from the roof tops and to bring people to meet each other.' When Winter was deported from Jan Smuts Airport (Johannesburg), Naudé was there to bid him farewell, 'like Abraham with arms outstretched in a great Calvinist blessing'.[32]

Just how defensive the state was becoming in the face of action by dissenting white Christians, was revealed by the rather different case of two Anglican priests living in the midst of Afrikanerdom at Stellenbosch. The Community of the Resurrection established a house in the town in 1968 with Fr Robert Mercer in charge of an integrated Coloured and white parish, and Fr Bernard Chamberlain as Anglican chaplain to the University of Stellenbosch. While their ministry was a search for dialogue and not a narrow denominational or evangelistic one, a crisis-point was reached within two years. A small Anglican Society was formed and provided facilities for an ecumenical presence on a campus where previously the NGK had held a monopoly. The Society also had the audacity to invite Beyers Naudé to speak. Then to complicate matters further, Elsa Treurnicht, the daughter of Dr Andries Treurnicht, started to attend confirmation classes at the chaplaincy — not a minor matter since her father was editor of the staunchly conservative publication *Hoofstad*, Assessor of the National Synod of the NGK and shortly to become chairman of the *Broederbond*.[33]

By the time Fr Chamberlain was deported without explanation in October 1970, his colleague Fr Mercer was also under attack. In this case the offence was revealed: Mercer had used the parish bulletin to raise the issues inherent in the WCC decision to provide funds to the liberation movements through its Programme to Combat Racism. White South Africans, he wrote, should not simply display 'righteous indignation towards the WCC', so defending the *status quo* in which they had a vested interest. Rather, he suggested, whites should try to learn from the motives behind what seemed to be an offensive commitment by fellow-Christians:

Might the [motive] have been something like this: 'Evolution is obviously better than revolution. But where there is no hope of progress, desperate situations demand desperate remedies. Violence is evil, yes. But the South African way of life is an even greater evil. Faced with a choice of these two evils, we must choose the lesser . . .'[34]

When Prime Minister Vorster misrepresented Mercer and attacked him in Parliament for 'besmirching the country' and stating his own point of view (when in fact Mercer had explored the motives of the WCC), he quoted the above passage, entirely omitting to place it in the wider perspective of Mercer's presentation.[35] In fact the parish bulletin went on to caution against any stoking up of revolutionary flames. Violence was 'likely to prevent that very multi-racial harmony it is meant to encourage. And it is certainly going to draw the white South African *laager* closer. Our demented racialism may have driven the WCC to this action. But their action can only increase our dementia.'[36]

An increasing number of black South Africans would have offered forthright support for the WCC and so have been in fundamental disagreement with Mercer's cautious approach. For Vorster, however, the mere invitation to think seriously about a decision to support the humanitarian projects of the liberation movement was too much. Mercer was deprived of his South African citizenship[37] and handed a deportation order. A petition signed by 2,000 prominent Cape Christians, and organised *inter alia* by Theo Kotze of the Christian Institute's regional office, failed to reverse the government's decision. That was not surprising. What was unusual and indicative of the acrimony in high places was that the Anglican Archbishop, Robert Selby-Taylor, wrote two personal letters to the Prime Minister in an effort to reverse the deportation order but did not enjoy the courtesy of an acknowledgement or reply.[38]

Five hundred people, half of them black, packed the small white-washed thatched church of St. Mary's on the *Braak* (Stream), Stellenbosch, for the farewell service for Chamberlain and Mercer.[39] Chamberlain, the first to go, was also given a resounding send-off at Cape Town's D.F. Malan Airport, an occasion which gave rise to an open letter to South Africans, a careful analysis of the parallels as well as some contrasts between the apartheid regime and Nazi Germany.

While there were differences, the open letter argued that in essence the 'dominant political ideology' in South Africa was a similar 'neurotic nationalism . . . a racialistic nationalism' driven by 'national messianism'. Hitler had 'called on the Germans to fulfill "the mission appointed for them by the Creator of the Universe" ' (*Mein Kampf*). Similarly, Dr Malan as Prime Minister had seen Afrikanerdom as the 'creation of God' and Afrikaner history as 'the highest work of art of the Architect of the centuries'. Hence, he concluded, 'no power on earth or hell can kill our nationhood because God created our nation.' Such national messianism, the open letter pointed out, was being 'constantly reiterated' at every celebration of the Day of Covenant. Moreover, the churches in South Africa fell into three categories comparable to those in Nazi Germany: a minority, faithful to the Word of God and working against the stream of government policies; a silent group condoning these policies or refusing to recognise political sin; and finally those who 'distort the Word of God' turning the Gospel into 'a theological appendage to . . . the Government's nationalist ideology'.[40]

The open letter had been an ecumenical effort, a damning analysis of the current scene that was signed by fifty Christians including prominent members of the Christian Institute in the Cape. It also pointed out that only a small minority of white Christians were prepared to speak and act out their dissent. Church protests were still essentially tame, short-lived and sporadic splutterings, even if a larger number of individuals and small groups were now acting courageously and with persistence. In fact the state's pattern of intensifying repression (which included action against ffrench-Beytagh, Moore, Winter, Chamberlain, Mercer and so many others) had been applied without any major outcry from whites. The campaign against Christian dissenters elicited formal protests from the multi-racial denominations, tough condemnations from the SACC and Christian Institute, the odd petition and an open letter, but precious little courageous leadership from the white hierarchy and hardly a murmur from white parishes. As Fr Cosmas Desmond expressed it before being silenced by his banning order: the security police had done the church a great favour by acting against clerics and church organisations, but 'they will have to be a lot more zealous in their efforts if we are to have a church-state confrontation in South Africa.' Church leadership, Desmond continued, did not reflect the reality of church membership — 75 per cent black — and for all their good intentions 'we cannot expect the hierarchies to give the lead in confronting the Government: they are too busy protecting their white interests.'[41] Desmond was right in so far as the vast majority of whites in the church hierarchies, like their white congregations, were still remote from black opinion, still essentially the captives of a white, capitalist and racist culture — even if their Biblical principles continued to inform their consciences, making them increasingly uneasy in apartheid society.

It was in this context of phlegmatic churches, intensifying intimidation and the repression of sporadic Christian dissent that the Christian Institute struggled to sharpen its analysis and to increase its tenuous leverage on the historical situation. This it tried to do by working against the sharply increasing polarisation taking place between blacks and whites. In other words, the Institute hoped to engender a new openness and flexibility among white church leaders and white interest-groups, while simultaneously supporting black pressures for change within the churches and within the wider society. By the late 1960s it was obvious that this strategy would involve an escalating confrontation between at least some Christians and the state; and in the longer run, perhaps, a major church-state confrontation. Such a confrontation, it was hoped, might yet save the country from the retributive violence which would inevitably follow should the injustices of apartheid continue. It was with these attitudes in mind that the Christian Institute and SACC launched their Study Project on Christianity in Apartheid Society (SPROCAS) in an effort to engender that new openness and flexibility among whites. As the following chapters point out, SPROCAS failed to do this, with the result that when black protests erupted in the 1970s they encountered white intransigence. As a result the Institute changed its strategy and was drawn more firmly into supporting black pressures for change.

NOTES

1. The statistics in this paragraph are taken from the South African Institute of Race Relations, *Annual Survey of Race Relations 1970* (Johannesburg, 1971), and 'An Open Letter Concerning Nationalism, National Socialism and Christianity', *Pro Veritate*, July 1971, supplement, pp. 1–12.

2. C. Desmond, *The Discarded People* (Harmondsworth, 1969).

3. 'An Open Letter', *Pro Veritate*, July, 1971, p. 5; *Daily Despatch*, 1 August, 1970; *Diamond Fields Advertizer* (Kimberley), 15 June, 1969.

4. Robert Wood for Christian Institute Information Service, *What Happens in South African Prisons* (Johannesburg), 27 June, 1974, pp. 1–2.

5. *Ibid.*

6. Author's interview with Rev. R. van der Hart, O.P., Oxford, 2 December 1972; A. Sampson, 'Behind the Black Curtain', *Observer* (London), 19 April, 1970; *Sunday Tribune* (Johannesburg), 14 March 1971; *Rand Daily Mail* (Johannesburg), 13 June, 1971; *Rapport* (Pretoria), 14 March, 1971.

7. As SACC's Programme for Social Change was to put it: 'I was hungry and you formed a Justice and Reconciliation Committee' (*PSC Newsletter*, 30 October, 1974, front cover).

8. O. Tiro, 'Injustice at a Black University', *Pro Veritate*, August 1972, pp. 20–1, being his graduation address.

9. *Rand Daily Mail*, 6 June, 1972.

10. P. Randall, *A Taste of Power*, p. 21; SPROCAS Background Paper 2, *Student Protest: the Conflicting Polarities* (Johannesburg, 1972.) pp. 3–4.

11. Christian Institute of Southern Africa, *Information Service News Digest* (Cape Town), 24 July 1974, p. 9.

12. *PSC Newsletter*, 3 October 1974, p. 6.

13. *Infra*, pp. 151–2, 217ff.

14. Institute for Industrial Education, *The Durban Strikes, 1973* (Johannesburg, 1974), p. 5.

15. *Ibid.*, pp. 10–11.

16. *Ibid.*, pp. 9–22.

17. Christian Institute of Southern Africa, 'Director's Report for the period 1st August 1971–31st July 1972' (Johannesburg), p. 4, typescript.

18. *Cape Times*, 17 September 1970.

19. 'Church-State Confrontation', *Pro Veritate*, April 1972, pp. 21–2; *Cape Argus*, 25 February 1971; *Rand Daily Mail*, 8 March 1972.

20. Christian Institute, 'Director's Report 1971–1972', p. 2.

21. *Ibid.*, *Pro Veritate*, April 1972, pp. 21–2; South African Institute of Race Relations, *Annual Survey of Race Relations, 1972*, pp. 40–1.

22. A.P. Walshe, *Church and State in South Africa; the Christian Institute and the Resurgence of African Nationalism* (London, Christian Institute Fund Trustees, 1978), p. 7.

23. Christian Institute, 'Director's Report, 1971–1972', p. 2; *Pro Veritate*, April 1972, pp. 21–2; South African Institute of Race Relations, *Annual Survey of Race Relations*, 1972, pp. 40–1; E. Regher, *Perceptions of Apartheid*, p. 98.

24. *Cape Times*, 9 August 1971.

25. *Southern Cross*, (Cape Town), 8 March 1972.

26. British Broadcasting Corporation (BBC) interview with ffrench-Beytagh, 24 September 1972.

27. *Ibid.*; South African Council of Churches, *Kairos* (Johannesburg), November 1971, pp. 1–3; *Sunday Times* (London), 1 August 1971; E. Regher, *Perceptions of Apartheid*, pp. 94–7.

28. *Ibid.*

29. S. Hayes, 'The Ovambo Strike', *Pro Veritate*, February 1972, pp. 12–14; C. Winter, 'Justice and South West Africa', *Pro Veritate*, December 1971, pp. 10–11.

30. Christian Institute, 'Director's Report, 1971–1972', p. 3.

31. 'Statement by the Diocese of Damaraland', *Pro Veritate*, February 1972, p. 15.

32. Author's interview with Bishop Colin Winter, Sutton Courtenay, 9 November 1972; BBC interview with Bishop Winter, 17 October 1972.

33. *Sunday Times* (Johannesburg), 4 October 1970; 7 October 1973.

34. *St. Mary's on the Braak Church Bulletin* (Stellenbosch), 13 September 1970.

35. *Hansard* no. 9 of 1970, col. 4204; *Sunday Times* (Johannesburg), 4 October 1970; *Cape Argus*, 3 October 1970.

36. *St. Mary's on the Braak Church Bulletin*, (Stellenbosch), 13 September 1970.

37. *Cape Argus*, 14 October 1970.

38. *Sunday Times*, 14 February 1971; Author's interview with the Archbishop, Cape Town, February 1973.

39. *Cape Times*, 26 October 1970.

40. 'An Open Letter', *Pro Veritate*, July 1971, pp. 1–12.

41. *Rand Daily Mail*, 16 April 1971.

8

SPROCAS I AND THE PROSPECT OF CIVIL WAR

The Study Project on Christianity in Apartheid Society (SPROCAS) was launched in 1969 as a two-year endeavour, a follow-up to 'A Message to the People of South Africa' which in the previous year had condemned apartheid as an anti-Christian ideology. Co-sponsored by the Christian Institute and the South African Council of Churches (SACC), SPROCAS was designed to move from the somewhat abstract 'Message' with its negative critique to practical suggestions and 'some vision of what South African society could be if Christianity was taken seriously'.[1] While the project was founded on Biblical principles, its policy recommendations were not envisaged as peculiarly Christian; rather they were designed to produce a common, non-racial society structured around the dignity of the human person. The hope was that SPROCAS would stimulate discussion in government circles and within political parties as well as in the churches by offering a humane range of alternatives to Christians and non-Christians alike.

Six commissions were formed with 150 'leading South Africans' as members and consultants. Each commission considered dozens of working papers and reports, many of them learned and well-informed, some of them provocative.[2] All ethnic groups and a wide range of occupations were to be represented. However, in practice the white professional class and particularly university faculty were predominant, with no more than token black representation on the commissions: the black/white member ratios were 5:26 in the Church Commission, 1:20 Economics, 1:14 Education, 1:13 Legal, 1:24 Political and 5:22 in the Social Commission.[3]

Although the Christian Institute was in the early stages of shifting to a more radical understanding of the processes of social change, one which was to recognise the central role of black leadership and black organisations, it had entered into yet another largely futile, white liberal effort to inform and to transform the politics of white interest groups. Nevertheless, it is important to maintain a perspective on the rather complex dynamics involved as the Institute entered SPROCAS yet simultaneously moved in a more radical direction. SPROCAS was a white initiative, but many of its leading figures had a strong sense that black pressures for change would be increasingly important. In the judgement of the Political Commission, these pressures would increase dramatically unless channelled into constructive constitutional politics. The alternative was an escalating race war which would engulf the whole region as a defensive white power structure erected a militaristic garrison state, an increasingly totalitarian system of white privilege.[4] This awareness of the potentially disruptive power of black frustrations and the acceptance of Biblical values — particularly those of social criticism or prophetic judgement in the style of the Jewish prophets — helped to keep SPROCAS self-critical, open to the future and exploratory in its recommendations. It was therefore able to adapt some of its strategies *en route*. As a result, a second initiative, SPROCAS II, was launched after the six commissions had reported. This in turn evolved into an important if short-lived Programme for Social Change which, with SPROCAS II, adopted a more humble and at last a listening relationship with black South Africans.

The start to all this, however, was not auspicious, even if the six commissions of SPROCAS I sold 20,000 copies of their reports by 1973. Each commission worked diligently to expose the ravages of poverty, racism, exploitation and repression.[5] But in the introduction to its 1972 report, the Economics Commission had to acknowledge 'the almost total absence of black participation, or of any significant guidance on traditional or modern attitudes from the huge, silent and under-represented majority within the country.' While this was honest enough, it also revealed the crippling racial divisions within the multiracial denominations. As the commissioners saw it, this absence of black input, let alone black leadership, was 'a weakness which we felt we could not remedy by any belated action on our part but which only too accurately reflects the lack of communication between black and white which characterizes most planning within the country today'.[6] Like its sister-commissions, the Economics Commission tried to rise above this impossible handicap so as to address both white and black communities. As we shall see, it made a brave attempt to diagnose the fundamentals of exploitation and to chart an alternative and Biblically-grounded course; but in the end the lopsided composition of the Commission led to a report, *Power, Privilege and Poverty,* which contained severe contradictions and could only hint at the more radical insights that were becoming commonplace within the black consciousness movement.

The five Biblical principles on which SPROCAS and its commissions were grounded were inherited from the theology of 'A Message to the People of South Africa'.[7] These principles also provided the foundations for an indigenous development of liberation theology — a theology that had been gestating within the Christian Institute and was simultaneously maturing as black theology within the black consciousness movement.[8] The first principle, that of change (II Corinthians

5.7; Galatians 6.16; Revelation 21.5), applied to personal redemption but also to the historical evolution of society; Christians were called to be 'active collaborators' in renewing all things, in seeking 'a new world'. This in turn required a concern for life (Matthew 11.4–6; 15.32, 25.36), which meant following Jesus in his compassion for the physically disabled (the sick, cripples), the economically exploited (the poor), those deprived of their freedom (prisoners) and those alienated from society (lepers, prostitutes, the mentally disturbed). But this Biblical focus on individual suffering had to be taken further in the light of 2,000 years of history and the disciplines of sociology, economics and politics. It was much clearer now in the latter half of the twentieth century that humanity had a new potential, a moral consciousness about the formation of its own social structures — structures which could crucify one's brothers and sisters. To love one's neighbour in the modern world implied a responsibility for public affairs and government policies.

With this understanding, it was argued, a third principle was revealed, that of Christian or rather human participation (Luke 10.1; John 15.15; Matthew 23.8), a sharing together in the ordering of the human community. This was seen as the antithesis of race domination or class exploitation and implied the fourth principle: stewardship (Matthew 25.14; I Corinthians 4.2; I Peter 4.10). As individuals were stewards of their own lives and abilities, so, as citizens, they were stewards of the land and its resources. Just as important, they were now stewards of the social processes by which a society's culture was conditioned and its political economy controlled. In other words, every human being had 'management responsibilities'. This was confirmed by the fifth principle of human worth which was rooted in the dignity of each person being created in the likeness of a loving God (Luke 12.6; Ephesians 2.10; Galatians 3.28). Each person, through Christ, had 'been freed to devote [herself or himself] to the renewal of the world . . . [a person] loved by Christ and free to love'. Such Christian love would denounce 'as false all that humiliates man, all that restricts his freedom, all that oppresses him, all that exploits him and all that alienates him from his fellows'.[9]

As suggested above, *Power, Privilege and Poverty*, the report of the Economics Commission, offers a good example of a SPROCAS commission working from these five principles yet constrained in its understanding by the limited nature of its overwhelmingly white membership. The report made a genuine attempt to envisage a more egalitarian society. It accurately described many of the structures of injustice and offered a series of recommendations which, if applied, would have gone a long way in eradicating racial discrimination in the economy and establishing a colour-blind welfare state. On the other hand, the Commission was apparently oblivious of the radical black critique of capitalism, and it made no attempt to present the insights and vision of what was becoming a black consciousness movement. It only hinted at the need for structural changes in capitalism itself. Moreover, it was over-optimistic in its expectation that white initiatives would be as important as black initiatives in dismantling apartheid and ushering in a new social order.[10]

The Economics Commission's goal was a 'Responsible Society'. By this was meant a political culture which produced a constant effort to broaden the participation of its citizens in decision-making processes, and which persisted in trying to narrow the gulf between rich and poor. The 'Responsible Society' was envisaged as one in which citizens were conscious of the need to create and nurture a humane culture which treated people as more than mere producers and consumers. Such a society would also exercise a sense of stewardship in working within the constraints of a fragile ecological system.[11] Put in slightly different terms, the 'Responsible Society' would have a nuanced understanding of 'development' as a much more complex possibility than economic growth. In addition to increased GNP, development would entail a more equitable distribution of income, a social security net for 'the helpless and the weak', self-reliance in decentralised organisations, and cautious technological innovation that was environmentally sensitive.[12]

Having surveyed the historical roots of apartheid and rejected 'separate development' as an illusion, a system of white privilege quite incapable of producing a 'Responsible Society', the Commission made its recommendations. The basic assumption was that a fundamental redistribution of power between whites and blacks was essential. For this to happen, 'for steps to be taken towards the Responsible Society, not only should initiative emerge among blacks to improve their position, but, equally important, whites controlling the organisational network should realise the role they have to play.' This process of black self-help and black political pressure, plus white adaptability, was to establish the preconditions for a Responsible Society: 'the right of all people to effective political power', legally recognised trade unions for all workers, a 'significant redistribution of land . . . wealth and income', a common non-racial social security system and 'radical changes to the existing educational system', including the 'right of all to equal access'.[13]

The Commission went on to make fifteen concrete suggestions, 'immediate steps' that would initiate these reforms. Each suggestion was followed by a list of organisations which might effect the specific change; for example, the following were judged to be political pressure-groups that could work for the abolition of migrant labour:

the Churches, the Federated Chamber of Industries, *Die Afrikaanse Handelsinstituut, Die Afrikaanse Sakekamer*, the Associated Chambers of Commerce, the Trades Union Council of South Africa, the Confederation of Labour, Industrial Councils, large employers of black labour, the (Bantustan) Territorial Authorities and Urban Bantu Councils. A comparable list was offered as a means towards 'an effective minimum wage level' which was to include farm labourers, mine workers and domestic servants. Although this second list made no reference to the Territorial Authorities of Urban Bantu Councils, it added: Agricultural Unions, the National Council of Women, the Union of Jewish Women, housewives' organisations, the South African Institute of Personnel Management, the Wage Board, Department of Labour, Rotary and the Junior Chamber of Commerce.

Several such lists of what were essentially white interest-groups were offered as the basis for 'appropriate action'. Apparently black input was to come through the institutions of separate development (a policy already rejected by the Commission) — the Territorial Authorities, Urban Bantu Councils, the South African Indian Council and the Coloured People's Representative Council. The two additional sources of black input suggested were the African Chamber of Commerce and the South African Students Organisation (SASO), both of which were mentioned as bodies that might co-operate in research on the role of multinational corporations. The African Chamber of Commerce was also expected to help in removing restrictions on black entrepreneurs, while SASO was seen as a potential pressure-group for a 'national body of works committees' which might prepare the way for trade unions.[14]

With all their goodwill, the white commissioners not only placed an extraordinary emphasis on government agencies, and Afrikaans- and English-speaking corporate structures; they also assumed that the very political institutions of apartheid could offer a black input in setting up the Responsible Society — those institutions which had been overwhelmingly and consistently rejected by black protest movements. In addition, the Economics Commission exhibited a serious weakness in assuming the untrammelled continuity of capitalist structures, something it was only able to do by giving scant attention to the popular forces of African protest with their predilection for some form of African socialism that would emphasise the value of communalism.[15] Nevertheless, the long-term, if largely unexplored, implications of the Commission's Biblically-grounded value judgements were radical. This was so in the sense that a redistribution of political power allied to egalitarian expectations would have had major economic and cultural repercussions and shattered the 'South African way of life'. At times the Commission glimpsed this reality, even if its internal contradictions prevented it from following through on such insights.[16]

These momentary flashes of radical insight involved the recognition that South African racism had been inter-twined with class exploitation; as a result, any shift in power towards blacks might well involve both dismantling colour-bar legislation and a reassessment of capitalist structures: 'Several writers have pointed out that in South Africa "race reinforces class and . . . race is employed as a rationalisation or justification of class" '.[17] Yet this crucial piece of analysis was not addressed in any systematic way. While the Commission rejected the argument that economic growth would 'inevitably bring about real social and political change',[18] and described the structures of apartheid as those of 'institutionalized violence' which placed 'economic objectives above social justice', so serving 'to entrench the yawning gap between rich and poor', it failed to explore any structural alternatives to the existing modes of capitalism. The Responsible Society had to work for a 'more equitable distribution of power amongst its members rather than concentrating all power in a few hands'; industry and commerce could not be left to be dominated by 'those who put money into an enterprise'. But then the argument faltered. There was 'much room for discussion amongst Christians' on restructuring economic life'; however, 'the problem of reconciling individual liberty with communal responsibility' was not an easy one and the Commission did 'not propose to attempt it'. In short, its vision was limited to bleaching racism out of the existing system in the hope that this would release political forces which might then press for gradual changes in the country's economic structures. A mere footnote referred readers to one commissioner's personal and socialist contribution to the debate: Richard Turner's, *The Eye of the Needle* (SPROCAS 1972).[19] Clearly the Commission found structural issues discomforting and potentially divisive; but like SPROCAS I in general, the reason it so easily sidestepped them was that it did not represent the oppressed, was not in touch with the poor and so was not under pressure from black organisations.

It can be argued that the Commission was intent on communicating with white South Africans and trying, through them, to initiate a non-violent re-orientation of public policy. It can also be argued that the Commission sat in a period when there were no obvious African political leaders other than those in gaol or in exile, when the ANC and PAC were outlawed and before the black consciousness movement had matured. There is even an excuse for placing some reliance on Bantustan leaders and institutions, for it was at this time that Gatsha Buthelezi, Prime Minister of Kwa Zulu, showed signs of being able to use the political institutions of apartheid to develop a black anti-apartheid power base. However, the central point is that SPROCAS relied on white expertise which was critical of racism but far less aware of its own predilections for the pervasive culture of capitalism. Strongly inclined towards a liberal cast of mind, seeing capitalist organisations as essentially progressive forces capable of incremental reforms, and with a strong faith in education, the great majority of commissioners had little understanding of, or stomach for, a process of change in which the poor were given power.

For most of the commissioners and consultants associated with the original SPROCAS initiative, the lack of control implied by an acceptance of black leadership and black initiatives for change was a barrier to more radical thinking. However, this was not so for the Director of SPROCAS, Peter Randall, and his co-directors, Beyers Naudé, Bishop Bill Burnett of the South African Council of Churches, and Alan Paton. With the staff of SPROCAS and the Christian Institute, they began to think more courageously. Rather than seeing black pressures for change as a problematical and even alarming reality that had somehow to be coped with, they were slowly coming to see such pressures as the sociological basis for a Biblically-inspired hope. Early signs of this shift in thinking are discernible at points in the Church Commission's report, *Apartheid and the Church*, and more obviously in the final co-ordinated SPROCAS report, *A Taste of Power*, of which Randall was the author. As Naudé put it in his annual report to the Christian Institute, 'more and more blacks will take the lead — not only in the Institute but in society as a whole. The slogan of SPROCAS, "The Future is Black", is taking on a new meaning if seen against this background.'[20]

The Church Commission called for confession, particularly on account of the tragic failure of the multi-racial churches 'to promote inter-racial contact, communication and dialogue on a large scale'.[21] Trapped in a web of apartheid legislation which stunted Christian fellowship, parish life had become flaccid, sunk in a torpor of conformism, racism, legalisms, wordiness, ecclesiastical self-concern and fear — a range of anti-evangelistic attitudes which the Commission saw as crippling the church's mission. What was now required of the church was humility, a preparedness to take risks and a willingness to open itself to the future. It was hoped this would lead to a renewal of the church's own life so that it might begin to witness to an alternative social order: salary scales of black and white clergy should be equalised by 1975 and congregations opened to all races. The Commission also raised the possibility of passive resistance in that it called for symbolic acts against all forms of racial discrimination and support for conscientious objectors. Most important of all, it went on to call for crash training programmes for black clergy and laity so that they could take over leadership positions — the beginnings of a shift towards an acceptance of black predominance in the life of the church.[22]

While the Church Commission called for the encouragement of black leadership within Christian communities, the implications of black predominance in the wider society were spelt out more emphatically in the final co-ordinated SPROCAS report, *A Taste of Power*. This not only encouraged whites to work for the emergence of black leadership, but recognised that South Africa was at a turning-point in its history in that a white control model for change had become an outmoded strategy, an unrealistic hope destroyed by white intransigence. The future of the church and indeed of the country itself was now essentially dependent on black initiatives for change. As we have seen, the six SPROCAS commissions made their recommendations on the understanding that white-controlled institutions might yet be flexible enough to respond to mounting black pressures — by quickly instituting processes of inter-racial collective bargaining. L. Schlemmer put it as follows in the 1971 report of the SPROCAS Social Commission: 'The greatest hope for peaceful change in South Africa lies in the possibility of there being opportunities, in the not too distant future, for blacks to exert constructive pressures on whites and within white-controlled institutions.'[23] Two years later in 1973, as SPROCAS I came to an end, Peter Randall recognised that the whole Project had been overtaken by events. A fundamental redistribution of power and resources was urgently required, but the country was 'in the early stages of a new historical phase . . . in which the initiative for change is passing into black hands.' Blacks had 'a taste of power' and whites could not indefinitely 'prevent them enjoying the full meal'. Henceforth the white oligarchy would be on the defensive. There were 'the beginnings of a transference of power'.[24]

Rather than responding flexibly to the SPROCAS call for negotiated change, Randall's analysis continued, the Afrikaner press and apartheid government had generally ignored the commissions' reports and occasionally attacked them with bitterness. Rather than re-examining apartheid, the power structure clung to white privilege and power, using parliament as the 'instrument of white solidarity and white supremacy, and of Afrikaner nationalist imperialism'.[25] In fact there had been a sharply increasing rate of polarisation between black and white in the early 1970s. At the same time there was polarisation within the white community as a small minority opposed the vast majority who were consolidating behind the Afrikaner National Party to defend the established order. This polarisation within the white community was symbolised in June 1972 'when short-haired Afrikaner policemen beat long-haired English students in the precincts

of [the Cape Town] Anglican Cathedral for protesting in public against
the educational inequalities suffered by blacks.' The black/white
polarisation was symbolised by the government's intransigence in
attempting to crush SASO and the Black People's Convention by
banning their leaders in 1973 — an act 'which can possibly be seen as a
continuation of the actions against the ANC and PAC in the sixties'.[26]
Given these events, there was no room for an iota of false optimism.
The white power structure showed no signs of accommodating 'the
need for a fundamental sharing of wealth, land and power'.[27] In
Randall's judgement the country's future now depended on black
pressures for change which the government was so desperately trying
to repress: from anti-apartheid 'homeland' leaders like Gatsha
Buthelezi, the reviving Indian Congress, the (Coloured) Labour
Party, and black trade unions. But most important of all, the initiative
had shifted to the black consciousness movement with its understanding of black theology, black drama and black poetry — to the
ideas generated by SASO and boosted by the formation of the Black
People's Convention in 1972. These ideas were no longer confined to
the black intelligentsia, but were spreading among students and
workers, so producing a 'new Black Solidarity'.[28] While white
supremacy was 'no delicate plant which will wilt in a slightly changed
political, social or economic climate', it had lost the initiative in a way
which suggested that the established political as well economic
structures were incapable of 'enabling the kind of fundamental
change' SPROCAS had hoped for. Indeed, the question now arose of
'whether we should be exploring far more vigorously the potential
alternatives offered by socialist forms of society, including those which
have been developed in other parts of Africa.' The black consciousness
movement had no hesitation in answering this question positively.[30]

There was no immediate prospect of power for black South Africans,
but the growth of a black consciousness movement and internal unrest
were beginning to wrest the political initiative from an intransigent
white power structure. As Randall and his SPROCAS staff
recognised, the country was entering a new stage in the long struggle to
end white supremacy, a struggle in which there was every prospect of
escalating violence and a major church-state confrontation. Having
interposed themselves between established white interests and the
organisations of resurgent black dissent, the Christian Institute and
SPROCAS were in the vanguard of that church struggle. Moreover,
by committing itself to the giving of power to the poor and dispossessed, the Institute was bound to be caught in the turmoil of what was
evolving into a situation of civil war. While SPROCAS had been
deliberating, these tensions were increased still further by the WCC
financial support for Southern African liberation movements, support

which raised in a more acute form an issue which had surfaced at a theoretical level in SPROCAS.

In 1970 the multi-racial churches were startled, as the South African government and the white DRC were outraged, by the unanimous decision of the WCC Executive Committee to give financial support to the liberation movements in Southern Africa. In *Pro Veritate's* judgement, it was 'a truly historical decision'.[31] What had occurred was the natural consequence of the WCC's Programme to Combat Racism and the latter's decision to establish a Special Fund. This was to 'strengthen the organisational capability of racially oppressed people, to raise the level of awareness about racism, and to support organisations that align themselves with the victims of racial injustice'.[32] In the first year, 1970, the sum of $200,000 was allocated for these purposes, and a comparable amount the next year; by 1975 the annual grant had risen to $475,000. Of this amount, just under a quarter went to Southern African organisations and their support groups. Nineteen organisations were assisted in the first year of operations with grants going, *inter alia*, to Aborigine groups in Australia, to Indians in Colombia, minority organisations in the U.S.A., the anti-apartheid movement, and black groups in Britain.[33] However, the most contentious grants were to the Southern African liberation movements, those in exile and those in control of territory through military action.

FRELIMO, in control of approximately one-fifth of Mozambique, received $15,000 for social welfare as its first development plan set out to expand the number of schools and clinics, to foster agricultural co-operatives and encourage exports of groundnuts, rye, cashew nuts, tobacco and rubber. SWAPO (the South West African Peoples Organisation) received $5,000, ZANU (the Zimbabwe African National Union) and ZAPU (the Zimbabwe African People's Union) $10,000 each, the MPLA (Popular Movement for the Liberation of Angola) and GRAE (the Revolutionary Government of Angola in Exile) $20,000 each, and UNITA (the National Union for the Total Liberation of Angola) $10,000. The ANC received $10,000 to launch a Lutuli Memorial Fund which, it was hoped, would influence world opinion though exploring alternatives to apatheid. $5000 was allocated to the Angola Committee and Dr. Eduardo Mondlane Foundation for a joint venture: a Foundation for the Promotion of Information about Racism and Colonialism.[34] These were modest sums and all recipients gave assurances that the funds would be used not for military purposes but for educational or organisational needs which included establishing social infrastructures in liberated areas. Nevertheless, at the centre of it all, and the source of some wellnigh hysterical outbursts in South Africa, was a decisive shift in mentality, one towards which the Christian Institute was edging its way — a determination on the part of the WCC 'to allow the powerless and the oppressed to control their own destinies'.[35] Given this commitment, South Africa became a priority 'due to the overt and intensive nature of white racism and the increasing awareness on the part of the oppressed in their struggle for liberation'.[36]

Many of the issues raised by the WCC action had begun to emerge in the SPROCAS commissions, and there is no doubt that the former had a stimulating effect on the latter. Certainly the WCC decisions, coming as SPROCAS was getting under way, added a note of urgency and perhaps banished some wistful thinking. Both the WCC and SPROCAS recognised the need to redistribute power and resources, that violence had many dimensions and that it was not the sole peroga-tive of oppressed, desperate people; violence inhered in the very struc-tures of injustice and could be ruthlessly used in their defence by the forces of 'law and order'. Both the WCC and SPROCAS also came to recognise that conflict might well accompany the search for reconcilia-tion, and that alternative, more humane models had to be found for society — without those models themselves becoming the source of a new idolatry or of new ideological fixations.

It was the SPROCAS Political Commission which directly addressed the issues of violence, reminding those who condemned the liberation movements on moral grounds to examine their attitudes to earlier anti-government activities; for example the Afrikaner rebellion of 1914 and pro-Nazi sabotage during the Second World War. The Commission's own judgements were an indication of the ambiguities which now faced the Christian conscience as the WCC decision trig-gered public debate. Revolutionary violence in itself, the Commission argued, negated the vision of hope and love. Yet the commissioners joined with Archbishop Helder Camara of Brazil, who had chosen to 'go the way of the pilgrim of peace', in respecting 'men who, driven by their own conscience, decide to use violence: not the cheap violence of a drawing-room guerrilla, but the violence of those who have testified to their sincerity by sacrificing their lives'. The Commission's conclusion was to adopt in theory a 'just war' stance, but in practice to judge it inapplicable:

In abstract and philosophical terms . . . violence can be justified in situations where there is no alternative means of changing an intolerably unjust situation in which violence is done spiritually and materially by unjust rule, *and* where there is a reasonable chance that violence may succeed in its aims and achieve a more just social order.

Such situations were 'exceedingly rare' and contained the 'great danger' that violent revolt would 'brutalise both sides and thus render oppressor and oppressed indistinguishable'. Moreover, there was no real possibility of revolution in South Africa and, in any case, 'the cost in terms of human life, suffering and bitterness . . . would be over-whelmingly great.'[37] Having made this judgement, the Commission then shifted ground, issued a warning and recognised that the historical situation could change dramatically, ushering in the brutality, suffering and bitterness it had spoken of. Unless white South Africa assured blacks of their dignity which was being violated by apartheid, the small 'bands of guerrillas and other revolutionaries', at present 'unrepresentative of the feelings of the African population', could gain support.[38]

The WCC decision, coming amid increasing internal unrest and guerrilla successes against the Portuguese, meant that these issues were not left in the pages of *Pro Veritate* and the SPROCAS reports but were planted firmly in the midst of church-state politics. Moving in step with each other, the government and the white DRC set out to discredit the WCC. In Prime Minister Vorster's view, the World Council had no interest in preaching the Gospel in South Africa as it was infiltrated by Communism and was solely intent on revolution.[39] The DRC agreed with this assessment and the Rev. Dr J.S. Gericke, Moderator of the NGK General Synod, saw the WCC's support for 'sabotage, subversion and terrorism' as 'one of the most atrocious offences which Christian churches can commit against the Word of God'.[40] By 1973, when WCC support for the liberation movements had been main-tained and gradually expanded, Gericke's successor as Moderator, the Rev. Dr J.D. Vorster, felt compelled to attack the WCC in terms almost identical to the Prime Minister's: it was a 'Communist front organisation . . . instigated by liberalism and Communism, intent upon consummating the revolution . . . an instrument of left-wing aggression [which had] subtly infiltrated and manipulated' the liberal churches and was intent on expanding 'the economic class-war into the churches'.[41]

Prime Minister Vorster's immediate reaction was to call on the South African churches to sever all ties with the World Council. As we have seen, he also deported Fr Mercer for daring to initiate in his Stellenbosch parish a serious discussion of the Council's action.[42] Vorster then turned on Beyers Naudé for participating in the Ulvenhout Consultation, an informal group of ten leading WCC personalities who gathered in 1969 in the Netherlands to discuss the Programme to Combat Racism and ways of effecting change in South Africa. Naudé, Vorster told Parliament, 'owed an explanation to South Africa' for participating in a group which had been prepared to 'make contact with African leaders of liberation movements'.[43] Vorster then blocked a planned consultation between the SACC and the WCC on the subject of the Programme to Combat Racism by imposing unacceptable conditions which included rewriting the agenda. The gathering, he insisted, was not to be a consultation on WCC grants to 'guerrilla forces . . . and the reactions' of the South African churches, 'but a confrontation by the South African member-churches with the World Council of Churches regarding their abhorrent decision re. the terrorists'. In addition, WCC delegates were to be confined to the International Hotel at Jan Smuts Airport.[44] The government followed this up in 1972 with the Schlebusch Commission which was to investigate the goals, activities and organisation of the University Christian Movement, the Christian Institute, the National Union of South African Students and the South African Institute of Race Relations. It was soon clear that this highly political parliamentary commission had little judicial intent; rather it was designed to manipulate the white electorate and to discredit at least the first three of these organisations, branding them as subversive.[45]

The South African churches in their turn responded to the WCC action with alarm. One by one they disassociated themselves from the grants decision and took what they saw as a non-violent stance. Yet, to the annoyance of the Prime Minister, they and the SACC did not with-draw from the WCC but took the opportunity to broaden their under-standing of 'violence' and once again to attack government policies. For instance, the cautious and socially conservative Presbyterian Church of South Africa was badly divided in voting 75–57 to maintain its membership of the WCC. While it then passed a resolution dissenting from the 'violence pursued by guerrilla organisations' and from the WCC grants to them, the Church nevertheless went on to 'dissent at least as much from the violence inherent in the racial policies of the Government'.[46]

Just how confusing and emotionally upsetting these issues of violence/non-violence were for white churchmen can be sensed from the initial reactions of two SPROCAS directors: Bishop B. B. Burnett, General Secretary of SACC from 1967 to 1969, and Peter Randall, chief executive officer of the project. Burnett argued that the conse-quences of a war of liberation would be worse than anything known at present and that 'Africans would be crazy to go for warfare.' Change, he argued, should be generated from within, by black power which already had a base in the Bantustans and by collective bargaining by African trade unions. On the other hand, if Africans and Coloureds were denied peaceful opportunities for fundamental change, then 'we cannot use high-sounding arguments from morality to forbid their use of force.' Burnett believed the WCC had made a 'great error of judge-ment', yet by 'our silence or inaction or passive support of a society based on racial inequality we are quite as much in error.'[47] Randall's initial response was even more emotive. Support for the liberation movements implied the WCC wanted 'to see these organisations succeed in their aim of taking over control of the white-led countries of Southern Africa'. He wondered if the WCC had considered the kind of society that they would like to see emerging in the region, for the aftermath of a guerrilla war did 'not augur well'. Had the WCC leaders exhausted every other approach 'before giving tacit approval to violence'? He hoped the WCC had considered these matters because 'even those whom the WCC would, by implication, like to see killed, have a call on the compassion of their fellow-Christians. Or have white South African Christians finally been written off as beyond redemption?'[48]

There was a good deal of angst being paraded and Randall's outburst was particularly revealing. Coming from a person with a subtle and penetrating mind, one whose thinking rapidly evolved over the next few years to the point where he came to see the future as essentially in black hands, it showed how deeply the WCC had upset some of the most committed white opponents of apartheid. His response may have been conditioned by the heavily repressed political situation, where any hint of contact or apparent willingness for dialogue with the liberation movements (the ANC or PAC) exposed individuals and organisations to political annihilation under the Suppression of Communism and Terrorism Acts. It also showed little understanding of the WCC's carefully marshalled arguments and fell short of the rigorous analysis Randall was to provide as he directed SPROCAS over the following three years. For the moment, however, like whites in general, Randall made the instinctive and tendentious leap from the WCC's support for the publicity and welfare activities of the liberation movements, to the assumption that this support involved a commitment to the use of violence for change in Southern Africa.

It is difficult to believe that black Christians were comparably upset. Only Bishop Alpheus Zulu, Anglican Archbishop of Zululand and one of the Presidents of the WCC, publicly raised his voice, and then circumspectly. The South African churches, he felt, had not been consulted, and the 'SACC should lodge its protest and demand to be heard.'[49] *Pro Veritate* had the good sense to see the Bishop as atypical and to 'wonder what the silent majority is thinking'; if frankness and openness were possible, which they were not in a society honeycombed with police informers, 'one may find that our black Christian brothers view the WCC decision very differently.'[50] This feel for the situation would have been confirmed by a visit to the Federal Theological Seminary in Alice where the students celebrated long into the night on hearing of the WCC grants.[51] How quickly the situation was changing

was also confirmed by the cautious Bishop Zulu who three years later
was to write:

Very few whites in this country are committed to non-violence and there is no
reason why there should be any more among blacks. After the disillusionment
which followed the quelling of the black passive resistance movement in the
middle fifties, it has become unreasonable to gain support for the hope of a
non-violent solution. The harshness with which discrimination is enforced by
law and custom makes a black man look simple and naive if he continues to
believe and talk of non-violence ever becoming effective. This is a fact even
though nobody speaks of violence.[52]

South Africa had been faced with the spectre of civil war. In this
situation the Christian Institute, like the multi-racial churches,
adopted what it called a non-violent stance and disassociated itself from
the WCC decision. The Institute also added a rider to its statements,
insisting that South Africans had no right to criticise the WCC while
their country's political, economic and social life was characterised by
institutional violence. Given these circumstances, law and order could
not be sacralised.[53] In Naudé's judgement Christianity traditionally
offered two options:

The first point of view is that the Church and the Christian have under no
circumstances the right to approve or to use violence. The other point of view is
that when all other means have failed, a Christian has the right to use violence
to change a situation of unbearable injustice and to bring about a situation of
greater justice.[54]

His own view was the first — that of a Biblical pacificism, which in
Naudé's case was informed and supported by respect for Mahatma
Gandhi and Martin Luther King. It was this commitment that Naudé
maintained in his discussions with the WCC and at the Ulvenhout
consultation.[55] He judged passive resistance to be the answer to
injustice and, like Gandhi, he believed 'that prejudice and fear could
only be removed effectively by justice and love expressed in all actions
of protest and resistance'. This, Naudé argued, had 'the double effect
of liberating both oppressor and oppressed from all falsehood and fear,
all bitterness and hatred.'[56]

Naudé's stance was in fact much closer to the WCC position than
appeared at first sight. The WCC judged the issues to be ill-served by
posing the question in a simplistic way as violence versus non-
violence.[57] Because violence permeated the structures of society and
was well established in human history, the question was not whether it
could be avoided by Christians. Individuals might abhor overt
personal, police, military or guerrilla violence, but life had to be lived
in a particular historical context. Rather, the problem was to 'reduce
the sum total of violence in the situation and to liberate human beings

for just and peaceful relations with each other'. This meant Christians had to 'humanise the means of conflict and build structures of peace'.[58] Clearly the WCC saw its support for the liberation movements as an attempt to minimise injustice and violence in the short and long run; in no sense was it pro-violence. Although Naudé and the Christian Institute adopted a pacifist position, in fact they shared the WCC view that action against injustice was urgently needed so as to reduce the level of violence both in interpersonal relations and in social structures. The question was one of method, of how to do it. In the WCC's judgement it was now a matter of supporting those activities and structures on either side of a civil war which might help to humanise the tragic conflict. Currently absorbed in the early stages of SPROCAS, the Institute still held out some hope that fundamental change might be initiated through the flexible response of white interest-groups. This, and the repressive security system of the apartheid state, may well have prompted the Institute initially to exaggerate its differences with the WCC.

That Naudé was well into a new analysis by 1971, and that this analysis had been pushed further as a result of the WCC debate, is clear from a lecture he delivered to the white students of Natal University in May 1971. It is worth quoting this address at some length for it was an important if rather awkward bridge-statement — an address linking the Institute's thrust for peaceful change through the educational impact of SPROCAS to its increasing sensitivity to black consciousness, and hence to its realisation (shared by the WCC) that the country was drifting into civil war. As Naudé argued, the economic, political and military power of white South Africans:

has strengthened their belief in the inherent and undisputed supremacy of their own kind; it has created a sense of security in their position and has developed an attitude of indifference to the suffering of blacks. [. . .] In this situation the political awareness, frustration and bitterness of blacks is gathering momentum and will take the form of a growing militant black power consciousness, accompanied by an increased psychological withdrawal from everything white. Existing black organisations will be gaining more support and new all-black movements will emerge. [. . .] Increasingly there will be an organisational and/or psychological link-up with black organisations in other parts of the world. [. . .] The natural strength of the idea inherent in the concept of Black Power, as strengthened by decades of discrimination and humiliation, will impel it forward into the hearts of blacks and force it to expression. If the pace of change towards full political, economic and social participation [is not quickly established, the eruption of violence is inevitable]. Organisations usually described as 'white liberal' or 'white-controlled' will face a period of temporary rejection or estrangement . . . until the black community feels that it is strong enough to move back as equals or until these organisations adapt rapidly and creatively to black pressures. Reconciliation will become increasingly difficult. To meet black anger with duplicity or delay is dangerous. To try to meet it with brute force is fatal. To talk about goodwill and tolerance without concerted action is futile. [. . .] I personally do not believe that we are going to avoid a confrontation of violence of some kind. But I do believe that the whites are still in the position of power to diminish the harmful and unpredictable results of such a conflict. There is still time — but time is running out. More than twenty years ago, one of South Africa's great sons and writers, with rare and prophetic insight, made a gentle black man in his *Cry the Beloved Country* say: 'I have one great fear in my heart that one day when they turn to loving, they will find that we have turned to hating.' The older generation of today is largely unwilling to comprehend, accept or heed the serious truth contained in these simple but profound words. It is up to you, gentlemen, the generation of today or tomorrow, to heed and to act to build a responsible society where there will be freedom and justice for all.[59]

It is true that student protests had erupted on the white English-speaking campuses; but a few thousand undergraduates — a fragment of 'the generation of today and tomorrow' — were in no position to usher in fundamental change. Moreover, the great majority of English-speaking students, in spite of NUSAS leadership,[60] were perplexed and ambivalent about radical reforms and black power. Their Afrikaans-speaking counterparts, with very few exceptions, were firmly committed to the structures of apartheid. To make matters even more discouraging, established white interests — 'the older white generation' — responded to SPROCAS with indifference (English-speaking South Africans) or with hostility (Afrikaners), so confirming Naudé's fear that apartheid would inevitably breed a countervailing violence.

By 1974 the Christian Institute and the South African Council of Churches realised that the country was entering a state of civil war. The result was a renewed sense of urgency. As the Portuguese were being driven out of Mozambique and Angola, as black consciousness was surging in South Africa and the ANC was beginning to re-establish its underground organisation in the country, young whites were drafted in increasing numbers to defend the apartheid state. In this context the debate on WCC grants to the liberation movements was transformed into an attempt to generate a movement of conscientious objection.[61]

The sense of urgency which led the Christian Institute and the SACC to take a more determined stand on conscientious objection, had been heightened by the experience of their delegates in May 1974 at the All African Council of Churches Conference in Lusaka. This proved to be a remarkable gathering in which blacks and whites discussed the most contentious issues with frankness and with a great deal of patience and goodwill. It was also a meeting which listened to representatives of the liberation movements. For most of the South African delegates, this was their first personal contact with exiled members of the ANC and PAC, and they discovered that many were committed Christians whose political ideals were formed in large part by their understanding of the Gospels.[62] In a penetrating if contentious address, the General Secretary of the Conference, Canon Burgess Carr, set the tone of the gathering in calling for a 'rebirth of hope', for the 'Christian Church in Africa to be identified as one of the movements of liberation God is using to renovate history', for the Church to 'be a redemptive influence upon all mankind'. The meaning of salvation and evangelisation, Carr argued, could only be understood in the context of human development — the search for dignity, justice and the full realisation of people. Unfortunately, he continued, the Church had not lived up to this; it had not become 'an agent of God's mission of liberation, justice and reconciliation'. What was it that made it so easy for Christianity 'to tolerate the socio-economic exploitation of racism and colonialism, but vigorously oppose the socio-economic institution of polygamy'?

The weakness of the Church, he suggested, was the lack of a theology to deal with injustice. Canon Carr went on to contrast the 'selective violence' of the liberation movements with the 'collective violence of the South African, Rhodesian and Portuguese regimes', and argued, in his most contentious passage, that this context made 'any outright rejection of violence . . . an untenable alternative for African Christians'. The liberation movements should receive 'unequivocal support . . . because they helped the Church to rediscover a new and radical appreciation of the Cross. In accepting the violence of the Cross, God, in Jesus Christ, sanctified violence into a redemptive instrument for bringing into being fuller human life'.[63]

If Canon Carr lost some of his audience, including the South African delegation, on the point of 'sanctified violence', there was no escaping his main argument: 'The Church, which has for so long sanctioned captivity, must now throw its weight on the side of liberation. Unless we do that we shall not be able to exercise the reconciling role we are commanded by the Gospel to fulfil.'[64] Most of the South African delegates, including those from the Christian Institute, were more comfortable with this, even if the awkward question remained: how were they to throw their weight on the side of liberation? One of the delegates was Jane Phakathi, an increasingly influential if recently appointed black staff member of the Christian Institute who was responding rapidly to the insights of liberation theology. In her judgement the Lusaka Conference had been an eye-opener, a 'time of emotional anxiety. We discovered that we had never really gone down to the roots of our Christian role — especially that of prophetic witness in the South African situation.' Carr had been 'controversial', but he and the whole

Lusaka gathering had challenged South African Christians to combat institutionalised violence and to formulate 'a programme for radical change by non-violent means'.[65]

It was with these issues swirling around, and in the hope of appealing to the black liberation and black consciousness movements as much as to whites, that the South African Council of Churches met in August 1974 at Hammanskraal near Pretoria. It called on all Christians not to be stampeded into the military defence of apartheid. South Africa was not being invaded by foreigners, as government propaganda insisted; rather apartheid was generating a civil war. The formal response of the conference was the 'Hammanskraal Resolution', an effort to find a 'third way' — not that of defending the *status quo* as 'law and order', nor that of countering the violence of unjust social structures and repression with revolutionary force. The hope was that a way could be found between the violence of white domination and the force of black liberation — a way of non-violence with conscientious objection and passive resistance as major components. When the Resolution was proposed, Beyers Naudé seconded it and the annual conference, which was now two-thirds black, passed it overwhelmingly. It was the united voice of black Christians being firmly expressed in the councils of the multi-racial churches — and it upset many whites.

The Hammanskraal Resolution acknowledged the one and only God 'who mightily delivered the people of Israel from their bondage in Egypt and who in Jesus Christ still proclaims that. He will 'set at liberty those who are oppressed' (Luke 4.18). Where the government failed to be ' "God's servant for good" rather than for evil and for oppression' (Acts 5.29; Romans 13.4), Christians should 'obey God rather than men'. The Resolution then went on to recall the mainstream traditions of both Catholic and Protestant theology, that the taking up of arms was 'justifiable, if at all, only in order to fight a "just war" '. South Africa was a 'fundamentally unjust and discriminatory society' and this was the 'primary, institutionalised violence which had provoked the counter-violence of the terrorists or freedom fighters'. It was hypocritical to deplore guerrilla violence while preparing 'to defend our society . . . by means of yet more violence'. The Resolution then turned to South African history and declared the injustices suffered by blacks to be 'far worse' than those against which Afrikaners waged war in earlier decades. The churches, therefore, should call on their members to 'identify with the oppressed' and consider 'becoming conscientious objectors'. In addition, the churches were asked to ensure that military chaplains did not provide support for injustice, and to accept pastoral responsibility for 'communicants at present in exile or under arms beyond our borders'.[66] In other words chaplains should be provided to both sides in the civil war.

If the Christian Institute and SACC had opposed and initially misunderstood the position of the WCC in making grants to the liberation movements, it was now their turn to be condemned and misunderstood in what was becoming an atmosphere of war psychosis. With predictable unanimity, members of the cabinet and leading DRC *predikants* attacked the SACC with cries of treason and a call to all loyal citizens to defend the country's borders.[67] Less predictably, the United and Progressive Parties condemned the Hammanskraal Resolution for undermining the security of the country. All these critics refused to acknowledge the basis of the Resolution — its diagnosis of an impending civil war. Perhaps more surprising, the same critical stance was adopted by Fred van Wyk, President of the South African Institute of Race Relations, and by many non-DRC white clergy.[68] According to these voices, the impending struggle was against foreign attack and the SACC was, at best, irresponsible in failing to condemn such military aggression. Taking advantage of this furore, the government moved to repress any incipient movement of conscientious objectors through a Defence Force Amendment Act: this made it an offence, punishable by five years imprisonment and/or a fine of R5,000, to encourage conscientious objection.[69]

In the Christian Institute's judgement, this hostile response from whites was a shocking revelation of how apartheid propaganda about the country being under attack, 'only by Communistic terrorism', had been 'swallowed hook, line and sinker'. Whites were not willing 'to listen to the authentic *black* voice in South Africa'; they were unwilling to adopt a third way which would neutralise military confrontation and remove the 'primary violence' of apartheid by establishing 'a government in which the black community receives effective representation and its God-given human rights such as the whites enjoy'. Naudé and his colleagues feared that the gulf between black and white was on the verge of becoming calamitous. Far from the Resolution 'alienating people from the church' — as the white Presbyterian congregation of Klerksdorp asserted — 'all the black Christians with whom [they had] discussed the matter expressed their joy over the Christian witness at Hammanskraal.'[70]

Naudé and the Christian Institute's staff had played an important part in preparing for the Hammanskraal Resolution and in the subsequent public debate. One by one, the member-churches of SACC called on the government to respect conscientious objection and to legislate for alternative non-military service. Some denominations offered lukewarm support, while others were enthusiastic and saw the Resolution as a 'truly prophetic judgement'. It was used as a study document for justice groups in a number of diocese and parishes. In addition the Roman Catholic bishops, led by the Archbishop of Durban, Denis Hurley, accepted the Hammanskraal analysis and offered the most vigorous support of all. The bishops made a strong plea for both universal and selective conscientious objection, the latter being the individual's right to judge a particular war to be unjust. In Hurley's view, whites had to 'recognise the right of liberation movements to react to the situation in this country'. Whites should seek a peaceful solution through negotiation with black leaders, including those in exile. Given the emerging civil war and the injustices of apartheid, the Archbishop saw the churches' duty as the encouragement of conscientious objection — if necessary to the point of open confrontation with the government.[71] The response of the white parishes, however, was distinctly unenthusiastic so that the attempt to encourage a white movement of conscientious objectors was not immediately successful.

In the aftermath of Hammanskraal, the Institute's modest membership within the white community began to diminish. This, Naudé suggested, was 'simply because many whites who are willing to be "liberal" are unwilling to be liberated.' In other words, liberal whites would not relinquish control. In principle they were prepared to move away from racial discrimination and permit blacks to enter the established economic and political structures under white leadership; but they balked at the risks involved in empowering the poor and oppressed majority. The Institute, Naudé argued, nevertheless had 'no option . . . but to continue to portray to the church and society its understanding of liberation as proclaimed and exemplified by Christ'.[73]

In fact the whole experience of the 'violence debate', from the WCC resolution in 1970 to the All Africa Conference of Churches and Hammanskraal in 1974, moved the Christian Institute into a more activist period — some would say, moved it out of the doldrums. SPROCAS I was essentially an intellectual and educational effort. Certainly it raised the theological, political and economic consciousness of those working on its commissions and those who read its reports. However, it was the concurrent debate on violence which created a heightened sense of crisis and deepened the Institute's understanding of black viewpoints. As a result, SPROCAS II and the Programme for Social Change took an activist direction in an atmosphere of some urgency.[74] These initiatives, allied to firm support for the Hammanskraal Resolution, in turn helped to increase black membership. Even more important, they gathered respect for the Institute within the black protest groups that were forming inside the churches and in the black consciousness movement.

The Institute continued in its efforts to find a third non-violent way, but it now recognised that with increasing black/white polarisation it had to take the option for the poor and do so with much greater determination. This required a firm commitment to black initiatives for change and a far greater sensitivity to black hopes for a more just society. In facing up to this requirement, the Institute was moving into a period of much closer contact with black organisations. It was preparing for a situation 'where more and more blacks will take the lead — not only in the Christian Institute but in society as a whole.'[75]

An important indication of this transition was the Institute's willingness to align itself with the spirit of the Lusaka Manifesto by endorsing its principles, if not its commitment to back guerrilla warfare should all peaceful efforts to dismantle apartheid fail. In April 1969 the heads of fourteen East and Central African states issued the Manifesto as a joint policy statement on Southern Africa. In this they committed themselves to assist in ending the region's 'system of minority control'. This liberation struggle, the statesmen argued, was not for a 'reverse racism'; it was a search for equal rights and human dignity for all — black and white. In this struggle the heads of state recognised that 'for the sake of order in human affairs . . . transitional arrangements' might well have to be made. By 1974 the Institute had come to see the Manifesto as a vitally important and 'relatively moderate document' indicating black aspirations; it was particularly impressed with the African leaders' willingness, even at such a late stage, to seek a peaceful alternative to civil war. As the Lusaka Manifesto put it:

If peaceful progress to emancipation were possible, or if changed circumstances were to make it possible in the future, we would urge our brothers in the resistance movements to use peaceful methods of struggle even at the cost of some compromise on the timing of change.

Unfortunately for the Institute's hopes and the hopes of those black statesmen who met in Lusaka, the apartheid regime was to become even more resolute and ferocious in its defence of white power and privilege.

NOTES

1. SPROCAS, *Five Biblical Principles* (Johannesburg, *c*.1971), p. 1.
2. 'Spro-cas Progress: Report to 2 April 1971' in P. Randall (ed.), *A Taste of Power. The Final Co-ordinated Spro-cas Report* (Johannesburg, 1973), pp. 117, 146.
3. P. Randall (ed.), *A Taste of Power*, pp. 113–16.
4. The Commission's hope was to avoid this disaster through a gradual dismantling of discrimination, initially under flexible white leadership. It also

argued for the constitutional entrenchment of civil liberties and of minority rights as well as the incorporation of black leaders and organisations into a common political system with whites. That system was to be built on decentralised communal authorities, optional segregation and a federal state. The Commission's analysis and recommendations were based on the premise that South Africa had polarised into conflicting racial groups and that constitutional engineering would have to recognise this; simplistic visions of an integrated society structured on the basis of individual liberties alone would not do. *South Africa's Political Alternatives* (Spro-cas, Johannesburg, 1973).

5. The six SPROCAS commission reports were entitled: *Education beyond Apartheid* (1971), *Towards Social Change* (1971), *Power Privilege and Poverty* (1972), *Apartheid and the Church* (1972), *Law, Justice and Society* (1972), and *South Africa's Political Alternatives* (1973).

6. *Power, Privilege and Poverty. Report of the Economics Commission of the Study Project on Christianity in Apartheid Society* (Johannesburg, 1972.), p. 7.

7. *Supra.*, pp. 60ff.

8. *Infra.*, p. 161.

9. D. van Zyl, *Five Biblical Principles* (Johannesburg, *c.* 1971), pp. 1–3.

10. That the Christian Institute itself still shared something of this cast of mind can be seen from the fact that both Naudé and Kotze were approached in January 1971 by the Progressive Party Leader, Colin Eglin, and asked to stand as Party candidates in the next general election (*Sunday Times* [Johannesburg], 6 January 1971). Both declined on the grounds of their pressing responsibilities in the Institute, but it did not seem an inappropriate possibility at the time. Within two years, however, such an approach would have become unthinkable as the Institute's leadership moved in a more radical direction with both Naudé and Kotze identifying closely with the black consciousness movement and black organisations.

11. *Power, Privilege and Poverty*, pp. 11–12. In developing this understanding of a 'Responsible Society', the Commission drew on a lecture by Dr W.A. Visser 't Hooft at the University of Cape Town in March 1971, and the writings of theologian Johannes Metz, Archbishop William Temple and R.H. Tawney.

12. *Ibid.*, pp. 12–15.

13. *Ibid.*, pp. 102–4.

14. *Ibid.*, pp. 104–10.

15. *Infra.*, pp. 149ff.

16. These insights appear to have been those of a small minority on the Commission, Richard Turner, author of *The Eye of the Needle*; Paul Goller, editor of *Challenge*; Martin Fransman, economics lecturer at the University of Swaziland; and Francis Wilson, economics lecturer at the University of Cape Town.

17. *Power, Privilege and Poverty*, p. 56, quoting L. Schlemmer, 'The Factors Underlying Apartheid' in *Anatomy of Apartheid* (Johannesburg, 1970), p. 22.

18. *Ibid.*, p. 70.

19. *Ibid.*, p. 13–16.

20. Christian Institute of Southern Africa, *Director's Report for the Period lst. August, 1972 to 31st. July, 1973* (Johannesburg, 1973), p. 4.

21. P. Randall (ed.), *Apartheid and the Church. Report of the Spro-cas Social Commission* (Johannesburg, 1971), p. 161.

22. *Ibid.*

23. L. Schlemmer, 'Strategies for Change', in *Towards Social Change. Report of the Spro-cas Social Commission* (Johannesburg, 1971), p. 161.

24. P. Randall (ed.), *A Taste of Power*, pp. 6–7.

25. *Ibid.*, p. 8.

26. *Ibid.*, p. 9.

27. *Ibid.*, p. 10

28. *Ibid.*, p. 7.

29. *Ibid.*, p. 11.

30. *Infra.*, pp. 155, 191–2, 219–21. When Richard Turner of the Economics Commission tried to explore these issues further in his seminal work, *The Eye of the Needle*, he and his work were quickly banned and Turner was subsequently assassinated.

31. 'The World Council Bomb', *Pro Veritate*, October 1970, pp. 1–2.

32. Community and Race Relations Unit of the British Council of Churches, *The Special Fund of the World Council of Churches Program to Combat Racism*, (London, *c.* 1971), p. 1. Hereafter *The Special Fund*. The Fund was set up as a separate entity so that only those choosing to support the Programme to Combat Racism would have their contributions to the WCC used for the Programme's purposes.

33. 'The WCC Decision. Special Issue', *Pro Veritate*, October 1970, p. 3; E. Regehr, *Perceptions of Apartheid*, p. 204.

34. *Ibid.*; *Cape Times*, 17 September 1970.

35. *The Special Fund*, p. 2.

36. 'Recommendations by the International Advisory Committee for the Programme to Combat Racism regarding the Special Fund', *Pro Veritate*, October 1970, p. 4.

37. *Pro Veritate*, April 1974, p. 14; SPROCAS Political Report, *South Africa's Political Alternatives* (Johannesburg, 1973).

38. *Ibid..*

39. *Cape Times*, 15 September 1970.

40. *DRC Newsletter*, July–August 1970, pp. 1–2.

41. *DRC Newsletter*, September 1973, pp. 1–4.

42. *Supra.*, pp. 97–8.

43. *Cape Times*, 15 September 1970; E. Regehr, *Perceptions of Apartheid*, p. 86.

44. Letter from the Prime Minister, the Hon. B.J. Vorster to Rev. J. de Gruchy of 8 May 1971, and the full correspondence between the Prime Minister, the SACC and the WCC, reprinted in *Pro Veritate*, July 1971, pp. 14–25. In 1974 the government expelled Dr Lucas Vischer, head of the WCC Faith and Order Commission, and placed a ban on all WCC personnel visiting the country. E. Regehr, *Perceptions of Apartheid*, pp. 65–6.

45. *Infra.*, pp. 174–9.

46. *Pro Veritate*, October 1970, p. 7.

47. *Cape Argus*, 16 October 1970.

48. *Pro Veritate*, September 1970, pp. 15–16.

49. *DRC Newsletter*, July–August 1970, p. 3.

50. *Pro Veritate*, September 1970, p. 2.

51. Author's interviews.

52. *Pro Veritate*, February 1974, p. 18.

53. *Fragmenten en citaten uit toespraken interviews en artikelen van Beyers Naudé uitgegeven ter gelegenheid van zijn erepromotie in die theologie aan de Vrije Universiteit* (Utrecht, 1972), p. 33. (Hereafter *Fragmenten . . . Vrije Universiteit*.) See too *Pro Veritate*, July 1970, p. 2, editorial.

54. International Commission of Jurists, *The Trial of Beyers Naudé*, pp. 84–5.

55. *Ibid.*

56. *Post* (Johannesburg), 5 October 1969.

57. *Pro Veritate*, March 1971, p. 4, being the statement on methods of achieving social change adopted by the Central Committee of the World Council of Churches at Addis Ababa, January 1971.

58. *Pro Veritate*, April 1974, p. 10, being the WCC Central Committee's 1973 report on 'Violence, Non-violence and the Struggle for Social Justice'.

59. *Fragmenten . . . Vrije Universiteit*, pp. 28–30.

60. The NUSAS executive, and Student Representative Council Presidents at the Universities of Cape Town, Rhodes and the Witwatersrand, associated themselves with the Hammanskraal Resolution. In doing so they accused the government of deliberately developing a 'war psychosis which blindly clings to militarism', rather than rooting out inequalities and permitting blacks 'to share equally in the political process and the wealth of the land'. *South African Outlook*, August 1974, p. 135.

61. While this response was an indigeneous phenomenon, it was encouraged by the success of the peace movement in the United States which opposed the war in Vietnam (E. Regehr, *Perceptions of Apartheid*, p. 265). Under the South African Defence Act, conscientious objectors were drafted for non-combatant military service; no alternative was allowed for non-military service. As such objectors had to be *bona fide* members of a pacifist denomination, there was no allowance for persons who refused to serve in what they considered an unjust war; in their case the penalty was 12–15 months' imprisonment. *Ibid.*, p. 269; South African Institute of Race Relations, *Annual Survey of Race Relations*, 1973, pp. 58–9.

62. E. Regehr, *Perceptions of Apartheid*, pp. 270–1.

63. Burgess Carr, 'The Engagement of Lusaka', *Pro Veritate*, June 1974, pp. 5–12, being the Secretarial Address to the assembly of the All African Council of Churches, Lusaka, Zambia, 12–21 May 1974.

64. *Ibid.*

65. J. Phakathi, 'The Liberation Issue', *Pro Veritate*, October 1974, p. 6.

66. *Pro Veritate*, August 1974, p. 6, being the SACC Resolution of 2 August 1974 at its annual conference at Hammanskraal.

67. Christian Institute, *Information Service News Digest*, 9 September 1974, pp. 1,6.

68. *Pro Veritate*, August 1974, p. 7.

69. E. Regehr, *Perceptions of Apartheid*, p. 272; South African Institute of Race Relations, *Annual Survey of Race Relations*, 1973, p. 59. The Church Insti-

tute and other church bodies continued to encourage conscientious objection. However, as there was no immediate groundswell of resisters, the authorities hesitated to use their new powers.

70. *Pro Veritate*, August 1974, pp. 7–8, 'White Reaction Evades the Issue', a Christian Institute statement signed by the Revs. Beyers Naudé, Brian Brown and Roelf Meyer. See too Tokatso Mofokena, 'Whites must provide an Alternative to Violence', *South African Outlook*, August 1974, p. 120.

71. *Cape Times*, 27 August, 5 September 1974; *Sunday Times* (Johannesburg), 8 September 1974.

72. For further analysis of the 'Conscientious Objection Debate' see J.W. de Gruchy, *The Church Struggle in South Africa*, pp. 138–47.

73. Christian Institute, *Director's Report for the Period August 1, 1973 to July 31, 1974* (Johannesburg, 1974), p. 8.

74. *Infra.*, pp. 139ff.

75. Christian Institute, *Director's Report for 1972/1973*, p. 5.

76. '*The Lusaka Manifesto*', *Pro Veritate*, January 1975, pp. 14–16. See too 'Press Statement re Lusaka Manifesto, 12 December 1974, *ibid.*, p. 16.

9

WHITE CONSCIOUSNESS AND THE
SEARCH FOR A NEW PRAXIS

While the Christian Institute was exploring the theoretical alternatives
to apartheid, agonising over the WCC grants and debating conscientious objection, it had also been searching for new modes of non-
violent action. As we have seen, several issues clarified by 1974 with
the Institute countenancing passive resistance, increasing its black
staff, moving closer to black organisations and nurturing black initiatives. However, there were moments before these new commitments
were accepted when the Institute appeared to some to be a spent force.
Certainly Naudé, his directors and staff were far less certain of themselves by the late 1960s and early 1970s than they had been
immediately after the formation of the Institute. Their faltering efforts
to build Christian community, to arouse and to challenge Christian
consciences, were nevertheless an important part of a process which
eradicated false hopes of easy grace. The experience of the mid-1960s
dispelled any illusion of painless reform and reminded those involved
in the attempt to dismantle apartheid that the Cross preceded the
Resurrection. At the centre of these efforts was the attempt to nurture
Christian fellowship through Bible study, a commitment on which the
Institute never wavered from its formation in 1963 to its banning in
1977.

The Institute's Bible study groups were ecumenical and inter-racial.
They met approximately nine times a year and were scattered throughout the country. Within two years of founding the Cape regional office
in 1968, there were a dozen such groups in the Western Cape, and the
beginnings of a comparable network existed in Natal by the early
1970s. In the Transvaal, where the activities of the Institute's headquarters had taken the limelight to the neglect of local regional leadership, the two dozen or more Bible study groups of the mid-1960s had
peaked as they ran into the patterns of resistance or indifference which
the Institute encountered throughout white society.[1] There was also
severe limits to black participation. For Africans these multi-racial
groups were generally suspect as white initiatives and were usually
seen as paternalistic in an era of rising black consciousness.

Staff members nevertheless spent a good deal of time fostering the
Bible study groups and preparing material for them: pamphlets and
booklets which emphasised the hope of church unity and a prophetic
ministry 'to warn society of dangerous paths, wrong directions and evil

systems'.[2] Theo Kotze, as Director of the Cape Regional Office, was one of the most active staff members in travelling widely to initiate and sustain these fellowships, moving in annual sweeps as far afield as Windhoek and Port Elizabeth. In the latter city, he and Beyers Naudé led a Bible study week in 1969; the following year Kotze worked with Dr G.W. Asby of Rhodes University to produce a week of discussion, meditation and prayer designed to lead to 'a new understanding of the great truths the Bible proclaims'. Rather than worship 'the gods of political might, technical genius and economic power', the central theme of the week called Christians to recognise the 'sovereignty of the God of the Bible'. As Kotze put it, 'most of us are sick and tired of pious resolutions made at conferences and church meetings.' The Bible week was for reflection *and* action. It was designed to overcome the 'absurd and tragic' divisions of race and church, and to support people who would work 'through their Christian way of life' to 'eradicate the deep injustices of the land'.[3] Unfortunately, what action should be taken was not always obvious.

The Institute prepared a series of Bible study aids designed to incorporate both the vertical (God-person relationships) and horizontal (inter-human relationships) dimensions of Christianity. According to these booklets, the task was to integrate worship, form human community and search for justice. Study sessions emphasised God's grace in history, the working out of Christ's gospel through the 'Spirit's world-wide power' to draw individuals and societies towards love, more just social structures and reconciliation. Christian mission was a 'struggle for history'; that is, it went beyond the overt fellowship of the church, beyond private and communal spiritual life to the social and political commitments of Christians. Mission involved the formation and renewal of cultures through the painful process of 'confrontation, conflict, strife and freedom'. Christ had called on humanity to reject the domination of powers and principalities, to break out of the stultifying limitations of family, tribe, race, caste and worship of the state or nation so as 'to participate in the tasks of the coming of His kingdom'.[4]

A Covenant Liturgy, which was used during the early 1970s, offers a further glimpse of the Biblically-based liberation theology that was slowly evolving within the Christian Institute.[5] The Act of Praise was to a God of love who created man in His own image, to Jesus Christ 'who went about proclaiming the good news of the kingdom of God; who came to proclaim release to the captive and liberty to those who are oppressed.' Thanksgiving was offered to a Father who called for bread to be shared with the hungry, for the poor to be housed and for 'the oppressed [to] go free and to break every yoke'. Following the sermon there was a prayer for forgiveness for the sins of omission as much as

those of commission, a part of the liturgy which reveals that in spite of
the Institute's evolving theology, its main focus at this time was still on
the raising of white consciousness rather than on the historically more
effective task of working with the poor. Penitence was necessary
because

> we have kept silent in the face of injustice; we have enjoyed prosperity in the
> face of our brothers' need; we and our families have lived together in security
> while others are separated from husbands, wives and children. Shame on us.
> We who make unjust laws and publish burdensome decrees, depriving the
> poor of justice, robbing the weakest of God's people of their rights.

These themes from Isaiah were followed by further admonitions from
the prophets and the New Testament; whereupon the liturgy drew to a
close with a list of intercessions, the call to love one's neighbour as
oneself, and the Lord's Prayer.[6]

Such liturgies as well as Bible study pointed to the need for action. As
we have seen, SPROCAS I with its six commissions of enquiry tried to
prepare for this at the intellectual level. As we shall see, this led to
SPROCAS II and the Programme for Social Change. However,
before these new ventures, an exploratory attempt was made in the
early 1970s to raise white consciousness on the devastating effects
apartheid was having on African family life. This involved two
initiatives, a 600-mile pilgrimage or walk to publicise the evils of
migratory labour (a pilgrimage for which the *Covenant Liturgy* was
written), and the personal witness of a courageous and prophetic
member of the Institute, the Rev. David Russell.

The 'Pilgrimage of Confession for the Healing of Family Life'
started in Grahamstown on the Day of the Covenant, 16 December
1972, with eight white members of the Institute setting out for Cape
Town.[7] This method of raising white consciousness had been readily
accepted by church hierarchies — perhaps to assuage their embarrassment at the lack of action in the wake of the WCC challenge. The
approach, it was argued, was one that whites could not easily smear as
'political'. The hope was that the pilgrimage would raise so basic an
issue that the hearts and consciences of whites, if they were ever to
respond, would do so on this matter of family life.

Grahamstown was selected as the starting-point because the
Voortrekker leader Jacobus Uys had been presented with a Bible and
an address of sympathy when he camped at the settlement in 1837 *en
route* to the interior. The intention was to focus once again on the Bible
as a source of inspiration — but this time to call the descendants of the
Voortrekkers, and all white South Africans, to confess their misuse of
power, and to inspire in them a renewed search for a Biblical understanding of justice. Whites, it was argued, had betrayed their steward-

ship in using their power to establish a system of labour control which was 'tearing husband and wife apart' and devastating the lives of 'countless thousands of voteless victims'. Claiming to act in the 'name of Christian faith', white Christians had identified with white power or become accomplices through 'the sin of omission', in effect trying to wash their hands of responsibility. Migratory labour was 'a cancer in the life of the nation', and white Christians should undertake 'effective and sacrificial action' to eradicate it. If they were not to be accused of the most 'hollow hypocrisy', whites would have to press parliament 'to make it legal for every South African husband and wife who wish to do so to live together with their children in a family home.'[8]

After weeks of hiking, stopping for liturgies and Bible readings, impromptu roadside discussions, press conferences and town meetings along the way, the small group was joined by a crowd of several hundred as it approached Cape Town. Beyers Naudé and Archbishop Denis Hurley were among those who joined the march as it headed for a final demonstration on Rondebosch Common. There a substantial if somewhat disappointing crowd of approximately 4,000 adopted the 'Charter for Family Life' and listened to speeches by Naudé, Hurley and a footsore Francis Wilson — pilgrim and economist from the University of Cape Town.

When the publicity died away, and spontaneous white support did not materialise, it was far from clear what further action should be taken. Rather than generating a movement of protest, the pilgrims and the Christian Institute were faced with a numbing anti-climax. White South Africans had other concerns. A Family Life Office was established to continue the effort to raise white consciousness, but it gained little support and was disbanded. There was talk of further pilgrimages in other parts of the country, but nothing came of this. Co-operating with SPROCAS and drawing on the carefully researched work of Francis Wilson, the Institute drew up a 'Memorandum on the Pass Laws, Influx Control and Migrant Labour'. This was submitted to the Deputy Minister for Bantu Affairs in August 1973 — a futile exercise.

The Memorandum presented a well-argued case for accepting the reality of a permanent African population in the urban areas and phasing out migrant labour. It also outlined the practical steps to achieve this goal: the staged elimination of the pass laws, provision of freehold tenure and a crash housing programme. In setting priorities and implementing these changes 'effective consultation with Africans themselves was essential'.[9] Like the Pilgrimage, the Charter and the Family Life Office, this direct approach to a government which took not the slightest notice was a total failure. The Christian Institute was as far as ever from engendering 'effective and sacrificial action'.[10] Indeed, it was becoming clearer and clearer that the sociological reality of racism, class privilege and apartheid ideology was only too effective in blocking out the Biblical call to justice.

This forlorn if prophetic struggle to move white opinion and so to shift government policy on one of the most basic of Christian commitments — maintaining family life — was symbolised, above all else, by the determined resistance of David Russell. The Pilgrimage had been only one of his efforts in a prolonged series of public protests. The son of an advertising executive and United Party MP who had broken away in 1959 to form the Progressive Party, Russell attended the prestigious Anglican high school, Bishops. He went on to Cape Town University and read history at Oxford before entering Mirfield Seminary in Yorkshire. Deeply influenced by Mahatma Gandhi and Charles de Foucauld, he returned to South Africa where he soon took direct action against the injustices of apartheid.[11]

In 1969, as the white assistant priest of an African pastor in the Transkei near Kingwilliamstown, Russell began ministering to the African 'resettlement area' of Dimbaza, one of the dumping grounds for dependants and redundant labour 'endorsed out' of the urban areas. Working with the destitute and burying the community's children, he asked repeatedly for official assistance. Receiving none, he moved to confront the authorities. Living in utter simplicity, a person of humility, dogged courage, few words and constant service, Russell was widely respected by blacks and an inspiration to his fellow-members of the Christian Institute. Because of his commitments to a church and a world 'turned upside down', to black leadership and a genuinely indigenised Christianity, he was able to remain on good terms with his friends in the black conciousness movement. This was particularly true of Steve Biko and Barney Pityana, both of whom played key roles in the formation of SASO and in establishing the value commitments of black consciousness and black theology. In Russell's understanding 'the Church was duty bound to be a disturbing presence', whether it be in 'Thessalonica or Pretoria, London or Lusikisiki'. Indigenisation certainly did not mean conforming to a given social structure or passively accepting an established tradition, whether it be black or white. The church could only become more indigenised by

identifying with and *becoming naturally part of* — rooted in — the plural society of Southern Africa. [. . .] The Church must now throw in its lot with the needy, the underprivileged, the insulted; it must be *poor* with the poor, but not in any patronising or romantic way. It must seek for every man what is due to him as a man; struggle for the freedom of all men in all the senses of that word, and be prepared to die in the struggle.

Whites, Russell argued, were just as much in need of freedom as blacks: 'freedom from their prejudice, and from a great deal of their wealth'.[12]

Dimbaza, with a population approaching 10,000, had negligible employment opportunities in the surrounding white areas. Those few women who found work received R5 to R7 per month; the few able-bodied men lucky enough to find casual labour tried to maintain their families on R20 per month. Pensioners received R5 per month. After serving this community for two years and burying thirty-eight children in the first two months of 1971, Russell wrote to M.C. Botha, Minister of Bantu Administration and Development, requesting a personal meeting to explain the situation. While he drew attention to the overall poverty and demeaning unemployment, the specific issue he raised was that of widows who were being dumped in the rural areas and denied the monthly R2.50 *per capita* maintenance grants for which they would have been eligible in the cities.[13]

Because Botha was not prepared to see him, Russell travelled to the steps of St. George's Cathedral close by Parliament in Cape Town. There he began a ninety-hour vigil and fast surrounded by his posters: 'Hunger is Violence'; 'Resettlement Widows Desperate'; 'Bible Demands Justice for Widows'. This time he was able to see the Secretary for Bantu Administration and for a moment was hopeful of some amelioration. However, the Department's cynical response was that the widows could receive their maintenance grants of R2.50 per month but they would have to forgo the resettlement rations. These were valued at R2.55.[14]

Russell returned to Dimbaza in April 1972 and attempted to live for six months on an African's pension of R5 per month. At the end of every month he wrote to Botha describing his experience. After two months he was bitterly cold at night in spite of his clothes and six blankets. He was also having to drink mugs of hot water to stave off hunger. 'At times,' he wrote, 'I feel quite limp and weary — listless and without zest for life. May those pause and wonder who charge the poor of "having no initiative", of "laziness" and of "not bothering to help themselves" '. After five months he was 'under a strain which I don't believe I could carry much longer. I feel a great tiredness deep within me. I just do not know how Africans "manage" '.[15] Not having heard from Botha, Russell now accused him of having hardened his heart, 'like Pharaoh', and explained that the final sixth letter would be sent to DRC ministers of the NGK — 'my colleagues in Christ's healing work'.[16]

It was when all this had been to no avail that Russell, talking things over with Francis Wilson and other close friends in the Christian Institute, decided to try the Pilgrimage to Cape Town. When that failed to generate a politically significant movement of white compassion,

Russell was as nonplussed as the other pilgrims. He continued his lone protest in later years and was arrested on several occasions, for example when entering African areas without a permit and when protesting at the destruction of African homes at Crossroads near Cape Town in 1976. After being banned in 1977 with other leading members of the Christian Institute, Russell broke his banning order the following year by working with the Crossroads community; again in December 1979 he defied the authorities by attending the Anglican Synod which was meeting at Grahamstown.[17]

These were lone protests, a personal style of resistance which Russell initiated in the late 1960s. As for the Christian Institute itself, in the anti-climax following the Pilgrimage there was much uncertainty over the strategy and tactics to pursue. The Institute's sense of ineffectiveness in the early 1970s was strong; the prospect of gaining significant leverage in the white community was increasingly remote; and neither its leadership nor its general membership were ready for a determined campaign of passive resistance. Some serious re-thinking was called for. Not only was the Institute failing in its mission to transform the Christian commitment of whites. SPROCAS, its educational effort, had drained the Institute's energies and had done virtually nothing to build bridges with black organisations.

Nevertheless, while the scene was bleak, by 1971–2 the Institute was on the brink of a major reorientation. When this shift took place, it reflected a new understanding of the historical forces at work in South Africa, at least by the Institute's leadership and those recruited to staff SPROCAS II. This new understanding prompted the launching of SPROCAS II in the particular form that it took, for at the heart of the new venture was the Black Community Programme — a commitment to give power to the poor and oppressed through supporting the black consciousness movement. SPROCAS II also involved a renewed attempt to raise white consciousness. Although this was again largely futile, it did encourage a small minority of whites to countenance passive resistance and to reject the capitalist underpinnings of apartheid. To understand the context which elicited this far more radical understanding of the Biblical call for justice, which in turn prompted the Institute to identify with the black consciousness movement and led to a critical analysis of the country's capitalist structures, it is important to set the scene in some detail, to use a microscopic lense for a moment.

By the end of 1971, Naudé in Johannesburg and Kotze in Cape Town, with their staff and the Institute's Board of Management, had come to a more profound understanding of the rapid polarisation taking place in South African society. Not only were the SPROCAS I commissions beginning to produce their findings, but 1971 was the year when African workers struck in Namibia and the incidence of black strikes began to rise in the Republic itself. Academic studies were detailing the inexorable movement of black labour into the urban areas and confirming the continued divergence of white/black wage differentials. The few opinion polls taken pointed to increasing African bitterness. SASO's leaders were speaking out with anger and eloquence; when Biko and Pityana addressed an inter-racial student conference at Cape Town University, they shocked their white audience with an assertive black consciousness. They also gave a directive to white liberals to leave blacks alone and to turn their attention to overcoming the fetid racism of their own community.[18] These attitudes were understood within the Institute, since several of its leading personalities formed important friendships with young black radicals, some of these friendships dating back to the University Christian Movement of the late 1960s. It was in 1971 that Naudé met Steve Biko and was deeply impressed by him. The Institute's painful and deteriorating relationships with AICA also alerted many to the dangerous mix of white goodwill and paternalism. The result was a capacity to listen — an institutional humility — a new sensitivity to the call for black solidarity as the essential means to liberation. The deep frustrations as well as the potentially disruptive and creative power of black Christians in the multi-racial churches also erupted during 1971. Segregated Roman Catholic seminarians challenged the autocratic white authorities at Hammanskraal (near Pretoria) and the institution was closed down. Shortly thereafter a group of black lay Catholics in Johannesburg, led by Drake Koka, called for the consecration of a black bishop, a black cardinal and an end to the institutional racism of the white-controlled hierarchy.[19]

If the Institute's leadership was influenced by these signs of impending industrial turmoil and rising black anger, 1971 was a year which also confirmed their deepening pessimism about the government's inflexibility, its adamant refusal to discuss the fundamentals of apartheid. Prime Minister Vorster continued to push ahead with his 'outward-looking policy' — his attempt to increase trade and to establish diplomatic relations with independent African states while tightening up repression at home. This was the year when President Banda of Malawi, whose capital city was being built with South African funds, provided the one overt success for Vorster when he exchanged ambassadors and was welcomed to Pretoria with pomp and ceremony. Official communiqués referred to the prospect of a constellation of Southern African states — a regional commonwealth of some sort. However, below the surface of this public relations campaign, Naudé and his colleagues knew Afrikanerdom to be hardening its apartheid stance in a determined drive to maintain an exclusive,

privileged and regionally dominant white nation. In Naudé's judgement, even the younger generation of Afrikaners, including those in
the universities, were shifting to the right within a militaristic *volk*
ethos. Young men were joining the police and army with rising enthusiasm.[20] Gatsha Buthelezi, Prime Minister of Kwa Zulu and a person
with whom Naudé was in serious dialogue at this time,[21] was scathing
in his condemnation of the hypocrisy of apartheid and the government's pan-African manoeuvres. His response was to call for a
national convention of blacks and whites, a new start and a re-writing
of the South African constitution rather than the impending civil war.
But, like Naudé and the Christian Institute, Buthelezi was not
optimistic: 'White South Africa', he suggested, 'was like a child who
plays with a time-bomb, caring very little what will happen when it
eventually explodes'.[22]

As we have already seen, the regime's response was to increase its
repression of the black consciousness movement and to intensify
harassment of dissident Christians.[23] 1971 saw Vorster's refusal to
enter into conversation with the World Council of Churches[24] and his
confrontation with the Archbishop of Canterbury who was visiting the
country. In sharp contrast with the patterns of injustice exposed by the
SPROCAS commissions, the Institute's fear of impending civil war
and Buthelezi's call for a national convention, the Minister of the
Interior, Theo Gerdener, expressed the cabinet's view: 'a small but
active group of church leaders [was] trying to bring about a massive
onslaught on the Government's policies, even if it could ultimately lead
to violence'.[25]

This was the historical situation in which the Institute and staff of
SPROCAS II began to draw more consciously on the political theology
coming out of Europe and on the liberation theology of Latin America.
In the process, as we shall see a little later on, they interacted with the
protagonists of black theology. The result was an indigenous South
African form of liberation theology which began to emerge both from
within the Christian Institute and from the black consciousness
movement.

The early stimulating influence of European and Latin American
theologians can be seen in the pages of *Pro Veritate* in the late 1960s, and
particularly from 1970 onwards. These influences can also be traced in
the internal memoranda of the Institute and SPROCAS II. It was at
this time too that *Pro Veritate* began to pay more attention to injustice
throughout the Third World. Although Metz and Moltmann were
prominent among the Europeans, and Camara the favourite among
the Latin American exponents of 'consciencisation' (the awakening
consciousness/conscience of an oppressed and exploited people), there
were others including de Chardin, Illich and Freire. Freire's

educational methods were used by the Institute's Transvaal
Community Organiser, Anne Hope, in the years preceding the confiscation of her passport and her one-way exit from the country in 1973.
Before leaving she prepared several bibliographies for the Institute
which introduced members to these writers as well as to black
American and black South African theologies of hope. Freire's
methods were also used by the Black Community Programmes that
were part of SPROCAS II.

The resulting 'consciencisation' within the Institute was carried
further by the visit in 1970 of Professor J. Verkuyl of the Free University in Amsterdam. Verkuyl was invited by the South African Council
of Churches, but he spent a good deal of time with members of the
Christian Institute. He also contributed a series of pamphlets on the
'theology of transformation' or the 'message of liberation today' which
the Institute published, distributed and used for Bible study groups. In
these pamphlets Verkuyl provided a concise introduction to the
theology of hope. History had 'become an open and dynamic arena for
God's mission and the mission of the church *en route* to the kingdom'.
But, to bear responsibility for such Christian mission, Verkuyl argued,
required a sense of the times, an understanding of structural injustices
acquired through the careful study of one's particular historical
conditions. In a previous age, in the days of Shaftesbury and
Wilberforce, the 'fulfilment of the times' required an attack on slavery;
whereas 'in our day the items on God's agenda are clearly the
relationship between the rich and the poor lands, relations between the
races, and the problems of modern war'.[26]

If Verkuyl helped to develop a theology of liberation, he also had a
word of caution for churchgoers. While the 'name of Jesus' was the key
unlocking the meaning of history, the name which 'fills time and
history with hope', the church had failed to 'show what liberation
means through liturgy, word, service and fellowship'. Unfortunately,
an 'open church with a clear spoken message in service to the world'
had been as 'rare as a white raven'. The hope was that New Testament
congregations would 'tear down the barriers between classes and races'
and form the new fellowship. But in reality Christians had to accept
with humility that much of Christ's work would in fact be done by
'groups which stood outside the official churches', often in a strained or
dialectical relationship with those churches.[27]

These themes were in step with the theology behind 'A Message to
the People of South Africa' and had been expressed, albeit somewhat
paternalistically, in the intentions of SPROCAS I.[28] As we have seen,
liberation theology was explored and analysed with increasing frequency by other writers in *Pro Veritate*; its themes were encountered as
well in the informal and formal contacts linking the Institute with an
international network of Christian fellowship in Europe, Britain and

North America. One consequence of this broadening experience was a growing sense within the Institute of being linked, through time, to figures like Dietrich Bonhoeffer in their struggle against the demonic and closed ideology of Nazism. Of even more importance was an increasing awareness of the new, worldwide Christian movement for human liberation which cut across denominational lines and confirmed the South African experience. As a result the Institute might be said to have passed through a transformation in consciousness which re-established its confidence and gave it new heart. The Institute then set out once again, some thought belatedly, to generate an increasing number of small Christian fellowships or basic communities. These groups were to work independently as well as catalytically within the churches, with Justice and Peace Commissions and Challenge Groups. Wherever possible they were to be directly involved with the poor and oppressed. In this way it was hoped the church might become a vital 'agent for real change', able to follow Latin American precedents where after years of patient organising effort 'the church suddenly provided crucial leadership.'[29] Initially SPROCAS II was planned as an effort to bring about these changes.

But Southern Africa was not Latin America, and SPROCAS II evolved in unexpected ways. It soon became clear that the initiatives which were to hold out any prospect of effecting radical changes in the apartheid order were not to come from within the formal organisations of white-dominated churches, or even from the efforts of black Christians to confront white hierarchies. Rather, the more effective of the SPROCAS programmes were those which became black initiatives and supported the new generation of black leaders as they struggled to establish their own cultural and political organisations.

That this priority was discerned and then incorporated in the final plans for SPROCAS II, late in 1971, was not only due to the rapidly changing South African situation. It was also due to the evolution of Peter Randall's strategic planning as he tied up the loose ends of SPROCAS I and turned to planning its successor. Randall had directed SPROCAS I, co-ordinating its many committees and publishing its reports, tasks which he carried out with imagination, competence and a remarkable capacity for teamwork. Nevertheless, as late as June 1971 he still thought of SPROCAS II as a predominantly white initiative designed to help blacks — a programme with a white consultative committee and 'specialist action groups', the latter being drawn from the overwhelmingly white SPROCAS I commissions. The projects envisaged at this time were rewriting the social studies textbooks for private schools, starting credit unions, drawing up a code of conduct to guide corporations in their dealings with black labour, and supporting adult education at the practical level of household budgeting, nutrition and improved agricultural techniques for African farmers. There were also to be 'community self-surveys' or decentralised research and remedial self-help efforts.[30]

This approach accepted the inevitability of black pressure but it was still paternalistic, a strategy rooted in the analysis of the SPROCAS I Social Commission Report which was written in 1970. While the Commission had been undecided as to whether the 'major lines of race conflict will be drawn between whites and all blacks collectively, or primarily between whites and Africans with other groups in a marginal position', its hope for peaceful change lay in 'organized and regulated bargaining' with blacks exerting 'constructive pressure on whites and within white-controlled institutions'.[31]

By October of 1971 this strategy had been transformed.[32] The result was that when SPROCAS II was launched in January 1972, Randall, with the backing of Naudé and the Institute, came out in support of the new solidarity which was emerging among blacks. Disillusioned by the inflexibility of whites, Randall put aside his serious reservations about the black consciousness movement and began to support it. This support took the form of Black Community Programmes which quickly became the central feature of SPROCAS II. As with SPROCAS I, the Christian Institute worked in co-operation with the SACC to sponsor the venture even if there were signs that the Council, under its General Secretary John Rees, was apprehensive at the radical trend now being set. The sponsorship and good offices of the SACC were to remain important, but financial support from member-churches stagnated at a very disappointing level. With less than one per cent of the SPROCAS budgets coming from South African churches, SPROCAS II was forced to rely on the Christian Institute's international contacts for its financial survival, almost half of the funding coming from the Netherlands.[33]

SPROCAS II, or the renamed Special Project for Christian Action in Society, was expected to run for two years (1972/3) with an anticipated budget of R130,000. As the Christian Institute and the SPROCAS staff soon realised, the programme was wildly optimistic in hoping to defuse the impending civil war by initiating a new direction in white politics while simultaneously encouraging the assertiveness of black organisations. In practice any group committed to a black viewpoint — to the hopes of the dispossessed — was excluded from influential white circles. Nevertheless the attempt was made to effect a 'dual thrust into both the black and white communities'.[34]

The Black Community Programmes (BCP) was to be staffed as a separate black initiative so that it could assist leaders who were already active in their African, Coloured or Indian communities.[35] When the BCP, as one of its first tasks, surveyed the network of organisations which emerged within black communities following the formation of SASO in 1968, it found over seventy black-controlled 'cultural, educational, political, professional, religious, self-help, student, welfare and youth organizations'.[36] Given this context, SPROCAS II, diagnosed its greatest temptation as the formation of still further new programmes for the poor — the danger of creating new dependences rather than giving power to leaders who were already active in existing black organisations. The BCP was therefore launched as a black initiative which meshed with the forces for change already welling up on the black campuses, in SOWETO and other urban centres. Its goals were 'to help the Black Community become aware of its own identity . . . create a sense of its own power . . . and organize itself'.[37]

The person chosen to direct this effort was Bennie Khoapa,[38] a black social worker who, after his graduation in 1959, worked as a personnel officer and then as Secretary for the African activities of the South African National Council of the YMCA. Khoapa was fully in step with the black consciousness movement. Although the BCP became formally autonomous only in March 1973, he insisted on and was given a free hand from the start. He was therefore able to attract other staff members of the calibre of Steve Biko, Barney Pityana and Bokwe Mafuna who quickly facilitated an important range of contacts and new opportunities for the black consciousness movement. In addition the BCP staff exercised a profound influence on the white staff of SPROCAS II and on the leadership of the Christian Institute. By the end of 1973, BCP was the vital centre of SPROCAS II; its share of the total budget had risen from 20 to 50 per cent and this was to increase still further as the White Community Programmes failed to generate a significant response and so were phased out.[39] The issue, as Randall pointed out, was whether whites would move from their reformist attitudes to the radical stance of supporting black organisations and leadership. Very few were prepared to do so. However, for those in the Christian Institute and in SPROCAS II, as well as for several key personalities in the SACC, it was now clear that 'fundamental change — a radical redistribution of power, land and wealth — [would] ultimately be initiated and brought about by blacks.'[40] At the very least, independent, organised black pressures were essential if spontaneous and increasingly widespread violence was to be avoided.[41]

The White Community Programme (WCP) was staffed by whites and intended to raise white consciousness; that is, the responsibility of well-meaning whites was now seen to be in their own community. There the task was to release individuals from their race and class biases, to free them from the morally stultifying grip of their own privilege so that they might 'respond creatively to black initiatives'.[42] However, little was accomplished, for unlike the BCP which could move with and support the tide of resurgent black protests, the White Programme faced an intractable sociology.

The WCP was planned as a broad range of catalytic efforts which would activate a critical social consciousness. This consciousness, it was rather desperately assumed, must be lying dormant among at least a small minority of whites in the multi-racial churches, opposition political parties, the business community, white trade unions and youth organisations. At first the 'target group' was to be the 'liberal, affluent establishment . . . with their hypocrisy and built-in racism/exploitation which they inflict daily through their institutions'.[43] Questionnaires were to be sent out to spur critical evaluation in the hope that the resulting surveys would spark a number of decentralised community efforts. While WCP staff might initiate these efforts, local groups, stiffened by Christian Institute activists, were expected to float free and pursue their own tactics for on-going reform.[44]

In trying to generate such activities, the WCP would 'not draw back from tactics of polarization where these seem to be creative and necessary'. The intention was also to work with justice groups which were being formed by some churches. If all went well, there was even talk of 'a new [white] political movement' which might emerge by the mid-1970s.[45] White consciousness was expected to rise, not through the efforts of some tightly disciplined political vanguard, still less through a conspiratorial clique. Rather there was to be an open, in practice amorphous and ultimately hopeless attempt to regenerate the culture of white society. As the Christian Institute suspected, even as the programme was being launched, there was insufficient yeast — no critical mass. Certainly the dough did not rise, despite the efforts of a few brave individuals.

One of the first white-focused efforts of SPROCAS II was a 'Labour Programme'. When this was initiated in August 1972, hundreds of letters and questionnaires were posted to employers' organisations, major corporations, trade unions, industrial councils and churches calling for a debate on black labour conditions. The response was patchy and the national debate on a 'Code of Employment Practices' never materialised.[46] In its introduction, the questionnaire sent to denominational schools quoted Johannes Metz's call to the church to mobilise 'that critical potency' inherent in the 'central tradition of Christian love'. When this love was activated, Metz continued, it led to an 'unconditional determination to bring justice' which moved beyond inter-personal charity into the social dimensions of public policy. The questionnaire then asked for information on black employees: cleaners, gardeners, kitchen staff, drivers and maintenance personnel. Again the response was patchy, but it indicated that within the white-dominated churches, wage levels, food rations, hours of employment, vacation time, family accommodation (or lack of it), length of contracts and methods of dealing with complaints were almost invariably those of apartheid society. The challenge of being questioned and the resulting publicity startled some school authorities and shamed a few into gradually improving these conditions. However, SPROCAS II only ran for two years and such amelioration did not affect the segregated structure of church schooling, nor did it change the essentially menial nature of black employment.[47]

Although SPROCAS increasingly diverted its limited funds from the White to the Black Community Programmes, it persevered in its attempt to stir up grass-roots ferment among whites. In this it had to rely very heavily on members of the Christian Institute who tended to form the nucleus of any new activity. To facilitate this, the Institute prepared Biblically-based study guides to the commission reports and to other SPROCAS I publications. It also focused its Bible-study groups on the goals of SPROCAS II. When fifty Capetonians formed a Citizen Participation Group which included several city councillors, municipal officials and university faculty, it was chaired by the Rev. Des Adendorff of the Institute's Cape Regional Office and launched with the help of Danie van Zyl, Communications Director for SPROCAS II. In this case the intention was to create a pressure-group in municipal government and to repeat the precedent throughout the country.[48] In practice the group slowly disintegrated.

A further example of SPROCAS II activity is provided by 'KEMPEG' an ecumenical organisation formed by Methodists, Anglicans and Roman Catholics in Kempton Park, a white suburb of Johannesburg. The group affiliated itself to the Christian Institute and set out to determine a programme of action. The outcome was symptomatic of the tendency for these small groups to falter on encountering massive white indifference, whereupon they either disintegrated or turned away from the radical intentions of SPROCAS II and consoled themselves by undertaking welfare services for blacks. In this instance KEMPEG's attempts to raise *white* consciousness evolved (should one say degenerated?) from study groups, multi-racial social gatherings and experimental justice liturgies into the provision of educational opportunities for black ministers and lay workers in the churches of nearby Tembisa Township. A combi van was hired to transport the participants to evening sessions at a Boksburg extension college where they attended shorthand and typing classes or prepared for their school-leaving certificates. One person eventually gained access to a university college.[49] All this may be considered admirable in itself and KEMPEG also fostered a feeding scheme; but it was not focused on raising consciousness in the white community. The temptation was still to do things *for* Africans.

In addition to nurturing such activities, staff from the Christian Institute and SPROCAS helped to conduct workshops for Roman Catholic Justice and Peace Commissions and Anglican Challenge Groups. Unfortunately these study groups in the white parishes tended to be apprehensive and unresponsive — ready for lengthy discussions on SPROCAS I publications but unable to empathise with the more radical perspectives of SPROCAS II. In these depressing circumstances Archbishop Denis Hurley of Durban provided a rare example of the type of follow-up SPROCAS II hoped for. Ecumenical in his approach to social justice, Hurley was a prominent member of the Christian Institute and he encouraged the Natal Justice and Peace Commissions to work with the staff of SPROCAS II. When, after two rather disappointing years, SPROCAS II ended and very few white Catholics, lay or clerical, were being radicalised, Hurley approached the Natal Council of Churches and with their co-operation launched *Diakonia* in 1974. This was an inter-denominational pastoral institute essentially designed to continue the dual thrust of SPROCAS II's white and black programmes.[50] Elsewhere the White Community Programmes had few successes, unless one associates the robust political activism of the Christian Institute's Cape Town staff with the new cast of mind of SPROCAS II. It was during the SPROCAS II years of 1972–3 that Kotze and his Cape Regional Office committed themselves to supporting student protests and took the Institute on to the streets of Cape Town. Nevertheless the sense of isolation among this small group of activists persisted. Even after Kotze was arrested on the Cathedral steps and, with his family, came under physical intimidation plus psychological harassment, there was no sense of steadily growing support from the white community. Solidarity had been established with student protesters, but the rest of white South Africa remained hostile, indifferent or incapacitated through fear.[51]

Even if the White Community Programmes were essentially a disappointment for those trying to bring about change, they were sufficient, in conjunction with the Black Community Programmes, to produce a sharp increase in police surveillance and repression. By September 1973 intimidatory police raids on the offices of SPROCAS and the Christian Institute had become regular occurrences and every executive member, of both the White and Black Community Programmes, experienced state action of some sort: Khoapa and his four black staff were banned; Kleinschmidt too was banned and his four colleagues had their passports confiscated.[52] Staff members were also prosecuted for refusing to testify before the Schlebusch Commission.[53]

As a result of this flurry of intimidation, but also because SPROCAS publications were selling well, a last-ditch attempt was made to extend the White Community Programmes for a year. Renamed the Programme for Social Change, the hope was that it might yet be possible to draw a larger number of potentially activist whites into confessing communities. This effort was long overdue, for such support groups were vital necessities if individuals were to sustain their nerve and commitment in the climate of intensifying repression. The Programme supported the goals of the BCP and set out to call conferences, provide source materials and 'promote radical alternatives to the existing social order' for as long as its meagre funds lasted.[54] The Programme for Social Change was launched in January 1973 with an advisory committee that included Beyers Naudé, Theo Kotze, Archbishop Denis Hurley, Bishop David Russell, Alan Paton, André Brink (the Afrikaner novelist) and Francis Wilson.[55] Once again Peter Randall was in charge as executive director, this time with a budget of R25,000 gathered together by the Christian Institute.[56]

The results were again disappointing and finally disillusioning. In the 1974 general election whites continued to move behind the apartheid regime with increasing numbers of English-speaking South Africans voting for the Nationalists.[57] When a white self-tax movement was started as a voluntary means of redistributing wealth in favour of a trust designed to assist black self-help projects, it failed to gather significant support. Only a few dozen individuals in each of the major cities participated and the venture faded out.[58] Perhaps the most shattering experience of all was when the Programme for Social Change tried to raise white consciousness about black detainees. This took the form of protest prayer vigils. There was also a fund drive for the dependants of political detainees arrested in 1974 on account of their black consciousness activities and held incommunicado for periods from 85 to 129 days.[59] A modest crowd of several hundred passed through St George's Cathedral in Cape Town during a twenty-four-hour vigil and the Christian Institute's Cape office continued to raise funds for the detainees and their families. Elsewhere trends were even less encouraging. In Johannesburg the bells of St. Mary's Cathedral tolled every day at 1 p.m. for five minutes as a call to prayer. Lunch-time services were held every Wednesday at Diakonia House, the Christian Institute's Headquarters, and the Catholic Bishops' Conference spoke out against arbitrary arrests, solitary confinement and detention without trial. However, when the Witwatersrand Council of Churches held its protest meeting, only thirty persons attended and the Council took no further action.[60] These events had not generated anything but a flicker of white political protest; the detentions did not stir the white parishes and it was only in the Cape where the Institute's Regional Office diligently nurtured the effort that the churches 'played an active role in providing emotional, spiritual and financial support for the detainees' families'.[61] The whole frustrating experience was symptomatic of the rapidly diminishing part which the small minority of radical whites could play in generating opposition to apartheid and its police apparatus.

By mid-1975 the Programme for Social Change had exhausted its modest budget and burnt itself out. The Schlebusch-LeGrange Commission might consider it a 'threat to the state', but Horst Kleinschmidt and the Programme's white staff were 'finding that the PSC does not have any real relevance to substantial change in South African Society'.[62] From now onwards the Christian Institute had no option but to view its own predominantly white membership as, at best, a vital but remnant fellowship: vulnerable, imperfect and ineffective yet a small clear voice of Christian hope. Fortunately stronger voices were being raised by the oppressed themselves and, paradoxically, as the Institute became more self-effacing, more committed to give power to others, more sensitive to the black consciousness movement, so its own life was to be renewed.

NOTES

1. *Cape Times*, 7 April 1971; Christian Institute, *Director's Report 1972/1973*, p. 6.

2. *Cape Times*, 7 April 1971, the Rev. Theo Kotze, 'The Christian Institute — What it is and what it does'.

3. *Evening Post* (Port Elizabeth), 24 October 1970. A particularly lively study group formed at Addo, one that embraced a significant number of blacks including illiterates.

4. R. Meyer, *Involvement:serve the King in this world* (Johannesburg, Christian Institute Bible series, 1972), pp. 1-43.

5. Unfortunately the terminology of this theology, and that of the Institute in general, was still thoroughly sexist.

6. *A Covenant Liturgy* (circa 1971), issued by SPROCAS.

7. The pilgrims were: François Bill, Trevor de Bruyn, Norman Hudson, Athol Jennings, Victor Kotze, David Russell, Augustine Shutte and Francis Wilson — an ecumenical group of clergy and academics.

8. *A Pilgrimage of Confession for the Healing of Family Life in South Africa, 16th December, 1972* (Johannesburg), pp. 1-2.

9. *Memorandum on the 'Pass Laws', Influx Control and Migrant Labour*, as reprinted in *Pro Veritate*, December 1973, pp. 211-12. See too F. Wilson, *Migrant Labour in South Africa*, pp. 212-15.

10. The Institute also threw its weight behind the movement to resist the destruction of District 6, the old and characterful Coloured area at the centre of Cape Town. This historic community was to be removed to the outskirts of the city and the area made available to white commercial developers. Once again the protests were ineffective.

11. *Sunday Times* (Johannesburg), 9 Decenber 1969; *Cape Times*, 1 December 1979.

12. D. Russell, 'Church Indigeneous,' *South African Outlook*, September 1970, pp. 37–8.

13. Rev. D. Russell to the Hon. Mr. M.C. Botha, the Ministry of Bantu Administration and Development, 2 April 1971, *South African Outlook*, December 1973, p. 201, 'Letters from Dimbaza'.

14. Author's interview with D. Russell, 26 January 1973, Cape Town; *South African Outlook*, December 1973, p. 201.

15. 'Letters from Dimbaza', *South African Outlook*, December 1973, pp. 212–16; *Cape Times*, 18 May 1972. See too *Pro Veritate*, October 1973, pp. 11–13, a medical report on the Dimbaza rations which were comparable to those Russell was trying to survive on. They were judged to be 'seriously deficient in calories and vitamin C, and deficient in niacin and tryptophan for women who were moderately active. The diets are more inadequate for growing teenagers, especially boys, for adult men and for pregnant, lactating or even very active women.' Signed A.S. Truswell, Professor of Nutrition and Dietetics, Queen Elizabeth College, University of London, 25 October 1972. See too D. Cleminshaw, 'Dimbaza Rations: a comparison with Boer War Concentration Camps', SPROCAS discussion paper, *c.* 1973, pp. 1–6.

16. *South African Outlook*, December 1973, p. 216.

17. *Sunday Times*, 22 September, 9 December 1979.

18. H.W. Van der Merwe and D. Welsh, (eds.), *Student Perspectives on South Africa* (Cape Town, 1972), p. 195.

19. When an Auxiliary Bishop was consecrated in 1972, Koka offered his congratulations but went on to 'warn our Black Bishop and priests not to fall into the comfortable seats of their white predecessors, [at] the expense of their own downtrodden Black brothers and sisters'. The 'hypocrisy of the supposed non-racialism of the white-dominated Catholic Church' had to end; it had to 'fall into the hands of the indigenous'. The Bishop was called upon to 'identify with us in our struggles and aspirations [and to] help us to bring Christ and Christian values back into the Catholic Church in South Africa'. Black Justice and Peace Vigilantes' Committee, Johannesburg, 22 October 1972, *Open Letter to His Lordship Bishop P.J. Buthelezi on His Consecration*.

20. Author's interview with Beyers Naudé, Cape Town, 6 February 1973.

21. Their relationship cooled later with disagreements, *inter alia*, on the role of foreign investment in the apartheid system.

22. *Sunday Times*, 27 August, 1972.

23. *Supra.*, pp. 93ff.

24. *Supra.*, pp. 113–14.

25. *Cape Times*, 9 August 1971.

26. J. Verkuyl, *Theology of Transformation or Towards a Political Theology*, (Johannesburg, Christian Institute of Southern Africa, 1971), p. 7.

27. J. Verkuyl, *The Message of Liberation Today* (Johannesburg, Christian Institute of Southern Africa, 1971), pp. 20, 22, 24.

28. *Supra.*, pp. 103ff.

29. 'Sprocas White Programs: Some Preliminary Working Notes', October 1972, pp. 3–4, mimeo.

30. P. Randall, 'SPRO-CAS TWO', 1 June 1971, pp. 1–8, mimeo.

31. P. Randall (ed.), *Towards Social Change. Report of SPRO-CAS Social Commission* (Johannesburg, 1971), pp. 49, 161.

32. 'SPRO-CAS 2: Planning Meeting: 15–16 October 1971' (Johannesburg), pp. 1–2, mimeo.

33. *Financing of SPROCAS:*

		Rand
1969	SPROCAS 1	13,810
1970	SPROCAS 1	12,258
1971	SPROCAS 1	17,071
1972	SPROCAS 1	1,094
1972	SPROCAS 2	45,606
	BCP	17,920
1973	SPROCAS 2	45,000.
	BCP	50,300
TOTAL	1969 — 1973	203,059

The major donors for the 3 SPROCAS projects:

	Rand
Kirchlicher Entwicklungsdienst	39,062
Landskirche Hessen-Nassau	30,969
Kom over de Brug	24,340
Church of Norway	23,781
Group Chairman's Fund	22,000
Christian Aid	20,099
Maurice Webb Trust	14,000
Christian Fellowship Trust	9,166
Church of Sweden Mission	7,500
HEKS	4,323
Rissik Trust	1,400
Vrije Universiteit, Amsterdam	1,400
Total donations received from South African churches, approx.	1,200

P. Randall (ed.), *A Taste of Power*, p. 129. See too Spro-cas 2, *Basic Principles and Aims* (Johannesburg, 1971), p. 13, mimeo.

34. Spro-cas 2, *Basic Principles and Aims*, p. 1.

35. *Ibid.*, p. 8.

36. P. Randall (ed.), *A Taste of Power*, p. 67.

37. Spro-cas 2, *Basic Principles and Aims*, p. 8.

38. In addition to Randall and Khoapa, the executive staff of SPROCAS II included the Rev. Danie van Zyl, Communications Director, who previously worked with the Institute and AICA. Neville Curtis, retiring President of NUSAS, was designated Organiser for White Programmes; towards the end of 1972 Horst and Ilona Kleinschmidt were appointed as Transvaal Organisers while Curtis concentrated on the Cape.

39. P. Randall, 'Spro-cas: Motivations and Assumptions', *Reality* (Pietermaritzburg), March 1973, pp. 2–4.

40. *Ibid.*, p. 3.

41. R. Meyer, *Poverty in Abundance or Abundance in Poverty?* (Johannesburg, Christian Institute of Southern Africa, 1973), p. 37.

42. Spro-cas 2, *Basic Principles and Aims*, p. 8. See too *Spro-cas White Programmes: Some Preliminary Working Notes*, pp. 2–6.

43. *Spro-cas White Programmes: Some Preliminary Working Notes, p. 5.*

44. *Ibid.*, pp. 1–6; *A Programme for Action for the Christian Institute* (Johannesburg, *c.* January 1973), pp. 1–5.

45. *Spro-cas White Programmes: Some Preliminary Working Notes*, pp. 2–3.

46. 'Spro-cas 2 Launches Labour Program' (Johannesburg, August 1972), press statement, mimeo.

47. 'Spro-cas 2 Questionnaire', and covering letters (Johannesburg, 1972), mimeo.

48. *Ecunews Bulletin*, 16 November 1972, p. 4.

49. *CI News*, November 1973, pp. 5–6.

50. The Anglican, Methodist, Presbyterian, Congregational, Lutheran and Catholic churches were involved. *PSC Newsletter*, March 1974, p. 9; *Pro Veritate*, May 1975, pp. 23–4.

51. *Supra*, p. 93.

52. *Star*, 2 December 1973; *CI News*, November 1973, pp. 1–3.

53. *Infra*, pp. 174–6.

54. Christian Institute of Southern Africa, *Director's Report for the Period lst. August, 1972 to 31st July, 1973* (Johannesburg, 1973), p. 4.

55. *CI News*, November 1973, p. 5.

56. The publishing activities of SPROCAS I and II were transferred to the independent Ravan Press, of which Randall also took charge. SPROCAS publications had been selling at almost three times the expected rate in 1972/3, with annual book revenue up from R9,000 to R20,000. Sales were particularly good to church organisations, but commercial outlets were increasing their orders too. P. Randall (ed.), *A Taste of Power*, pp. 125–6; author's interview with P. Randall, Johannesburg, 13 March 1973.

57. The opposition United Party lost four seats to the Nationalists and five to the Progressives, and then disintegrated. Peter Randall stood in Johannesburg as a member of the Social Democratic Committee. Given his socialist platform, his commitment to a fundamental redistribution of power, wealth and land in favour of blacks, he did well not to lose his deposit and to hold his United Party opponent to a 3,000 majority. *C.I. Newsdigest*, 26 April 1971, p. 1.

58. *PSC Newsletter*, March 1974, pp. 8–9; *Pro Veritate*, May 1975, p. 22.

59. *Infra*, pp. 90, 181.

60. Programme for Social Change, *3rd Report on Arrests, Detentions and Trials of Members and Supporters of: South African Students Organization, Black Peoples Convention, Black Allied Workers Union, Theatre Council of Natal, Black Community Programmes*, (Johannesburg, 18 April 1975), pp. 1–15.

61. *Ibid.*, p. 10.

62. H. Kleinschmidt, L. Crawford and M. McCarthy, 'Program for Social Change' (Johannesburg, July 1975, form letter to supporters).

10

BLACK CONSCIOUSNESS AND THE SEARCH FOR A NEW PRAXIS

If the white consciousness programmes failed to make any noticeable headway against the sociological reality of white privilege and racism, the SPROCAS II Black Community Programmes (BCP) had an easier task in moving with the currents of a resurgent black nationalism. However a word of caution is necessary, for even here it is easy to exaggerate the BCP's impact. It did not initiate a new protest movement; rather it set out to support the black consciousness movement which had its independent origins in the late 1960s. Moreover, its over-optimistic and even grandiose plan to function as a catalyst in establishing and co-ordinating networks of black churchmen, youth organisations and trade unions was frustrated by limited resources, the immensity of the task and state repression. Nevertheless the BCP did provide a significant boost for black organisations as they approached a point of confrontation with the state. In addition it became a conduit for the flow of ideas from the black consciousness movement into the Christian Institute, a factor which, when allied to the appointment of black staff members in the Institute, helped to transform the thinking of Naudé and his colleagues.

The resurgence of African nationalism, usually described as the black consciousness movement, can be traced in an organisational sense to the formation of the anti-apartheid and multi-racial University Christian Movement (UCM) in 1966. The UCM was soon riven by internal tensions because black-white co-operation was increasingly difficult in the aftermath of Sharpville and in the context of repression as well as impending civil war. Given this racial polarisation, police informers, police intimidation and the military draft for white students, it became apparent that the old liberal model of a non-racial student organisation could not withstand the pressures of disillusioned and outspoken black undergraduates. Nevertheless the UCM attracted a rising number of such students from the isolated and segregated African (tribal), Coloured and Indian colleges. In part, this was because it started to function as a matrix within which inter-black contacts could grow. By 1968 a black caucus emerged with Steve Biko and Barney Pityana at its centre, a caucus which was determined not only to understand the long history of black protest in South Africa, but also to draw on the current writings of black Americans, for example Baldwin, Carmichael, Cleaver and Cone. One result was that the

UCM started to focus on black theology and its Biblical foundations — the Scriptures' call for the liberation of the poor and culturally
oppressed.[1] It was from this black caucus that the initiative came to
form the South African Students Organisation (SASO) in 1968; and it
was SASO which played a leading role in arousing black student unrest
in the 1970s. It was SASO too which took the initiative in drawing
together a wide range of groups to form the Black People's Convention
in December 1971[2]: student, church and clerical organisations
including AICA and the Interdenominational African Ministers'
Association, and social and cultural groups like the Association for
Educational and Cultural Advancement of African People. This
attempt to fill the political vacuum included a number of somewhat
rusty politicians of an older generation. Of these, perhaps Dr Willy
Nkomo was the best-known personality. With Anton Lembede,
Nelson Mandela and others he had been a leading figure in the formation of the African National Congress Youth League in 1943.[3]

The black consciousness movement, with its component of black
theology, was a diverse phenomenon ranging from SASO and other
student groups to the BCP and the umbrella organisation, the Black
People's Convention. It was also strengthened by the activities of
several small cultural organisations, the most aggressive, radical and
influential of these being drama groups. When the 1973/4 round-up of
black leaders took place, five of the thirteen brought to trial[4] were from
this world of black theatre: Saths Cooper, Strini and Lingam Moodley,
Sadecque Variava and Solly Ismail. While active in SASO, in 1969
they founded the Theatre Council of Natal (TECON) on the Indian
campus.[5] TECON became an important part of a 'black renaissance',
a flowering of drama among young people whose own lives were often
the stuff of tragedy. This was the case with Abraham Tiro and Mthuli
Shezi. Tiro was a member of SASO and played a dramatic role in the
student unrest of the early 1970s. Speaking as President of the Student
Representative Council at the University of the North (Turfloop), he
delivered an uncensored, honest and hard-hitting speech at the 1972
graduation ceremony. His resulting suspension triggered mass student
protests.[6] Following his expulsion, Tiro took up a teaching post but was
sacked on the insistence of the Department of Bantu Education. After
working as a full-time organiser for SASO, he left the country late in
1973 with several other members of SASO and sought asylum in
Botswana. There he was killed by a parcel bomb in February 1974.
The package bore the stamp of the International University Exchange
Fund;[7] it blew off Tiro's hands and disembowelled him.[8]

Like Tiro, Mthuli Shezi joined SASO and worked hard behind the
scenes to draw the Black People's Convention together. Six months
after his election as Vice-President of the BPC in July 1972, Shezi died

in highly suspicious circumstances. All indications were that he had been pushed under a train after protesting to white railway officials about their handling of several black women passengers. Shortly before his death, Shezi had written a play which was produced by several of the black drama groups. Entitled *Shanti*, it told the story of a love affair between an African man and an Indian woman. It was set in a military training camp for freedom fighters.[9]

In addition to TECON, other political theatre groups included the People's Experimental Theatre (another Natal initiative) and the Music, Drama, Arts and Literature Institute (MDALI) which was formed in Soweto in 1972.[10] The MDALI message was 'black selfhood and self-respect'. It was not interested in portraying the corruption of black life through comedy or tales of unfaithful women, dissolute men, broken homes, thuggery and social decay. That type of theatre, the Institute declared, 'leaves the people broken and in despair'; rather 'we tell the people to stop moaning and to wake up and start doing something about their valuable and beautiful black lives.' In 1971 TECON produced a free adaptation of *Antigone* which explored the theme of confrontation with apartheid. It opened with a hanging, used newsreel footage and included a chorus of black women. A later show was presented at the 1973 SASO conference and entitled *Black Images* — an intense political collage of music, poetry and one-act plays. It opened with a call to black unity,[11] scorned the 'non-white' Uncle Toms — 'You who give your master a blue-eyed faithful look' — and attacked the township thugs who preyed on their own kind. Other scenes focused on the exploitation of black workers and reaffirmed traditional music and art forms. The powerful finale used 'staccato music', drumming, flashing lights and angry background voices to create a sense of urgency before moving into the praises of black leaders from Tshaka and Dingaan to Mandela, Sobukwe and SASO personalities including Biko and Tiro. It ended with the challenge: 'Everyone says Yes to FREEDOM. Everyone says Yes to BLACKNESS. But how many are prepared to die?'[12]

When the thirteen black consciousness leaders were eventually brought to trial in 1974, those who used black drama as a 'liberating weapon' faced Charge no. 7: conspiracy to 'stage, present, produce and/or participate in inflammatory, provocative, anti-white, racialistic, subversive and/or revolutionary plays or dramas'. In spite of such repression, black theatre continued to evolve for a short while, if in a more circumspect way. The Black Renaissance Convention of 1974[13] made a brave effort to co-ordinate this remarkable release of suppressed talent, but by the end of 1975 continued bannings and detentions had purged the struggling drama movement of its more overt black consciousness messages.[14]

The SPROCAS II Black Community Programme was therefore launched as the black consciousness movement was moving out from the campuses to the black townships, into the school-age population, black parishes and the black working class. As a result the BCP became part of this much wider movement, this revival of African political resistance to apartheid. While it had neither the desire to eclipse SASO and the Black Peoples Convention, nor anything approaching a capacity to control the movement, the BCP set out to function as a catalyst, as a facilitating, consciousness-raising team of full-time black organisers — an unheard-of luxury in African political life. Certainly the modest budget of R18,000 for 1972 (which ran into an overdraft of R10,000 with the Christian Institute) and R50,000 for 1973[15] precluded any illusions of grandeur. Yet, if the BCP's initial goals were modest, in that they involved working with existing scattered groups and producing black consciousness material for seminars and conferences, in the longer run it hoped for more dramatic developments. Having helped the 'Black Community to become aware of its own identity . . . to create a sense of its own power, to organise [and] analyse its own needs', the next phase was to be a national mobilisation under new black leadership.[15] Whenever possible, local and regional initiatives were to be taken in conjunction with SASO so as to establish a country-wide network of contacts. These contacts were expected to form the basis of youth and trade union movements. The BCP was also to work for the formation of a black caucus within each of the multi-racial churches.[16]

If its achievements fell short of such widespread mobilisation, the BCP nevertheless took several important initiatives. These are difficult to assess in terms of their ideological impact within the black community, but they contributed in a significant way to the growth of a new, more confident and assertive black leadership. This was in part because of the quality of the BCP's own staff. By the end of 1972 the BCP executive comprised Bennie Khoapa as Director, Steve Biko the founder-president of SASO and Bokwe Mafuna an ex-journalist and trade-union organiser. They were joined for a brief period in 1973 by Barney Pityana before the entire staff was banned in March of that year.[17] Although this was a stunning blow, a good deal was achieved in less than two years.

The BCP set out at once to become a registry for black community activities which meant, as a first step, surveying the range of cultural and political organisations already in existence. Several important publications followed. Given the absence of a black-controlled press, these books and pamphlets provided a forum for black thought and political analysis — an intolerable security risk for those in charge of the apartheid state. The first annual survey, *Black Review 1972*, was a major achievement. It reported cultural and political events, trials and sporting activities, so raising black confidence and giving some intimation of the extraordinary ferment taking place. A quarterly, *Black Viewpoint*, printed speeches and articles by the new black consciousness leadership, its first number appearing in September 1972 with Biko as editor. Working in co-operation with Peter Randall at Ravan Press, several other works were printed of which *Cry Rage* (published in December 1972 and banned in March 1973) became the most famous. A collection of invective, anguished poetry and indomitable hope, it sold over 4,000 copies in its brief three months of legal circulation.[18]

Such a cultural and political renaissance, such a publishing phenomenon, had to be stopped in its tracks. Biko was banned after the publication of *Black Viewpoint*, vol. 1, and so his editorial had to be torn out of all copies. When Khoapa was banned, all 230 pages of *Black Review 1972* had to be withdrawn from distribution. In addition, of course, the banned BCP leadership could no longer be quoted in any South African publication.[19] Nevertheless, the ramifications of this short BCP publishing effort were incalculable. By mid-1973, and in spite of the severe restraints imposed by the bans, *Black Review 1972*, *Black Viewpoint, A Handbook of Black Organizations* and *Cry Rage* had sold a total of 12,300 copies.[20] These circulated widely and were mostly read by many more than one person.

While these publications were in preparation, Khoapa and the BCP had also been organising literary classes, seminars, black caucuses and conferences. Their first major initiative was the May 1972 three-day 'Conference of Black Church Leaders' at the Edendale Ecumenical Centre near Pietermaritzburg. Approximately eighty participants — mainly clergy — gathered on this occasion and a further twenty-three at a second conference in August. Both conferences or workshops were designed to co-ordinate the efforts of 'black church leaders in the so-called multi-racial churches'. The goal was to 'increase their effectiveness' as black leaders, to gain 'control over [those] churches whose membership is mostly black', and to use such power to change priorities. This meant re-orienting the churches 'towards the needs of the black people'.[21] A recurring theme was the need to form caucuses within particular churches and to broaden such black solidarity through strengthening the Interdenominational African Ministers' Association. In this way blacks were to transcend denominational divisions — those artificial barriers introduced and maintained by 'the missionary churches'. It was time, the BCP argued, for blacks to take up new responsibilities, to lobby and purge the churches of racism; black leadership was essential, and black theology should be introduced into the seminaries. The BCP also hoped to raise additional funds and to co-ordinate a countrywide network of adult education centres that would make use of church buildings — an ambitious project which never really got underway. More modestly, BCP staff underwent training themselves and started several literacy classes in co-operation with SASO.[22]

These conferences, and the caucusing that followed, signalled the emergence of a more assertive black leadership within the churches. This led, *inter alia*, in the late 1970s to the election of the Rev. John Thorn, Bishop Desmond Tutu and the Rev. Sam Buti to top positions in the SACC. Pressures for black advancement were mounted within all the multi-racial denominations, and in the NGK a serious confrontation developed between the 'daughter'-churches and the white 'mother'-church.[23] If, at first, this caucusing led to a great deal of misunderstanding and friction, it also engendered a heightened sense of urgency among white hierarchies and produced some innovations. One such case involved the Church of the Province of South Africa. In this instance a campaign was mounted for a stronger black voice in church policy and a change in the method of electing synod representatives. As a result, the old basis of parish representation, which gave a disproportionate voice to relatively small white congregations, was replaced by representation on the basis of communicants.[24]

Although the BCP encouraged and may be said to have legitimised black caucusing within the churches, its easiest rapport and most successful entrée was with youth groups. Co-operating whenever possible with SASO as it tried to reach a wider constituency in the townships, Khoapa, Biko and their co-opted assistants set out to address high school students and recent school-leavers. By providing an element of on-going organisational capacity, the BCP drew would-be activists into training sessions and directed their energies into student-parent discussion groups, literary classes and the handful of medical clinics that became a symbol of community service. Existing youth organisations, for example in the parishes, were judged to be effete; they lacked a 'meaningful philosophy', were without any 'direction in their programmes' and were condemned for having focused on the narrow interests of their members.[25] To be more specific, they were given over to picnics, games, dances and 'non-directional' Bible study classes which were judged to be pious and irrelevant given the desperate needs of the oppressed community. The BCP Youth Programme set out to draw representatives from such groups into local training sessions and regional conferences with a view to launching a national youth movement sometime in 1973.[26] The full-scale co-ordination that was envisaged could not possibly have been achieved before the 1973 bannings. Nevertheless, in the short space of just over a year, new contacts were made, ideas spread and expectations were kindled.

Working from a headquarters in Durban, it was natural for the BCP to concentrate its initial youth work in the townships around Durban and Pietermaritzburg while SASO paid more attention to SOWETO. A series of ten training sessions was held in the region during 1972. Towards the end of the year, as confidence grew, workshops were held further afield: on the Witwatersrand, in the Transkei, in the Eastern and Western Cape. A typical 'Youth Leadership Conference', held at the Edendale Ecumenical Training Centre on 19–20 August 1972, drew forty-three registrants and was organised by Steve Biko and Harry Nengwekhulu. Within the next few years at least half of those attending were to be detained by the security police for their organisational efforts in the townships — efforts which, after the brutal repression that was about to be unleashed in the second half of the 1970s, came to rely on decentralised and more informal networks rather than vulnerable, centralised organisations like the BCP itself.

While the training programme set out to raise consciousness on matters of race and class exploitation, its terminology was certainly not that of a well-honed doctrinaire Marxism. Rather, one discovers an understandable obsession with the white man as problem and a straightforward outrage at grotesque economic inequalities. There was also alarm at the prospect of a black minority being co-opted in defence of the existing structures of injustice. The thrust of apartheid was presented as the deliberate nurturing of ethnic divisions so as to maintain a situation where blacks, with Africans in the lowest echelons, formed the base of both the socio-political and economic pyramids. Members of the small black middle class, it was argued, owed their relative wealth to the existing social order and would be 'unwilling to relinquish what they have'. They attached 'a lot of importance to a wrong value system, white equals valuableness' and so were turning their backs on the problems of their black communities. Having set the scene in general terms, the 'forces working against the black community' were then analysed in some detail: the legislation behind segregation, influx control and population removals; patterns of police intimidation and the ultimate sanction for oppression — the military; an economic system designed to secure the existing distribution of land, and to maintain the powerlessness of black workers through low wages, weak or non-existant trade unions, job reservation and the continued flow of money into the coffers of white-owned corporations and the apartheid state.[27]

With this analysis in mind, the workshops turned to overcoming black passivity. This was attributed to a culture of ignorance, a paucity of community organisations, informers and an escapist other-worldly religiosity which provided individuals with 'false comfort [in which they] found salvation for the soul in the world beyond, while sheepishly submitting their minds and bodies for slaughter in the present world'.[28]

The point was clear. Black leaders saw themselves as having to change the culture of intimidated communities. What was required, they argued, was some understanding of the historical situation, a rejection of the system of apartheid plus the study of black culture and black identity. Group and community consciousness had to be raised, not only through workshops like the one at Edendale, but through a country-wide dispersal of young leaders trained to start local discussion groups. In addition there were to be newsletters, drama and the formation of simple community centres — in some cases as simple as vacant garages. In all this, it was emphasised, a determined effort should be made to close the generation gap and to reach out to the illiterate and poorly-educated.[29]

As with the church leaders' conferences, it is difficult to assess the full impact of the Youth Programme. What is clear is that the BCP was able to build on SASO's pioneering efforts and assist in raising black consciousness within the townships. In this way it contributed in a significant if frustrated way to the growth of confidence among blacks in their teens and in their twenties, a confidence which was to produce the resurgence of mass protest in 1976 and the subsequent, continuing unrest.

A rare example of a supportive church-based training programme, which continued in a formal way to nurture black leadership as the state immobilised Biko and his colleagues, was the National Youth Leadership Programme. This was begun in 1970 by Dr Alex Boraine, General Secretary of the Education and Youth Department of the Methodist Church. There was also some Anglican support for the Programme. Its staff had close ties with the Christian Institute, and the project was taken over in 1972 by Derek Kotze, son of the Institute's Cape Regional Director. Under Kotze's guidance the Leadership Programme evolved from a white initiative into a fellowship of equals with an increasingly confident and, for whites, discomforting black input — the voice of black consciousness. Volunteers were invited to give a year to the church, the first part of which entailed three months' training in the Christian heritage, social awareness, community development techniques and communications: writing, drama, music and the use of audio-visual materials. Individuals then served in a parish or church project for a further nine months.

Situated in Durban, the Programme co-operated with the BCP, although its model of community was different. Rather than empha-sising separate black and separate white consciousness, like the Chris-tian Institute's Bible Study Groups, it struggled to transcend the existing reality of racial polarisation and set out to witness, through its own fellowship, to a future non-racial society. In each three-month period, a group of approximately twenty-five white and black trainees made a brave effort to nurture a microcosm of the hoped-for society while recognising the necessity of black leadership for achieving this. Mervyn Kemp provides an example of what the Training Programme hoped to achieve. A Coloured man of Indian extraction, he became a key figure in pulling together the black caucus within the Church of the Province of South Africa. Kemp also participated in the first church leadership conference sponsored by the BCP. In addition to nurturing such leaders, there were at least two other signs of the Programme's potential: the arrival of police informers and the fact that its graduates developed an activist reputation, with the result that the general run of white clergy were unwilling to accept them as church workers in their parishes.[30]

If the BCP had some success with its church and youth projects, it achieved very little with its imaginative but over-ambitious attempt to form a Black Workers' Council; that is, to organise black workers in 'sheer anger and revulsion at the hordes of God's people who are taken for granted and pushed around by whites'.[31] The Council was envisaged as a resource and educational centre that would foster black consciousness while serving the fledgling trade union movement. In addition to training union organisers and monitoring the anti-union activities of corporations, the Council was to foster a literacy movement among workers by enlisting black students as voluntary teachers.[32] BCP co-sponsored the project with SASO, each organisation committing an organiser for a ten-month period during which contacts were established with black workers. Regional seminars or 'motivation circles' were to follow in an effort to form local cadres. This leadership was then to be drawn in June 1973 into a national conference, from which it was hoped that the Black Workers Council would emerge.[33]

These hopes were not fulfilled. The Black Workers' Project sponsored several 'motivation circles' and a faltering start was made to the literacy programme; but overall the Project was a failure. While the circulation of black consciousness literature may have contributed to the labour unrest of 1973,[34] the Workers' Council never materialised and the Project was overtaken by events. Not only were BCP's funding and staff inadequate given its ambitious and diverse range of commitments — it simply tried to do too much — but other groups had already established their presence among the small number of African unions, for example NUSAS and the Institute for Industrial Education. Moreover, black workers were already restive and it is clear that the 1973 strikes received their essential impetus from deep-seated anger at the colour bar, the migratory labour system and low wages in the face of inflation.[35] It also seems likely that middle-aged labourers and the few experienced unionists within the black working class maintained a residual politicisation which owed more to the tradition of ANC protests and the earlier efforts of organisations like the South African Congress of Trade Unions than to BCP and SASO. Although SASO inspired the black consciousness movement among students, it never quite overcame its image as an intellectual, élitist organisation. For all their good intentions, the leaders of SASO and BCP were usually one step removed from the daily sweat and grime of the black working class.

While the BCP had been co-sponsored by the Christian Institute and the SACC as part of SPROCAS II, it evolved as a genuinely independent black initiative — tangential to, but separate in its organisation from the staff, membership and Bible study groups of the Institute. This did not prevent the BCP's organisers — particularly Khoapa and Biko — from exercising a real influence on the Institute's staff and Board of Management. It is true that in contrast to the BCP's exclusively black focus, the Institute's organisational model continued to emphasise inter-racial fellowship; the hope was that by transcending the racial divisions of apartheid, and even the dichotomy of white and black consciousness, the Institute might still witness in a prophetic way to the possibility of a transformed society. What had changed, however, was that the BCP's method of achieving such a society had been accepted: support for the black consciousness movement and for black leadership within the churches as well as in politics. An economically, politically and socially integrated society, one freed from apartheid's systematic thwarting of human fellowship, would have to be on black terms. Ideally speaking, when liberated, non-racial groups emerged in the future, they would be initiated by blacks.

In reality, of course, the Institute was constrained by its own history from adapting to this understanding — it had been a white-controlled organisation and a predominately white initiative from the start. Belatedly it now tried to adjust, not only by supporting black consciousness organisations like the BCP but by welcoming tough-minded black leadership into its own ranks. In mid-1973 the Rev. Manas Buthelezi was appointed Regional Director for Natal and Jane Phakathi Community Organiser for the Transvaal and Orange Free State. Additional black clerical staff were recruited for the Cape Town and Johannesburg offices. At the September 1974 annual general meeting of the Institute, eight of the twelve new members appointed to the Board to Management were black.[36]

Naudé's explanation for these events was that he had 'been forced to go through another metamorphosis', made to face a 'totally new set of black attitudes'. His first metamorphosis resulted from what he termed 'a re-learning of theology' during the late 1950s which, at the

Cottesloe Conference, led to his public rejection of the Biblical justification for apartheid. This earlier change in his thinking had gone hand in hand with a sense of *noblesse oblige*, a sense that 'I, the white man, [will] lead you, the black man, to a more just society.' With the advent of the black consciousness movement, Naudé had come to realise that the answer was 'not for the white man to play missionary, but to make way for . . . black thinking. Meaningful and truly equal relationships [could] only be achieved through black initiatives.'[37]

This change in thinking at the centre, when taken in conjunction with backing the BCP and a stronger black presence within the Christian Institute, helped to ensure that the process of radicalisation continued. It was at this time too that the Institute moved into a more overt confrontation with the state by refusing to co-operate with the Schlebusch Commission. All this led to a sharp decline in white membership during the mid-1970s and to a gradual increase in black membership. There was also an attempt to re-organise the Institute as a more de-centralised network of self-reliant Christian fellowships — a prophetic remnant.[38]

The appointment of Manas Buthelezi as Regional Director brought the country's leading exponent of black theology to the centre of the Institute's affairs. Buthelezi studied at the Lutheran Seminary at Oscarsberg, Natal, from 1958 to 1961, after teaching in a high school for three years. During this time he gained his BA through the correspondence system of the University of South Africa (Pretoria). He then served as a pastor before travelling to the United States in 1963 where he acquired a MA from Yale Divinity School and a doctorate from Drew University. On returning home in 1968 (as 'A Message to the People of South Africa' was published), he lectured at the Lutheran Theological Seminary at Mapumulo before serving as pastor to the Lutheran congregation in Sobantu, Pietermaritzburg, a position he held until he was seconded for three years to the Christian Institute.[39]

Buthelezi's views began to turn the world of the churches upside down. He not only worked from an understanding of mission comparable to that which was evolving within the Institute, but his analysis went further in that he demanded a new maturity of black Christians — that they not only live out their faith in ways which liberated them psychologically, spiritually and politically from oppression, but that they work simultaneously for the conversion and liberation of whites. For Buthelezi it was partly a matter of agreeing with his colleagues in the Institute that whites had betrayed their Christian mission, failed to offer Christian fellowship, grabbed the country's wealth and were now threatened by the coming wrath of God.[40] Certainly the church in South Africa had witnessed 'the systematic apostasy of the white man'. This lack of stewardship (and Buthelezi suggested that selfless Christian stewardship might have given the white presence some legitimacy) had 'violated the integrity of God's love and justice'. Whites had ignored the call to an equitable distribution of resources which was inherent in the Covenant, and likewise ignored the 'communal life of sharing . . . [the] communism of the New Testament Church'. Like his colleagues in the Christian Institute, Buthelezi argued that in the face of 'this spiritual vandalism' the church had to promote its black constituency and 'cease to be a satellite of white power politics in order to become a forum of communion for the whole people of God'.[41] But it was at this point in his analysis that Buthelezi went on to break new ground in demanding of black Christians that they bear the full responsibility of their faith. Black people had not preached the Gospel to all nations — not yet. Rather they seemed to 'have been conditioned into thinking of themselves as third-grade *kaffir*[42] ambassadors of Christ'. Had it ever occurred to the black man that if

white people are lost . . . he may be held responsible? [. . .] God will ask: 'Black man, where were you when the white man abandoned my Gospel and went to destruction?' When the black man answers, 'I was only a *kaffir*, how could I dare to preach to my *baas* [master]?' God will say: 'Was Christ's resurrection not sufficient to liberate you, black man, from that kind of spiritual and psychological death? Go to eternal damnation, black man, for you did not muster courage to save your white brother.'[43]

This attempt to bring about a psychological shift in black consciousness needs to be interpreted with some care. The rise of African nationalism in the form of the African National Congress had given voice to black hopes for over half a century. Moreover, in arguing for an alternative non-racial political order, this voice had been formed in part by Christian values, and the movement was often led by persons of Christian conviction.[44] What Buthelezi was now calling for was a *comparable* black maturity *within* the churches, a willingness to bear responsibility for the future, to witness to new forms of Christian fellowship, to confront injustice where necessary and so to start the healing of society. His method was to call for 'the establishment of a black Christian mission to the whites of South Africa', with white church buildings being made available as mission stations. Such a mission would be fulfilled by blacks who gave glory to God for being black, who had a special understanding of God's love as a result of being oppressed and who would preach love to the white man so that he might see 'that his security [was] not tied to his rejection of the black man'.[45]

As for the Christian Institute itself, Buthelezi had no illusions. He saw it as a fringe group that had been unable to liberate whites. Those blacks who heard of it doubted its chances of success and many of the younger generation suspected it was offering 'a placebo' — the 'discarded spiritual values of the white community'. This might no longer be true; but if it was to be disproved, if the Institute was to have any significance for blacks, it would have to be through 'the power of the theology of the cross'. The Institute, Buthelezi felt, was beginning to live this, beginning to live a theology blacks could understand 'because they have always lived it, [a] theology of power beyond words . . . the hope of the resurrection [as] power beyond power.'[46]

Shortly after his appointment as the Institute's Director of the Natal Region, Buthelezi attended the Bangkok Consultation on Black Theology and Liberation Theology. As a person with an increasing international reputation, the occasion offered him the fellowship of Third World theologians and an opportunity before a wider audience to renew his call to the church in Africa to become a mature partner in world mission.[47] In doing this Buthelezi stood in the mainstream of liberation theology. Methodologically speaking, black theology was simply a formula 'whose genius consists in . . . [recognising] that theological honesty cannot but recognise the peculiarity of the black man's situation.' The starting point for theological reflection had to be the 'existential situation in which the Gospel finds man'. For blacks this meant speaking from their own experience of exploitation, speaking from 'the dust and sweat of their daily lives'.[48] Dialogue was therefore an essential part of black liberation, that is of coming to see 'blackness as a gift of God instead of the biological scourge which the white man's institutions had made it'.[49] For Africans, this black theology might also be informed by the understanding of God in traditional religion and by the wisdom of traditional values: a respect for and a certain awe of nature, communal values and the sharing of accumulated wealth. This, he warned, should not deteriorate into an attempt to re-establish an idealised past; black theology was not a withdrawal from the broader currents of human history. Likewise, to limit the quest for black theology, to interpret it 'purely in terms of the awakening of Black nationalism or the consolidation of Black Power forces, [was] to trifle with one of the most fundamental issues in modern Christianity.'[50] Ultimately it was a search for a deeper understanding of a common humanity through the struggle for justice in a particular historical context. For the black man, this context required 'the retrieval of Christian love from the limitations of the white man's economic and political institutions'. It was the task of the black theologian, a person 'equipped to interpret the Gospel out of the depths of the groanings and aspirations of his fellow black people', to encourage this retrieval.[51]

Buthelezi's opportunity to pursue this understanding of black theology from his base in the Christian Institute was soon curtailed. In December 1973, a mere six months after his appointment, he was banned for five years under the Suppression of Communism Act.[52] As usual there was no explanation from the Minister of Justice. In the words of the Executive Committee of the SACC, the government's 'shocking act' had silenced 'a renowned theologian and respected Christian leader who has been in the forefront of a dynamic movement which has sought to make Christianity relevant to Black people' — a man who had made a 'strong stand for non-violence'.[53]

To the surprise of most observers, and in contrast with the treatment of other black leaders, Buthelezi's banning order was soon lifted. It is likely that this was the result of a bizarre performance by *To The Point*, a recently-established magazine that was subsequently revealed to have received financial assistance from a government slush-fund set up to support pro-apartheid politicians and front organisations in South Africa and around the globe.[54] Shortly after his banning, the February 1 issue of *To The Point* printed a false and malicious editorial suggesting reasons for the banning and designed to smear Buthelezi's character. Claiming to have access to 'certain facts' from 'the banned man's own circle, or that part of it which understands his Black Theology preaching but stops short of supporting bloodbath ideas', the editorial declared that Buthelezi encouraged radical change by violent means. Soon after his return from a visit to the United States and Europe, the editorial continued,

this compassionate and conciliatory man of God demonstrated his version of reconciliation. In a speech made at Elisaser, Mapululu (Zululand), he said that while he was out of the country in 1966 he had heard with pleasure of Prime Minister Verwoerd's assasination, a method that had worked in America and must be successful here too. He said he wished John Vorster, along with others, might die through a bomb that would blow up Parliament. He regretted he had no personal means to kill these leaders, but would not hesitate to assassinate them if he had.[55]

In the face of a world-wide outcry against the banning, this crude and over-zealous performance may have been an embarrassment for some in the apartheid regime. In any case, Buthelezi sued *To The Point* and was unbanned. A year later, finding that the case was of the same level of seriousness as that of Geyser and Naudé versus Pont,[56] the Supreme Court awarded damages of R13,500.[57]

After a further brief period with the Institute during which he took time to analyse and condemn the findings of the Schlebusch-Le Grange Commission, Buthelezi was asked by the Lutherans to take up the newly-created position of Associate General Secretary of the Federation of Evangelical Lutheran Churches in Southern Africa; shortly thereafter he was consecrated Bishop. At this point his official involvement with the Christian Institute shifted to the Board of Management.[58]

The appointment of Jane Oshadi Phakathi as Community Programme Organiser brought a different set of talents to the Institute — those of an energetic, articulate and determined social worker. While she was passionately opposed to apartheid, she was not yet, like Buthelezi, a confident exponent of black liberation theology. Hailing from Pietersburg in the Northern Transvaal, she completed her General Nursing at King Edward VII Hospital in Durban and in 1956 her Midwifery at Edendale, Pietermaritzburg. At first she nursed at Baragwanath Hospital near Johannesburg, and then in 1958 accepted a position with the Pretoria City Health Department, working first as a child welfare nurse and later as a health visitor. After joining the Institute in 1973, Oshadi Phakathi's political consciousness increased steadily as her black and white contacts widened — a process of radicalisation that was profoundly affected by her experiences at the May 1974 All Africa Conference of Churches meeting in Lusaka. Attending as an observer, Oshadi was surprised but pleased by the blacks' easy acceptance of white participants and by the Conference's capacity to discuss contentious issues, including the WCC grants, without lapsing into bitterness and racial hostility. She was also surprised by the views she encountered on the liberation struggle, views that differed markedly from those peddled by the South African press and radio. From Lusaka, the apartheid state was seen as the source of violence and the South African churches as unwilling 'to stick their necks out' — over-cautious as a situation of grotesque and deepening injustice was leading to civil war. Challenged by the provocative address of the Conference General Secretary, Canon Burgess Carr,[60] Phakathi had to wrestle with the issues of violence and passive resistance. In the process she came to realise that the primary, institutionalised violence in the situation was indeed that of the apartheid state. As with most of the other South African representatives at Lusaka, she also encountered members of the liberation movement for the first time and to her astonishment found that many were committed Christians.[61]

Oshadi Phakathi returned to South Africa to become part of a movement within the churches which a few months later, in August 1974, produced the SACC Hammanskraal Resolution on conscientious objection.[62] She also deepened her understanding of black theology and set about her community development work with a new zest. Having attained a wider perspective, she now saw her own effort as but one, non-violent, contribution within a much wider range of forces which were raising consciousness and working to destroy the institutionalised violence of apartheid.

By late 1975, after two years of persistent effort, Phakathi had made an important start in bringing the Christian Institute directly into the lives of at least a few black communities in the Transvaal. She experienced a ready response. Three literacy projects were meeting in the vicinity of Pretoria — projects which elicited the co-operation of black pastors in the townships and were geared to raising political consciousness. Self-help initiatives, for example day-care centres, and political action followed. A black women's petition was organised calling for the release of detainees held under the Terrorism Act: they should be charged or set free. Public services were held on behalf of detainees and their families; one held in May 1975 at St Peter's Seminary, Hammanskraal, drew over 600 people from the townships around Pretoria. As a result of these efforts, the black ministers of the area formed a community development agency with Phakathi and the Institute's staff as consultants. After these successes and several exploratory meetings, plus a workshop, Phakathi was invited by the Anglican parishes to start another community development programme in SOWETO.[63]

Further afield, a study group of fifteen community leaders was formed in the 'Homeland' of Lebowa. They were 'to evaluate the policy of separate development in the light of the Gospel and to educate the people to discover [their obligations] as Christian citizens'.[64] This was simply a low-keyed way of describing the start of an adult education effort in the Bantustans that would awaken black consciousness and encourage that divine discontent which was so objectionable to the purveyors of 'separate development'. Another related project in the Northern Transvaal was designed 'to educate political victims of the government's resettlement programme' — again a matter of some concern to the security police as domestic and international protests against the 'dumping grounds' were intensifying. By 1976 approximately 2 million Africans (essentially women, children, the aged and the disabled) had been 'endorsed out' of the urban areas and left to rot physically and psychologically in their 'homelands'.[65] Phakathi also made skirmishes into the Transkei to give four short literacy courses to community organisations. In Sekhukhuniland (N. Transvaal) a comparable course was broken up by the police. In addition to these efforts she addressed a number of organisations ranging from the Mother's Union of South Africa to the University College of Ngoye, St Bedes Theological Seminary, Roman Catholic societies, YWCA's, the National Child Welfare Society and the African Methodist Episcopal National Missionary Women's Society. Her themes give some sense of a continuing concern for community welfare, for hygiene, sanitation, dietetics and child care. By 1975 her speeches also reveal a firm commitment to black consciousness and an understanding that the movement might become a vital source of Christian renewal in the churches. Examples of her topics included: 'How do we change the present church system to the church of Christ?', 'Black Theology', 'A black view of the emancipation of women,' 'What people expect from priests' and 'The challenges facing Christian women today.'[66]

As the Christian Institute committed itself to assisting the black consciousness movement, and as it was shaken up by the advent of black leaders within its own executive ranks, the pattern of its membership changed. As has been mentioned, the number of whites declined.[67] On the other hand, black membership, which had fallen marginally as the number of black consciousness organisations mushroomed in the early 1970s, edged slowly upwards again. However, the overall trend was a fall in membership during the mid-1970s which left the Institute in a numerically weak position. It was also in a financially vulnerable state in that its inability to generate white support meant a continuing reliance on overseas funding.

In cold numerical terms it was a depressing picture. Membership shrank from about 2,000 in 1970/1 to about 900 in 1975. The only consolation was that the proportion of black members increased over these years from the vicinity of 10 to 20 per cent.[68] A further indication of the narrow base of hard-core support was the circulation of *Pro Veritate*, the Institute's mouthpiece, which had 1,272 South African subscribers in 1975, a further 749 in surrounding territories and 934 overseas for a total circulation of just under 3,000.[69] A special fund-raising drive for South African donations had been underway since 1972 in the hope of avoiding reliance on overseas support.[70] However, by the time the Institute was declared an 'Affected Organisation' in May 1975 and so was cut off from outside funding, it still received 75 per cent of its R200,000 annual budget from overseas churches.

Having been declared an 'Affected Organisation', severe retrenchment had to take place including a drastic reduction in staff: eleven in Johannesburg, five in Cape Town and one in Natal. Putting a brave face on it, the hope was to downgrade the importance of full-time executive staff in the life of the Institute and to rely increasingly on decentralised voluntary membership groups. The executive staff who remained took salary cuts and simplified their life-styles even further. Some, like the Kotzes in Cape Town, had housing loans from the Institute which they repaid by selling their homes so as to replenish the organisation's funds. (The Kotzes then built their own small dwelling.) A renewed and desperate effort to raise financial support, which absorbed a large slice of Naudé's time and that of his remaining staff, patched together a remarkably substantial budget of R140,000 for 1975/6 — only R60,000 or 30 per cent, less than the previous year.[71]

The key to this modest success was a burst of sympathy for the Institute in the aftermath of the Schlebusch-Le Grange Report. This produced a number of personal donations from individuals of varying denominations. (In contrast, corporations remained extremely wary of Naudé and his colleagues given their increasingly radical commitments.) The financial pressure was also relieved by floating off several of the BCP's development projects to alternative sponsors, for example to the Cape Town diocese of the Anglican Church which co-operated with the Institute on an *ad hoc* basis.[72] In the month after the Institute was declared an 'Affected Organisation', the Johannesburg headquarters received R6,883 from all over South Africa in subscriptions and donations from 141 persons and organisations; the Cape office received R2,500 from fifty-three donors and Natal gathered R1,495. These figures more than doubled in July and included a cheque for R15,000 from a supporter in Pretoria and another for R500 from the Roman Catholic Archbishop of Cape Town, Owen McCann, who, in a letter to all churches in his diocese, urged Catholics to support the Institute. A further R600 came from the National Federation of Catholic Students, while Rolf Friede, who directed the Christian Centre in Windhoek until expelled from Namibia, donated the proceeds from selling his caravan: R2,000. Some individuals gave jewellery, and many small donations of R1 to R10 boosted the total. In addition to McCann, other church leaders called upon their members to support the Christian Institute, for example the Anglican Archbishops of Natal and Cape Town, Philip Russell and Bill Burnett, as well as the Rev. Desmond Tutu, Dean-elect of Johannesburg, and the President of the Methodist Church, the Rev. Vivian Harris.[74] While the flow of funds was hardly an avalanche — only a few hundred individuals were involved and most churches merely offered verbal support — it meant survival, at least in the short run. By the following year, 1976/7, revenue had declined by a further 30 per cent to R97,000[75] as the Institute refused to bend to the pressure of moneyed interests and maintained its liberation commitments. It was a precarious situation, but the small flurry of donations heartened the Institute even if it alarmed the state. It was at this time too that the Institute's membership bounced back to around 3,000.[76]

Clearly an organisation's budget limits its effectiveness in society, and the Institute's had shrunk. On the other hand, the size of formal membership is seldom an accurate guide to an organisation's impact. This was particularly true in the case of the Institute which had come to exercise a quite disproportionate influence through the complex matrix of its wide-ranging contacts. These not only extended to the

SACC, the multi-racial churches, seminaries and black DRCs. They also included such organisations as SASO, the Black People's Convention, IDAMASA, AICA, NUSAS, the Young Christian Workers, Roman Catholic Justice and Peace Commissions, Anglican Challenge Groups, campus groups, the SAIRR, the Progressive Reform Party and others. As a result, the Institute's witness and liberation theology remained at the cutting edge of Christian protest in South Africa, disturbing white complacency while inter-acting with the black consciousness movement and black theology.

Although the Institute functioned in this seminal and prophetic way, and enjoyed a recovery in membership during 1975/6, it entered the final years of confrontation with the state as an organisational midget — a David who had foregone his weapon in the face of a Goliath armed to the teeth with modern weaponry and electronic surveillance devices. As (civil) war loomed closer, David was found searching rather desperately in the desert for an alternative to his sling. The hope was to find a 'third way', to support resurgent African protests and the black consciousness movement while refusing to meet the violence of apartheid with the countervailing force of guerrilla war. Periodically, an oasis with a tent and a round negotiating table appeared on the horizon; but in the heat of the desert it was simply a mirage.

NOTES

1. The Rev. Basil Moore (Methodist) and the Rev. Colin Collins (Roman Catholic) were important in encouraging this focus within the UCM.

2. G.M. Gerhart, *Black Power in South Africa* (Berkeley, 1978), p. 292.

3. P. Walshe, *The Rise of African Nationalism in South Africa*, p. 352.

4. *Supra*, pp. 90, 181.

5. International Defence and Aid, *Black Theatre in South Africa*, (London, 1976), p. 6.

6. *Supra*, pp. 89–90.

7. The Fund was infiltrated by the South African security police in the person of Williamson.

8. *CI Newsdigest*, 12 February 1974.

9. International Defence and Aid, *Black Theatre in South Africa*, p. 5.

10. Well known but more humorous and less fiercely political groups included the Serpent Players (New Brighton, Port Elizabeth); they nurtured John Kani and Winston Ntoshona who with Athol Fugard took *Sizwe Bansi is Dead* to Britain and North America. The equivalent Johannesburg company was the Phoenix Players, and in the Cape Adam Small inspired the Cape Flats Theatre. *Ibid.*, p. 2.

11. 'We must stand firm . . . Learn from their mistakes . . . The black fist of power is small but it is lethal . . . Our blood is hot but our actions cool, calculating . . . Let us take small not giant steps . . . And our passion must be gentle, our mothers and fathers, our family, must be treated with care, with love, with tenderness. Our sweat is for our family, our people, our tomorrow.' International Defence and Aid, *Black Theatre in South Africa*, p. 4.

12. *Ibid.*, pp. 4–5. See too B. Khoapa (ed.), *Black Review* (Johannesburg, Black Community Programmes, 1973.).

13. For the papers presented at the Convention, see S.P. Mkhatshwa (ed.) *Black Renaissance* (Johannesburg, Ravan Press, 1976).

14. *Ibid.*, p. 7.

15. SPROCAS 2, *Black Community Programmes* (Durban, 1972), p. 2.

16. SPROCAS Black Community Programmes, *Budget Proposals, 1973*, pp. 3–8.

17. *Ibid.*, p. 10; P. Randall, *A Taste of Power*, p. 131.

18. SPROCAS 2, *Staff Discussions, 27–28 January 1972* (Johannesburg), pp. 2–3, mimeo; P. Randall, *A Taste of Power*, pp. 126, 191–6; SPROCAS Black Community Programmes, *Budget Proposals — 1973*, pp. 8–9.

19. By 1975 Ravan Press was estimated to have lost over R20,000 as a result of these banning orders. *Financial Mail* (Johannesburg), 18 July 1975; E. Regehr, *Perceptions of Apartheid*, p. 98.

20. P. Randall, *A Taste of Power*, pp. 125–6. The other radical work banned at this time was Richard Turner's *The Eye of the Needle*, an incisive socialist analysis of the South African present and possible future. It sold 3,470 copies. Turner was banned in March 1973 and later assassinated.

21. SPROCAS Black Community Programmes, *Budget Proposals, 1973*, pp. 4–5. Black Community Programmes, 'Report of Follow-Up Conference of Black Church Leaders held at Lay Ecumenical Centre, Edendale, Natal on 15th–18th August 1972' (Durban, 1972), pp. 1–12, mimeo.

22. *Ibid.*, p.

23. *Infra.*, pp. 187–9.

24. Author's interview with M. Kemp, Elgin, 3 February, 1973. The black caucus numbered approximately 100 representatives and was supported on this issue by Archbishop Selby-Taylor.

25. Black Community Programmes, 'Report on Youth Leadership Conference held at Edendale Lay Ecumenical Centre, Pietermaritzburg, 19–20 August 1972' (Durban, 1972), p. 9, mimeo.

26. SPROCAS BCP, *Budget Proposals — 1973*, p. 5.

27. BCP, *Report on Youth Leadership Conference, 19–20 August 1972*, pp. 4–5. The format of these sessions may well have been influenced by UCM methods and those used by Christian Institute organisers, particularly Anne Hope who studied with Paulo Freire.

28. *Ibid.*, pp. 5–6.

29. *Ibid.*, pp. 6–7.

30. National Youth Training Programme, 'Budget Proposal for 1973–1975' (Durban, 1972), pp. 1–5, mimeo. Author's interviews with: Rev. E. Bartmann (black), Co-Director with the Rev. A. Jennings (white) of the Methodist Youth Programme, Durban, 8 March 1973; M. Kemp,

community worker, Elgin, 3 February 1973; D. Kotze, Director of the National Youth Leadership Training Programme, Durban, 8-10 March 1973.

31. BCP, *The Black Worker's Project: a Proposal* (Durban, 1972), p. 4.

32. *Ibid.*, pp. 5-8.

33. SPROCAS Black Community Programmes, '*Budget Proposals 1973*', p. 6.

34. *Supra.*, pp. 90-1.

35. Institute for Industrial Education, *The Durban Strikes, 1973* (Johannesburg, Ravan Press, 1974), pp. 89-101.

36. *CI News*, June 1973, pp. 1-2; October 1974, p. 4. Ten of twenty members of the Board were now black; previously there were five blacks on a Board of eighteen.

37. *Daily Despatch,* 11 October, 1973.

38. Christian Institute of Southern Africa, *Director's Report for the Period 1st. August, 1972 to 31st July, 1973*, p. 4.; *CI News,* December 1975, p. 1.

39. *CI News*, June 1973, pp. 1-2.

40. M. Buthelezi, 'Christianity in South Africa', *CI News*, June 1973, p. 5.

41. M. Buthelezi, 'Change in the Church', *South African Outlook,* August 1973, pp. 128-9, an address given at the University of Cape Town.

42. A derogatory term comparable to 'nigger'. Originally an Arabic word for infidel, *kaffir* was taken over and used in a racist way by white South Africans.

43. M. Buthelezi, 'Christianity in South Africa', *CI News,* June 1973, p. 6.

44. P. Walshe, *The Rise of African Nationalism in South Africa*, chapters 5, 8 and 13.

45. M. Buthelezi, 'Christianity in South Africa', *CI News*, June 1973, p. 7. If Buthelezi's immediate concern was the churches, he was very much aware of the long, heartbreaking struggle of Africans to offer an alternative to apartheid. Now, in the context of resurgent African nationalism, he offered the hope that black solidarity, infused with Christian values, might be a step towards wider unity; that if the black consciousness movement could survive government pressures, 'it may be a first necessary step towards [a] greater South African nationalism initiated by black people.' M. Buthelezi, 'The Ethical Question Raised by Nationalism,' in T. Sundermeier (ed.), *Church and Nationalism in South Africa* (Johannesburg, Ravan Press, 1974) p. 103.

46. M. Buthelezi, 'The Christian Institute and Black South Africa', *South African Outlook*, October 1974, pp. 162-4.

47. M. Buthelezi, 'Black Theology in Bangkok: Relevance for South Africa', *South African Outlook*, September 1973, pp. 155-6.

48. M. Buthelezi, 'An African Theology or a Black Theology', in M. Motlhabi (ed.), *Essays on Black Theology* (Johannesburg, 1972), p. 9. (The volume was re-published with additional material in London in 1973, with the title *Black Theology: the South African Voice.*)

49. M. Buthelezi, 'Black Theology in Bangkok', *South African Outlook*, September 1973, p. 154.

50. M. Buthelezi, 'An African Theology or a Black Theology', in M. Motlhabi (ed.), *Essays on Black Theology*, pp. 3–9.

51. M. Buthelezi, 'Black Theology in Bangkok', *South African Outlook*, September 1973, p. 156.

52. Buthelezi was the second official of the Institute to be suppressed in this way, the first being David de Beer who was banned in 1972 after working with Bishop Colin Winter in Namibia and becoming Administrative Secretary of the Christian Institute in Johannesburg. *CI News*, December 1973, p. 2.

53. *Ibid.*, p. 1.

54. *Infra.*, pp. 181–2.

55. *CI Newsdigest*, 12 February 1974, pp. 5–6.

56. *Supra.*, p. 50.

57. *CI Newsdigest*, October 1975, p. 6.

58. *Ibid.*, p. 1. The Rev. Brian Brown took over as Acting Regional Director in Natal for the next year before he moved into full-time Methodist ministry in Clifton Parish, Johannesburg. Brown had been National Administrative Director of the Christian Institute, working as one of Naudé's confidants and supplying a great deal of low-keyed administrative efficiency in the Johannesburg Headquarters. Like Buthelezi, Brown took up responsibilities on the Board of Management. However, his absence from day-to-day affairs was a serious loss, even though his parish was conveniently situated in the vicinity of Diakonia House. Brown's move was designed in part to relieve the financial stress in the Institute after it was declared an Affected Organisation in mid-1975. *Infra.*, p. 179.

59. *CI Newsdigest*, June 1973, p. 1.

60. *Supra.*, pp. 24–5.

61. J. Phakathi, 'The Liberation Issue', *Pro Veritate*, October 1974, pp. 6–7. E. Regehr, *Perceptions of Apartheid*, p. 271.

62. *Supra.*, pp. 120–2.

63. *CI News*, October 1975, p. 3.

64. *Ibid.*

65. M. Nash, *Black Uprooting From 'White' South Africa* (Johannesburg, 1980), p. 1. See too C. Desmond, *The Discarded People* (Harmondsworth, 1969); F. Wilson, *Migrant Labour in South Africa* (Johannesburg, 1972). The government was planning to move at least another one million.

66. Phakathi's range of contacts was also increased by her election in 1975 as President of YWCA in South Africa.

67. Bishop Colin Winter of Windhoek, Namibia, experienced a comparable phenomenon in that he virtually lost the white members of his Cathedral congregation when he set out to integrate the Diocese. The fact that he spent six years in pastoral ministry to whites, visiting their homes, visiting the sick and attending the dying, did not convert them to his understanding of fellowship. Like his colleagues in the Christian Institute, Winter came to the conclusion that the future lay with the poor, with African political organisations and African leadership within the churches; whites would have to focus on their own communities in an effort to eradicate racism and prepare for political change. Yet, while black and white consciousness had to be encouraged, Winter argued that the church should nurture 'Abrahamic communities' or

basic communities that transcended race — a witness the Christian Institute was also committed to. (Winter was encouraged to think along these lines by the writings of Archbishop Helder Camara of Recife, Brazil.) Just as Naudé and his colleagues found a staggering inertia within the hierarchies of the multi-racial churches, so Winter encountered the Anglican equivalent. An instance of this occurred at the height of the Ovambo strike in 1971. After three of his black priests had been beaten up by security men, and many workers had been subjected to arrest and torture, Winter had to sit, at a gathering of his fellow-bishops in Cape Town, while they discussed for an hour and a half, *inter alia*, the appropriate age for bishops to retire. Only then did they turn their attention to the travails of his people. (Author's interview with the Rt. Rev. Colin Winter, Sutton Courtenay, 9 November 1972.) Of course this did not indicate indifference, but it did say something about unexamined routines, customary attitudes and priorities. Unfortunately this response was typical of the lack of passion in white hierarchies.

68. *CI News*, October 1975, p. 4; December 1975, p. 2.

69. *CI News*, October 1975, p. 4.

70. Christian Institute, Director's Report, 1 August, 1972 to 31 August, 1973, p. 6.

71. 'The Director's Report 1975/1976', *Pro Veritate*, October 1976, pp. 16–17.

72. *Ibid.*

73. *CI News*, August 1975, pp. 3–4.

74. A reminder of the timidity and underlying resistance in the white community that was still being experienced by the Institute can be gauged from the response of the Methodist Church, a denomination which remained overwhelmingly under white control. At their annual conference, held shortly after the Institute was declared an Affected Organisation, the Methodists passed a cautiously-worded resolution expressing dissatisfaction with the Schlebusch-Le Grange Commission's findings and commending the Institute's commitment to reconciliation and non-violent social change. The conference then urged individual Methodists to examine the aims of the Institute to see whether they could support it. However, when an amendment was moved that the Conference vote R1,000 as a sign of support, this was rejected by 50–17 votes. *CI News*, December 1975, p. 4.

75. The Christian Institute of Southern Africa, 'Director's Report for the Period August 1, 1976 to July 31, 1977' (Johannesburg, 1977), p. 2, mimeo.

76. *Pro Veritate*, June 1976, p. 8.

Part IV
APARTHEID UNDER PRESSURE: THE CHRISTIAN INSTITUTE AND THE CRISIS OF 1976–1977

11
THE CHRISTIAN INSTITUTE AND LIBERATION

Although the Christian Institute was not a large and expanding organisation but a rather small and vulnerable one; and although it had not sparked a passive resistance movement among whites and was obviously not responsible for the black consciousness movement, from the point of view of those in charge of state security it had to be discredited. This viewpoint was shared by those who controlled the white DRCs, by National Party politicians and by many in the effete opposition United Party.

There was indeed something for these elements to be concerned about. The Institute had already contributed both directly and indirectly to the political destabilisation of the apartheid order. It had shattered the regime's aura of legitimacy insofar as this had been nurtured by the DRCs. It was disturbing the multi-racial churches as well as the black DRCs, and was assisting the black consciousness movement. It had extensive international Christian contacts. Furthermore its future influence was unpredictable. Draft resistance might spread. If a militant white Christian minority emerged and turned to passive resistance, the government would be seriously embarrassed, domestically and internationally. Dealing with a mere handful of resolute protesters like David Russell had been difficult enough, but should such white resistance escalate in conjunction with the rising tide of black discontent, there would have to be an even more overt use of repressive force which would complicate the task of South Africa's image-builders abroad, making it more awkward for the international banks and transnational corporations to supply capital and technology to the apartheid system. If the full force of the police and military machine had to be unleashed to contain political protest (particularly white protest), South Africa's image as a pro-Western state hounding a batch of Communist-manipulated guerrillas would be very badly tarnished. Beyers Naudé and his colleagues may not have enjoyed spectacular successes in their struggle against the apartheid state, but in the context of a rapidly changing Southern African scene they were an alarming phenomenon to those who were prepared to develop a totalitarian system in the defence of Afrikaner power and white privilege.

The initial move in a approach to repressing the Institute by stages had been to set up in 1972 the Commission of Enquiry into Certain Organisations — the Schlebusch Commission.[1] As a parliamentary commission composed of seven National Party and three United Party MPs, its brief was to investigate the UCM, NUSAS and the SAIRR in addition to the Christian Institute.[2] It was not a judicial commission but a group of partisan white politicians who sat in camera, withheld the names of witnesses, denied defendants the right to cross-examine their accusers, and did not publish evidence. As a result, the Institute refused to testify and was supported in this by the staff of SPROCAS II and the SACC.[3] Had they testified, the Institute's staff would not have known what they were accused of — a matter of some importance as the Prime Minister and MPs had already predjudiced the Commission by statements made in the House to the effect that there was a *prima facie* case against the Institute.[4] It was anybody's guess what the case was. Quite correctly, Naudé and his colleagues judged the Commission to be a public relations operation designed to prepare the electorate for the repression of the white and black protest organisations which emerged in the late 1960s and 1970s. This judgement was confirmed during the period of the Commission's hearings when the leaders of NUSAS, SASO and the BCP were banned. By January 1974, forty young South Africans were being held without trial under the Terrorism Act in an attempt to crush the black consciousness movement.[5] Later in the year, a further group of thirteen SASO members were added to the list after they attempted to organise a celebration of FRELIMO's victory in Mozambique.[6]

It was of course clear that the Institute had supported the black consciousness movement. But, unlike the *Broederbond*, the Institute had nothing to hide in that it was an open organisation whose documents were available to the state. (Indeed, Naudé offered to give the police a set of keys to the Institute's offices.) It would have willingly given evidence 'before a public, impartial, judicial tribunal'.[7]

However, the main issue was not simply the prejudiced nature of the Schlebusch-Le Grange Commission, its secrecy and failure to observe judicial procedures; it became a matter of 'Divine or Civil Obedience', the right and duty of churches 'to resist un-Christian governmental authority in the name of Christ'. Citizens did not owe 'blind obedience and servile submission' to the state. Rather, they had a responsibility to test public policy against Biblical values. These values led to a perspective where 'the state exists for the benefit of man.' Drawing on the writings of Reinhold Niebuhr, the Institute argued for democratic procedures and the rule of law: the search for human community and human dignity. In Niebuhr's words, the 'human strivings towards justice [made] democracy possible, but the human inclination towards injustice [made] democracy *essential*.' There did not seem to be much justice or respect for democracy in the Commission's proceedings. Rather, the Commission was seen as symptomatic of a movement towards fascism, an instrument of a government which sought to dominate, not to serve, 'to govern by means of arbitrary power and to control by force'. Such a government

becomes idolatrous because everything has to flow out of, and through the National State (cf. Revelation, 13). [. . .] Anything opposed to the will or policy of such a Government is then regarded as subversive or as dangerous to the State. Freedom is regarded as a concession from the Government and not the normal way of life. In this the Government as well as the Commission will have to answer to God in regard to the bannings and also in regard to the punishment which may follow for those who refuse on grounds of conscience to testify before the Commission.[8]

When the State prosecuted those who refused to testify, three years of costly legal wrangling ensued. Naudé's case was fought by the Attorney General all the way up to the Appeleate Division of the Supreme Court on the technical question, raised by the defence, of whether the Commission with only four of its members present was properly constituted when Naudé refused to testify. The Transvaal Provincial Supreme Court found in his favour, whereupon the state appealed successfully to the higher court. With this technicality decided, namely that the Commission was adequately constituted, Naudé's case reverted to the Transvaal Provincial Supreme Court. There his defence argued that the State President did not have the power to require that hearings before the Commission be held in secret and therefore that Naudé had 'sufficient cause' not to testify. The outcome in October 1976 was that Naudé was given a fine of R50 or one month in jail and three further months suspended for three years.[9]

Naudéchose to go to jail and was taken off to the maximum security section of Pretoria Central Prison. There he dressed in his baggy convict's garb, had his first prison meal, read the Book of Amos three times, slept 'like a top' in his cell, and was half way through the morning walk in the exercise yard when 'he was abruptly returned to the pressures and punishments of normal Christian Institute life.' His local NGK minister, J. H. P. van Rooyen, had paid the fine without

Naudé's consent and against his wishes. Naudé was chagrined. He knew only too well that his sentence had been a light one, but it allowed him to identify in some small way with the 'thousands of fellow-citizens' jailed for their beliefs, for their pursuit of justice.[10] Of the others who refused to testify, the Rev. Theo Kotze (Cape Director) received four months without the option of a fine, suspended for three years; Peter Randall (SPROCAS II Director and editor of Ravan Press) received a comparable sentence, but of two months; Dot Cleminshaw (a staff member of SPROCAS II) was fined R20 or ten days and given a two-month suspended sentence; and Ilona Kleinschmidt (of the Programme for Social Change) was fined R50 or one month. All these fines were paid by third parties, so that it was Naudé alone who saw the inside of a prison cell. The charges against the Rev. Brian Brown (ex-National Organising Secretary of the Institute), the Rev. Roelf Meyer (ex-editor of *Pro Veritate*) and Horst Kleinschmidt (of the Programme for Social Change) were all withdrawn.[11] The state had made its point in prosecuting, but the process stopped short of creating martyrs.

While all this had been going on, the Commission was busy producing its report on the Christian Institute. This was published on 28 May 1975. As the Johannesburg *Star* summarised it, the Commission found that the Institute was 'a danger to the State, that it supported violent change in South Africa and that it was working towards a Black-dominated socialist system achieved by way of race conflict.' The *Star* also warned that 'one cannot take seriously the Commission's findings' given the politics of its members and its secret proceedings.[12] The Commission also found that the Institute modelled itself on the WCC and received funds from that body;[13] that it had been corrupted by Marxist propaganda; that it was not part of a Christian church but had become 'a completely political body with a political destination'; and that foreign financial support led to the Institute being manipulated from abroad.[14]

Speaking in parliament, the Minister of Justice J. T. Kruger told the House of Assembly that the Commission's Report was a solidly factual document which 'ripped the mask of Christianity from the face of the Institute'.[15] Professor Colin Gardner, Chairman of the Institute's Board of Management, thought differently. The Commission's Report, he insisted, was 'a patchwork of outright lies, half-truths and facts taken out of context'.[16] Certainly hard evidence was lacking, and there were endless inaccuracies,[17] a great deal of innuendo and the coarsest use of guilt by association. In a virtuoso display of wilful ignorance, liberation theology was equated with Marxism — which itself was presented in a crudely distorted way. A search for truth and a serious analysis of the Institute's theology and commitments had never been the purpose of the Commission. Having argued that the Institute was modelled on the WCC, the Commissioners felt it was:

important to note that a line of thinking which appears in Marxist and neo-Marxist ideology and which justifies revolution has been adopted by the ecumenical Christians of the World Council, particularly since 1966. By means of Biblical concepts, stripped of their original meaning, this line of thinking is then represented as the content of the Christian message. What the ecumenical Christians do, therefore, is to propagate Marxist and neo-Marxist ideology by means of Biblical concepts, that are invested with a different meaning. [. . .] [In the Commission's judgement, *Pro Veritate* was] propagating in disguised form the basic principles, ideas and objectives of Marxism and neo-Marxism, not only by attacking apartheid, but also by constantly stressing the necessity for Marxist-orientated structural change. [. . .] [This was designed to produce a new socialist order] in which the place and future of the White man would change radically.[18]

On the issue of violence, the Institute and *Pro Veritate* were supposed to have taken an ambivalent stance in public while deliberately keeping the debate alive so as to foster acceptance of the WCC position (which supposedly favoured violence).[19] Naudé, the Commission claimed, condemned 'armed defence against terrorist insurgents' but approved of 'violence against the existing order in an attempt to change it'. The fact that the Commissioners' evidence came from inaccurate reports of speeches made in the Netherlands in 1974 — reports for which the newspapers concerned had publically apologised to Naudé — seems not to have concerned the Commissioners.[20] As Francis Wilson, the editor of *South African Outlook*, put it, only 'sick or very frightened societies accuse the man who rings the fire-alarm of starting the fire which he has seen.'[21]

When it attempted to analyse black theology, the Commission simply reiterated several of its preconceived themes: there were insidious foreign influences in the background, particularly the WCC; Christianity was being corrupted by socialist and Communist doctrine; the intent was to achieve black power through violence. In fact 'Black theology [was] nothing but the theological arm of Black Power' which had been introduced into South Africa from the United States by the University Christian Movement.[22] It was also 'clear to the Commission that, in the propaganda for a Black theology, the American Social Gospel [had been] carried through to its logical conclusions.' This same Social Gospel had corrupted the WCC and entered South Africa at the Cottesloe Consultation in 1960. Communists were now busy using the church as a channel for their propaganda which was being absorbed by 'well-meaning but uninformed Christian believers'. The result was a distorted theology which emphasised 'only the "horizontal aspect" (the relationship between

people), doing so at the expense of the "vertical aspect" (the relationship between people and God). Throughout, this method and
approach form the basis of Black theology as a theology of "liberation", in its sociopolitical sense.'[23]

Insulated by ignorance and driven by its pre-established political
commitments, the Commission had produced a simplistic analysis of a
complex issue. Genuine Christianity, it asserted, gave precedence to
the 'vertical relationship'. In having to reject this stance, which Naudé
and his colleagues saw as Gnostic and Docetist (i.e. dualistic, seeing
matter as inherently evil and so without an understanding of the historical implications of the Incarnation), the Christian Institute was forced
to articulate the essence of its own evolving liberation theology. The
analysis is worth quoting at some length. To give the 'vertical'
relationship precedence over the 'horizontal' was

a profound denial of the incarnation of Jesus Christ who in Himself and in His
life on earth has reconciled God and man. He established the Kingdom of God
and his direct involvement in all spheres in the world. *The Christian has no knowl-
edge of God or a 'spiritual' world without Jesus Christ who in reality is part of the
horizontal world because He revealed God therein.* God's revelation to and
relationship with men is here on *earth and in history*, and thus it is, as it were,
bound to the horizontal. According to the Gospel there is not a vertical world
as opposed to a horizontal world. God, however, is simply God over against
the world in its horizontal dimension.

In actual fact in the Bible the relationship of man to his neighbour
sometimes takes precedence over man's service to God through sacrifice (see
Matt. 5.23–24). — not that man's relationship with his neighbour is more
important than his relationship with God but because man's relationship with
his neighbour determines and is intrinsic within his relationship with God. In
no event can man maintain a relationship with God other than in an historical
earthly framework, nor can He be known in the spirit. God can only be known
or denied in the context of man's earthly life, his society, his personality, his
politics or his social life.

The Bible goes further and says that he who does not love his neighbour,
does not know God (for God is love) (1 John 4.7–8). According to the Gospel
there is an ineradicable bond between man's relationship with God and his
relationship with his neighbour, between the Kingdom of God and politics,
between the revelation of God and history, between redemption and forgiveness of sins and the incarnation of Jesus, the Christ.

*The 'spiritual life' cannot be separated from the political, community, cultural,
individual, economic and social life.* Life forms a unity and cannot be differentiated
into 'spiritual' and 'earthly' spheres because the earth and its inhabitants are
essentially the creation and work of God, and because the 'spiritual' is an
aspect of the created earthly humanity. It is thus clear that humanity does not
stand in a vertical relationship with God and in a horizontal relationship with
his fellowmen or with politics.

Continuing to use this terminology, it may be said that man stands in a vertical *and* horizontal relationship to both God and his fellowmen. According to the Gospel man's religion has political, social and individual meaning *and* man's political, social and individual life has religious meaning. God has created but one world and the entire creation falls within His sovereignty.[24]

Two days after the publication of the Schlebusch-Le Grange Report, the Institute was declared an 'Affected Organisation' and so deprived of all overseas financial support. As the Board of Management saw it, the state had directly attacked 'the universality of the Christian church . . . preventing one member from assisting another where there is need'.[25] In fact the crudeness of the Report's attack, as well as this attempt to isolate and cripple the Institute, worked in some ways to its advantage. The Institute's credibility increased among blacks, and it experienced renewed moral support in international church circles. As we have seen, there was a sharp increase in domestic funding and the Institute's membership bounced back from 900 to approximately 3,000.[26] Encouraged by this local response and a flood of letters and telegrams from abroad, Naudé and his staff re-dedicated themselves to the struggle against apartheid, to co-operating with the black consciousness movement and with the black DRCs.

However, in practice it was to prove just as difficult as before to mobilise the Institute. To gain more members was one thing; steadily to expand and vitalise this membership, to maintain its morale in the face of the brutal repression about to be unleashed on blacks, and to generate increasing political activism among fellowship groups was another. There were exceptions — lively, mutually supportive, activists. But in general the hoped-for network of decentralised basic communities had not been created in a systematic way by the time the Institute was banned in 1977. Naudé, with his focus on central admini-stration, his flair for public speaking and his capacity to explain the Institute's position to overseas audiences, must bear some respon-sibility for this. Perhaps, at this time of increasing state repression, he should have spent more time strengthening grass-roots cells and branches. Of course, the correct balance in such matters — in directing energies to fund-raising and public relations as against the nuts and bolts of local organisation — is always difficult to establish. Nevertheless, many in the Christian Institute felt that Naudé had not got the balance right. Distracted by the desperate struggle for financial survival, he relied for the moment on a series of public addresses.

He started with a grim, prophetic warning. While the Institute, he argued, was not in itself important, its ability to survive and co-operate with other organisations, including the churches, for non-violent radical change was crucial for the future of South Africa. This was because blacks were 'watching very carefully and waiting to see' what the outcome of the Christian Institute's confrontation with the state would be. 'I believe', he went on,

that it is essential for all of us to heed very carefully . . . the feelings of the black community. Because if they come to the conclusion that the peaceful efforts of bodies like the Christian Institute are not heeded, understood or supported, then one cannot predict what the despair in their hearts may bring forward. May the day never come when there is such a loss of faith in people acting with moral conviction, that the majority of our community will turn against us.[27]

Many felt that such a day had already arrived. If it had not, the state violence unleashed in the next few years confirmed Naudé's deepest fears.

While unable to abandon hope, Naudé was even now very pessimistic about the prospects of achieving at best a 'very turbulent' but 'reasonably peaceful' dismantling of apartheid. Given the deep divisions between the white DRCs and the multi-racial churches, the tensions between black and white Christians and the depressing record of all denominations in failing to eradicate racism within their own ranks, Naudé had little hope that the white-controlled churches as institutions would take the lead in bringing about fundamental changes. He feared they would not take the risks required to head off civil war.[28] As the Institute had realised for some time, hope now lay with black leaders and black pressures, although the damage inflicted by apartheid on the social fabric had made the future problematical under any circumstances. In Naudé's judgement, it would 'only be after the events of liberation that the full picture of the terrible damage which has been inflicted upon the humanity of both black and white by the idolising of the idea of separateness of people of different cultures, colours and races, will emerge.' In the face of this tragic inheritance, black leaders, he hoped and prayed, would have the magnanimity to 'start laying the foundations for a new and liberated South Africa where all racial and ethnic considerations will be made subservient to the common allegiance which all its citizens will be inspired and challenged to give to the country of their love'.[29]

As the Institute re-dedicated itself to peaceful confrontation in the struggle against apartheid, it did so amid signs of mounting black discontent in the major urban areas. Interacting with recurrent labour unrest and increasing anger as tens of thousands of dependants were 'endorsed out' to the rural dumping-grounds, the black consciousness movement had helped to focus a resurgence of African nationalism the like of which had not been seen since the 1950s. By continuing to support black demands in this turbulent atmosphere, while becoming more radical in its own analysis of racial and economic oppression, the Institute remained on collision course with the state.

The Institute had no doubt that it was facing an increasingly ruthless police state in that the Affected Organisations Act and the Riotous Assemblies (Amendment) Act of 1974 were refinements of a system of surveillance, bannings and detentions which had already destroyed the rule of law. These new statutes were simply extensions of executive power which had been unleashed over the previous twenty-five years by, *inter alia*, the Suppression of Communism Act, the General Laws (Amendment) Acts, the Terrorism Act, censorship and the whole panoply of unfreedom enshrined in every piece of apartheid legislation. The Institute had been declared an 'Affected Organisation' and now the Riotous Assemblies (Amendment) Act (the state's response to student protests)[30] removed the residual safeguards against the use of police violence in dispersing protesters. The Act also gave magistrates the power to prohibit any gathering for up to forty-eight hours and the Minister of Justice the power to do so for any length of time.[31] By mid-1974 twenty persons detained under the security laws had died in prison. Solitary confinement was commonplace and a culture of police brutality and torture was well established. When the thirteen black consciousness leaders were belatedly brought to trial in 1974, there were still at least twenty-six of their colleagues languishing incommunicado. Moreover, the number held without trial was to increase dramatically as the black student demonstrations of 1976 were crushed.[32]

As with other anti-apartheid organisations that had not as yet been banned, the Institute was struggling to survive within a web of repressive legislation, intimidatory surveillance and unbridled executive power. By 1975 it also seems to have become the target of yet more insidious practices which were financed from a government 'dirty tricks' or slush fund. As we have already seen, *To The Point* surreptitiously received an infusion of state funds and, *inter alia*, launched a scurrulous attack on the Rev. Manas Buthelezi — an attempted character assasination which backfired on the editors.[33] In 1974, however, a more sophisticated approach was adopted when the Christian League of Southern Africa was launched. Well funded, it soon had twelve full-time staff and volunteers in every major city. The League's purpose, in its own terms, was to 'warn Christians against the infiltration of Marxism and the destruction of the Christian faith throughout the free world'.[34] In the South African context this translated as saving the multi-racial churches from a 'pseudo-gospel' of liberal and Communistic values, and saving the country from a black Marxist revolution. More specifically, the League's task was to counter the influence of the Christian Institute, the SACC and WCC. The result was a steady flow of invective and propaganda from the League's mouthpiece *Encounter*. Its themes were the same patchwork of innuendo, distortions and half-truths peddled by the Schlebusch-Le Grange Commission. There were also bizarre embellishments, as when the SACC was supposed to have used overseas funding to 'distribute kits with directions on how to make bombs'.[35]

It took several years for the true nature of the Christian League to be publically revealed by what came to be known as the Muldergate Affair. In 1978, the year after the Christian Institute was banned, a major scandal broke, revealing that the Department of Information had been deeply implicated. At first it transpired that the League received an infusion of funds from the American financier John McGoff who, it was alleged, in turn received $10 million from the South African government for this and several other manoeuvres. These included an attempt to take over the *Washington Star* and the financing of United States electoral campaigns targeted against liberal anti-apartheid Congressmen and Senators, for example Senator Dick Clark. Later it emerged that the League had been a part of this wider strategy and that it received at least R280,000 per year from funds manipulated by the apartheid regime.[36]

A glimpse of the League's wide range of contacts was offered in 1978 when its National Chairman — the Methodist minister the Rev. Fred Shaw — led a group of five whites to the United States for a month of speaking engagements. Shaw's hosts included leaders of the evangelical caucus 'Good News' and Edgar C. Bundy of the 'Christian radical right' who controlled the Church League of America. In addition to leading this tour, Shaw was also an organiser of the right-wing International Christian Network which met in London in July 1978 to counter what it saw as the dangers of politicised Christianity and the horrors of liberation theology. When this carefully selected group of forty individuals gathered, it was under the chairmanship of Professor Peter Bayerhaus, director of the Institute of Missionary Studies at Tübingen.[37] Bayerhaus was the leader of an intensely political move to counter the spread of political and liberation theology in Europe and the Third World.

As the Christian League was being formed in 1975, the Institute came under further pressure from informers, one of whom appears to have been close to Beyers Naudé. Indeed the indications are that this informer was taken into Naudé's confidence and travelled abroad on his behalf on several occasions before the Institute was banned in 1977. Although the suspect was indeed treated with considerable suspicion by several of the Institute's executive staff, he seems to have allayed Naudé's suspicions until several years after the banning.

As this new campaign was mounted against the Christian Institute, the white DRCs re-asserted their defence of apartheid in church structures and within society. The Institute, with its countervailing views, was condemned as a source of heresy. This renewed attempt to isolate Naudé and his supporters was in part a defensive response to the Institute's increased contacts within the black DRCs. It was also bound up with the white DRCs' alarm at their intensifying confrontation with the international community of Reformed Churches following the 1968 Luntern meeting of the Reformed Alliance.[38] When the Alliance of Reformed Churches met at Nairobi in 1970 and the Reformed Ecumenical Synod sat in Sydney in 1972, these gatherings called once more on their sister-churches in South Africa to abandon apartheid, so posing at an international level the same Biblical challenge which the Christian Institute posed domestically. Led by the NGK, the Afrikaner churches turned their backs on both challenges. They broke their international ties with the Reformed churches and moved behind the apartheid state as it took steps to confine and then crush the Institute. Having isolated themselves from the WCC and then from their own denominational fellowship, the white churches of Afrikanerdom were able to look on with equanimity as the Christian Institute was declared an 'Affected Organisation' in 1975 and banned two years later.

The large NGK delegation of thirteen which attended the 1970 Nairobi meeting failed in its attempt to present apartheid as a humane and Biblically acceptable policy. Rather than endorsing this view, the Alliance of Reformed Churches responded by expressing its deep concern at the practice of racial segregation by the South African DRCs 'in their own church life'; it also regretted their apparent support for the government's 'policy and practice of racial segregation and white supremacy'. In the Body of Christ there was neither Greek nor Jew (Galatians, 3.11), so that 'racial segregation as a law of the Church's life' contradicted the 'very nature of the Christian Church.' The South African delegation, whose own NGK synod in 1966 had declared the Christian Institute a 'heretical movement', was further mortified by the conference's very last resolution which singled out the Institute 'for wholehearted and prayerful support' as a 'hopeful sign of reconciliation in South Africa'.[39]

In the Christian Institute's understanding, reconciliation required confession, repentence and action in the search for more just and non-racial structures. Rather than accepting this approach, the white DRCs adopted the face-saving device of relegating the awkward matter of the Institute to the on-going 'Ad Hoc Commission on Racial and Ecumenical Affairs' (the Landman Commission) which had been set up after the Luntern Conference of 1968. A further official condemnation would have been too embarrassing given the Institute's growing support overseas and the already severely strained relations between the white DRCs and the Reformed Alliance.

This was particularly true in the case of the NGK's 'mother-church', the Netherlands Reformed Church, many of whose leading person-alities were firm supporters of Naudé and the Institute. In this context, the Landman Commission was in no hurry to report. It took six years over the enquiry and only gave its verdict in 1974.[40] In the interim, the NGK tried to regain this lost ground, both at the 1972 Reformed Ecumenical Synod in Sydney and at its own South African Synod in 1974. In each case it set out to gain support for its segregated structures and for the government's policy of apartheid.

Two issues focused the discussions in Sydney: mixed worship and mixed marriages. In the former case the Reformed Ecumenical Synod insisted that 'no person may be excluded from common worship solely on grounds of race or colour.' Holy Scripture, it argued, did not pass judgement on mixed marriages, but neither the church nor the state should prohibit them 'because they have no right to limit the free choice of a marriage partner on the grounds of race or colour.' Marriage was a personal and family concern.[41] Again the white DRCs dissented, and this time they were contradicted by the delegates of the black DRCs.[42] Just how resolute white Afrikanerdom was became clear in the aftermath of Sydney. When the NGK Synod met in South Africa during 1974, Professor Ben Marais proposed a resolution urging that church doors be opened to all races. It was overwhelmingly defeated.[43] The only form of mixed worship white DRC communities were prepared to tolerate was household services where servants might attend family prayers. The same 1974 Synod accepted that there were no explicit scriptural condemnations of mixed marriage; however, scripture also upheld 'the ethnic separation of the human race'. Conse-quently, mixed marriages were to be condemned as destroying 'the God-given diversity and identity of men'.[44]

It is worth exploring a little further the political attitudes and theo-logical pre-suppositions behind these decisions, for this reassertion of segregation led to a sharp increase in tension between the black and white DRCs. Dr J. S. Gericke, Assessor of the NGK, feared that the opening of church doors to people of any race might lead to political demonstrations by blacks; that is, demonstrations in the white parishes.[45] Dr J. D. Vorster, the NGK Moderator, rejected all forms of mixed worship. The Reformed Church in Holland and most other churches, he argued, made the error of placing 'the concept that all men are equal above the concept that there are differences between men'. He regretted the prospect of a break with the churches in the Netherlands, but if they did not accept the South African outlook, he could see this happening. 'Then', he continued, 'we will just have to stand alone. What have we to lose, in any case, if the Reformed Churches.in Holland break with us? I think nothing.' The world was wrong; South Africans knew they were right and would 'not budge one inch from [their] interpretation to satisfy anyone.'[46]

These polemical responses by high-ranking members of the NGK do not, of course, give the nuanced official position of that church — even if they reveal the assertive, close-minded attitudes that were alienating the black DRCs. Nevertheless, when the NGK expressed itself very carefully in an attempt to avoid giving umbrage, its defence of ethnic churches and apartheid structures was still deeply offensive to blacks. When the Landman Report finally appeared in 1974, it propounded a theory of differentiation which concluded that 'under certain circumstances and conditions, the New Testament allows for the ordering of existence between different peoples living in one land by means of separate development.'[47] Certainly there was no Scriptural basis for racism, that is for white racial superiority; but, it was argued, there was a Scriptural foundation for the maintenance of ethnic diversity. While the 'curse of Ham' might not be relevant to an understanding of race relations in the late twentieth century, and the Afrikaner *volk* were not to be identified with the Israelites, apartheid was not in conflict with the norms of Scripture.[48]

The key to understanding this cast of mind is to be found in two propositions underpinning the Landman Report and the resulting statement from the NGK General Synod: *Human Relations and the South African Scene in the Light of Scripture*.[49] The first proposition recognised that 'the Scriptures teach and uphold the essential unity of mankind and the primordial relatedness and fundamental equality of all peoples.' However, the second proposition asserted that 'ethnic diversity is in its origin in accordance with the will of God' and should not be seen as in conflict with the 'fundamental equality of all peoples.'[50] In other words, the Synod defended a fundamental human unity transcending the historical reality of existing cultural, social and political institutions. At the same time it insisted that this reality was and should remain one of ethnic differentiation: 'the church should avoid the modern tendency to erase all distinctions among peoples.'[51] This God-given diversity, it was argued, preceeded the diaspora following the collapse of the Tower of Babel; it was a wholesome part of creation, a sign of God's mercy and not simply the result of sin. Such diversity, such differentiation, could only be overcome through the intervention of God's grace at the end of time. Consequently 'separate development . . . [or] co-existence of various peoples in one country' was in keeping with the Scriptures. Therefore the church's responsibility was to nurture justice between these groups and love of one's neighbour, given this reality of differentiation.[52] Insofar as the NGK differed from other churches, it was not due to a different view of moral concepts and values or of Christian ethics, but to a different view of the situation in South Africa and the teaching of God's Word in this regard. There is no difference in ideals and objectives, but merely disagreement on the best methods of achieving these ideals.[53]

The presumption that the ethnic diversity of South Africans should be legalised, rigorously maintained by public policy and so form the basis of the segregated structures of church and society, was, of course, anathema to the Christian Institute. By the mid-1970s, this presumption had also become unacceptable to the black DRCs. In their judgement, differentiation (apartheid) was the product of white racism and the means to sustaining the grotesque economic inequalities that nurtured white privilege. Far from 'separate development' being the basis for justice and concern for one's neighbour, it perpetuated injustice, retarded the growth of Christian community and was rapidly destroying the remnants of non-racial fellowship that struggled to survive.

The Landman Report and the NGK Synod of 1974 had done their ingenious best to expunge any racist exegesis from DRC theology. All 500 members of the Synod put the best possible interpretation on differentiation, but it was no good. Amid the realities of apartheid the arguments were essentially self-serving. This was highlighted when the Synod refused to address the central issues of migratory labour and the destruction of African family life which the Landman Report drew to its attention.[54] These might be awkward issues for white churchmen, but they were tragic matters, quite literally of life and death for black communities. Far from defusing tensions, the Report and the Synod's declarations brought the fundamental disagreements into an even sharper focus, isolating the NGK still further from the black DRCs and the World Alliance of Reformed Churches. Speaking as observers at the white synod, but also as Assessors of their own general synods, the Rev. E.T.S. Buti (*Kerk van Afrika*) and the Rev. E.G. Mannikam (Indian Reformed Church) warned their NGK colleagues that the black churches might well take different decisions on a range of issues that troubled the 'Mother-Church'; for example, relations with the Netherlands Reformed Churches, mixed marriages and mixed worship. As Buti put it on the latter issue; 'a Christian church cannot be a *volk* church. If it is a *volk* church we would not go into it whether its doors were open to us or not.' He also warned that the growth of the black DRCs was seriously threatened by the NGK's close ties to the apartheid state.[55]

To make matters worse, the NGK chose the moment of the 1974 Synod to move even more obviously into step with the government in that it again condemned the Christian Institute as a source of heresy.[56] At the same time, its loyalty to the apartheid state was re-asserted through an ultimatum to the Reformed Churches of the Netherlands over their decision to support the WCC Programme to Combat Racism:[57] they would have to rescind their decision 'to support terrorism on our borders . . . not later than the first session of the next synod' or the NGK would regard all ties as broken.[58] The Netherlands churches refused to be browbeaten. They continued to support the Christian Institute as well as the Programme; moreover, in the context of Luntern, Nairobi and Sydney, they again asked the NGK to reconsider its whole stance on race relations. As a result, the NGK Synod of 1978 declared 'the close bonds which existed between us and the [Netherlands DRC] as severed.'[59]

In the year following the crucial synod of 1974, the estrangement of the NGK from the black DRCs grew rapidly as the latter asserted their independence, rejected apartheid, joined the SACC and established still closer informal ties with the Christian Institute. When the white NGK took its intransigent stand, the sense of frustration and disappointment within the black DRCs ran deep. During the early 1970s, there had been considerable discontent, but it was allied to the hope that the international community of Reformed Churches would succeed in persuading the NGK to re-examine its entire stance on race relations. The Landman Report followed by the Synod of 1974 destroyed any residual optimism of this sort.

Whereas in the 1960s the principles (if not the practice) of apartheid were accepted, and black dissent was contained within the family of Reformed Churches, as the 1970s progressed a public debate erupted. By 1973 informal and tense discussions were taking place in several circuits of the African, Coloured and Indian DRCs. Most white NGK missionaries in these black churches still thought of their congregations as insulated from black theology and black consciousness. These 'threats' were supposed to be problems for the white-dominated and hypocritical multi-racial churches which had never faced up to their own ideals, never lived as integrated Christian communities. In reality however, the black clergy of the DRCs were beginning to revise their theology and their politics. Black theology and black consciousness did not seem inappropriate for humiliated and powerless people oppressed by the structures of apartheid; nor did they seem inappropriate for segregated black churches which did not share power with the 'Mother-Church' and were still under the control of white missionaries and NGK funding. Indeed the very terms 'Mother-' and 'Daughter-' Churches were being rejected by some bold individuals. They were asking whether the black churches did not have a missionary responsibility to convert the white DRCs from their corrupting racism. There were other questions too. Whites were often in black pulpits; why not a regular flow of preachers in the opposite direction? How could segregated churches witness to a common humanity? Why were black and white, African, Coloured and Indian congregations not sharing *nagmaal* (communion) together? Why was there not a Federal DRC Synod that was more than advisory, a Synod in which black churches, under black control, would exercise considerable power? Why was the NGK cutting itself off from the wider Christian community, from the SACC, the WCC and even isolating itself within the Alliance of Reformed Churches? Why was the Christian Institute being persecuted by the white DRCs and the state? Was apartheid a blasphemous attack on the process of building Christian fellowship? Was the segregated structure of the DRC itself blasphemous?[60]

It was in the midst of this ferment that 100 African ministers and their wives side-stepped the circuits and synods to discuss 'A Theology of Development and the Independence of the NGKA' (*Nederduitse Gereformeerde Kerk van Afrika*). They met twice in 1973 and finally condemned apartheid as unchristian. In addition they called upon all black clergy to 'conscientise the people in the Theology of the Liberation of the Whole Man'. What was needed was a 'theology of hope and not of despair'. All forms of violence and bloodshed should be avoided, but Christians had a responsibility to resist injustice and its fruits: 'social-class and race-conflict'.[61] To Naudé and his colleagues who had been cultivating their ties with the black DRCs since the formation of the Institute in 1963, this stand was a major 'breakthrough for the Kingdom of God in South Africa' , the beginnings of a black witness which might yet convert the white NGK from its 'tribal gods' and its 'glorification of Afrikaner nationalism', from its 'nationalist and heathen view [that] observes mankind in terms of race and birth'.[62]

When in 1974 the white NGK Synod dug its heels in and refused to listen to these voices, the new black leadership in the DRCs became more assertive. While black consciousness and black theology were a part of this ferment, the stance taken was a nuanced one which managed to link the thrust for black dignity, equality and leadership to the vision of an intergrated non-racial DRC. Dr Alan Boesak, a young theologian of the *Sendingkerk* who left his ministry in Paarl to further his studies at the University of Kampen in the Netherlands, welcomed what he saw as the coming confrontation — as long as it was honourable. This meant an open and honest if tough exchange of views. Boesak, who was to become one of the country's leading theologians and a revered figure in the Coloured community, did not favour ultimatums. But if such a style was to be adopted — as in the NGK's confrontation with the churches of the Netherlands — then the *Sendingkerk* was badly remiss in not facing the white NGK with an ultimatum 'over its unchristian behaviour.'[63] In Boesak's view, the

Landman Commission was a shocking instance of this, a supposedly objective church enquiry which forced 'the Christian ethic into the framework of apartheid and subjected it to the national ideology, instead of subjecting the ideology to the critique of God's liberating Word'. The commissioners and the NGK Synod had been blind to the 'bitter realities in which black people have to live . . . [unable] to see how the poor are being sold for a pair of sandals (Amos,2.6).' Nowhere had there been a 'sign that black people who suffer under this system have had the right to voice their opinion before the Commission'.[64] Blacks were not going to wait any longer for an invitation to express their views.

The result was quickly apparent. By 1975 the world of the white DRCs was being turned upside down. As the Christian Institute had recognised for some time, the future of Christianity and of South Africa itself now lay in black hands. Beyers Naudé, Roelf Meyer and Theo Kotze had observed this transition at close quarters, not least within the black DRCs where they had many friendships. In addition, Naudé often preached at the invitation of black pastors. Given this intimate personal involvement, it was not inappropriate for him and Roelf Meyer[65] to be invited (as observers) to attend the 1975 NG *Kerk van Afrika* Synod when it met in Worcester. The atmosphere at this Synod was symptomatic of the changes that were afoot. For the first time in its history, the *Kerk van Afrika* elected a black Moderator, the Rev. Ernest Buti of Alberton in the Transvaal. The *Kerk* also accepted the 1972 resolutions of the Reformed Ecumenical Synod in Sydney which condemned racism and declared differentiation, apartheid and separatism to be contrary to Scripture. The Synod's decision to eliminate tribal divisions in its seminaries was followed by a vote of 82 to 17, with white missionary clergy abstaining, in favour of eliminating the category of missionary and of dropping the condescending term 'Daughter-Church'. White ministers would still be welcome — as full members of the *Kerk van Afrika* and as brother-ministers but no longer as missionaries subject to the discipline of the NGK. In turn the NGK was asked to open its doors to black ministers.[66]

It is not surprising that in what seemed a highly contentious synod, several white ministers protested against the presence of Naudé and Meyer. Buti, however, quickly took charge, publicly welcomed his guests and invited Naudé to address the gathering. Naude did so, taking reconciliation as his theme: reconciliation between the Institute and the NGK, and reconciliation between blacks and whites through justice in the wider society.[67] As there was no prospect of this, Naudé's forlorn hope had therefore to become a prayer 'that God may use one or more of the Black Dutch Reformed Churches to be instrumental in effecting a true and lasting reconciliation between the white NGK on the one hand and the Christian Institute on the other'.[68]

When, as Moderator, Buti's turn came to address the Synod, he explained amid prolonged applause, singing and dancing that the *Kerk van Afrika* would be joining the SACC.[69] He then went on to describe the NGK's major problem as its close ties with the government; blacks were leaving the DRCs saying 'the NGK and the government are the same'.[70] Before the year was out, Buti followed up this judgement by co-operating with the Indian Reformed Church and the *Sendingkerk* in a major initiative which he hoped would transform all the DRCs, not least the NGK: a series of discussions designed to prepare for full union, for the establishment of one multi-racial church with one multi-racial synod. Not unexpectedly, it was the white NGK which ended the proceedings when its Moderator rejected this call for organic unity. It was, he said, impossible at this stage, and the black churches should not try to force unity 'down our throats'.[71]

By the end of 1975 the Christian Institute's pessimistic judgements about the NGK had been amply confirmed. On the other hand, the black DRCs were being transformed as they encountered liberation theology and struggled to establish a new understanding of Christian mission. Potentially, they were powerful forces within the black consciousness movement. Moderator Ernest Buti was forthright in praising black theology as an inspiration to blacks because it called them to reflect on their own historic reality and to become their own theologians. He also defended black consciousness as a source of dignity, so long as its long-term goal was not separatism.[72] However, Buti's measured words do not give the full flavour of the radicalisation and new leadership potential emerging within the black DRCs. This could only be sensed in the younger generation of ministers, men of the calibre of Alan Boesak and Sam Buti (the son of the Moderator) who were to face the apartheid state during the agonising years of bloodshed that were around the corner. Boesak, in a major contribution to liberation and black theology, put the matter in his usual, concise way:

Any theology which does not take God's liberation of the poor and the oppressed as a central point of departure, thereby excludes itself effectively from being a witness to the divine presence in the world.

This, he suggested, was the problem with the theology of Afrikanerdom, which had degenerated into an ideology.[73] Sam Buti's contribution was to outline the concrete political consequences of this position. Horrified by the slaughter of black school children in the SOWETO demonstrations of June 1976,[74] he joined Naudé,[75] the Netherlands Reformed Church[76] and others in calling for a round-table conference between blacks and whites with the black delegates including political prisoners, exiles and Bantustan politicians. At the same time Buti called on blacks to identify with black consciousness organisations, particularly with SASO and the BPC.[77]

Once again, the Christian Institute had placed itself in direct confrontation with the Afrikaner establishment. Having defied the Schlebusch-Le Grange Commission and having been declared an 'Affected Organisation', it was now seen to be intimately associated with what was becoming a nightmare for the NGK — the radicalisation of the black DRCs. While all this would have been sufficient to explain the eventual banning of the Institute in 1977, there was yet another dimension to its confrontation with the apartheid state. By the mid-1970s Naudé was leading the Institute into a more trenchent analysis of injustice, attacking the ethos and structures of capitalism and condemning foreign investment in the apartheid system. It is possible that these were even more dangerous waters to sail into, for the Afrikaner state had become intimately meshed with the structures of domestic and international capitalism.

A foretaste of the Institute's more critical approach to capitalism had already appeared in the 1973 final SPROCAS Report, *A Taste of Power*.[78] The themes raised at that time were expressed by staff members with increasing frequency in the middle 1970s as the Institute interacted with the black consciousness movement. *Pro Veritate* also reflected this shift into a structural criticism of capitalism and a search for radical alternatives to the existing economic order. When *The Principles for Which the Christian Institute Stands in Southern Africa* was published in 1973, it called on Christians to identify with 'the poor, the outcast, the exploited and the rejected'. In addition, it attacked 'the South African system [which] perpetuates poverty, exploitation, rejection and deprivation'. Christian commitment meant 'immediate care for those in need, and a radical change in the structures of society which cause it'.[79]

By 1975 Naudé was pushing this analysis further and doing so for two reasons. The Institute had come to its own conviction on these matters, but Naudé knew only too well that white South Africans were dangerously ill-informed on black politics. Isolated by apartheid and bemused by government propaganda, the vast majority of whites were abysmally ignorant of the real feelings, policies and judgements of black leaders. In addressing the Convocation of the University of Natal in August 1975 at Pietermaritzburg, Naudé argued as follow:

The vast majority of our African, Coloured and Indian community will never voluntarily accept the present economic system of distribution of wealth and land which the capitalist system, buttressed by a myriad of apartheid laws and regulations, has imposed on them . . . The recent developments in Mozambique have focused the attention of many Whites and Blacks in our

country on the whole issue of capitalism and socialism. The ruthless suppression by the Government, especially since 1960, of the freedom of the
organisation and expression of black thought which could seriously threaten
either the Nationalist policy of separate development or the present capitalist
system with its major profits always going into white pockets, has created a
situation where the majority of whites live in dangerous ignorance regarding
the real feelings and hopes of the black community on the issue of capitalism
and socialism. [. . .] the black leadership which will eventually decide the
political future of South Africa, does not voluntarily accept and support the
present economic system in South Africa and will never do so. The whole
concept of African socialism as, for instance, a leader like Nyerere in Tanzania
has accepted and promoted — and more recently the leadership of
FRELIMO has started to implement in Mozambique — has fired the
imagination of many South African blacks, and, I believe, that it would be
correct to state that a substantial number of blacks would, if they obtain the
power to do so, reject the present capitalist system in favour of a form of socialism which is much closer to the African concept of communal rights, communal freedoms and communal responsibilities than the present capitalist
system.[80]

A few months later, Naudé was to argue that it was 'imperative that
objective studies' be allowed within South Africa

to assess the role of capitalism on the one hand and historic communism on the
other hand, especially to ascertain to what degree the emerging form of African
socialism could provide a more adequate and just answer to the problem of
affluence and poverty which both the first and third world is currently facing.

Of course, the government 'with its terrible fear of Communism'
would not permit such discussions; but this, Naudé argued, was where
the challenge lay for Christians, this was where the 'perspective of the
Gospel' might create a vision of justice which would offer new insights
for a 'more just economic system.'[81]

Shortly after this the Institute condemned foreign investment in
South Africa. In doing so it placed itself at the head of an incipient campaign against any further involvement of the transnational corporations in apartheid. This was alarming enough for the government as it
was already trying to neutralise an international movement against
investment in South Africa which, with the support of church and anti-
apartheid groups, was gaining considerable momentum in North
America and Europe. The last thing Prime Minister Vorster wanted
was a comparable domestic protest movement which might move into
step with overseas efforts to initiate sanctions against his regime.
However, the Institute's stance was potentially even more disturbing;
for as it condemned further investment in apartheid, it remained in
contact with black organisations and continued to publicise its radical
critique of the ethos and structures of capitalism itself.

The Institute's position on these matters had evolved from its attempt in 1973 to develop a code of conduct, a set of minimum guidelines as criteria for any further investment in South Africa: full trade union rights, equal pay for equal work, the scrapping of job reservation and a steady move to provide the same fringe benefits to blacks and whites.[82] This attempt to prise a better deal for blacks from the existing system was reassessed over the next three years with the result that in October 1976 the Institute came out against any further investment in South Africa.[83] This shift was prompted by several factors.[84] The great majority of corporations had been unco-operative and intractable — the code of conduct had failed. More important, the black consciousness movement declared its position unequivocally. In December 1974, 300 delegates at the Black Renaissance Convention voted unanimously against any further foreign investment. This too was the stand taken by the SASO and the BPC, a stand which hardened still further after the SOWETO massacres of June 1976.[85] In addition, the Institute's own analysis of capitalist exploitation, and the increasingly ruthless nature of the apartheid regime, led to the conclusion that codes of conduct, or marginal concessions, would not 'relax the grip of capitalist control enough to enable the oppressed masses to discover and express their own dignity and self respect'.[86] In the Institute's judgement, the argument commonly used in corporate circles — that economic growth would undermine apartheid and produce fundamental changes — had been proved false. The argument that blacks would suffer most if foreign investment ceased was also unacceptable. The Institute was convinced that the great majority of politically conscious blacks opposed investment while recognising that an economic recession and unemployment would cause them suffering. However, the essential point was their willingness to endure temporary distress rather than 'the unending suffering caused by the continuation of apartheid'.[87] According to the Institute, the investment debate went far deeper than fair business practices to 'the very nature of an international system which exports something as potentially exploitative as present-day capitalism'. Leaders of the black consciousness movement realised this, were seriously questioning the system, and the Christian Institute 'wished to be part of [that] search for a new social order'.[88]

So it was that by 1976 the Institute's confrontation with the Afrikaner state was no longer simply a matter of challenging the civil religion of the white DRCs while condemning the racism of apartheid. The very process of confrontation, allied to an increasingly sophisticated analysis of the economics of apartheid, had led to a deepening understanding of structural injustice and social sin. As a result, Naudé and his colleagues did not withdraw into an otherworldly, dualistic religion when faced with the intransigence of white power and the tragic prospect of civil war. Rather, they had the courage to take the option for the poor, to support the black consciousness movement and black theology, so entering into a learning experience which gave rise to an indigeneous liberation theology.

While these developments were in themselves sufficient to call down the full wrath of the state, the Institute's growing influence with the black DRCs, its support for conscientious objection and its rejection of South Africa's capitalist economic order meant that the final confrontation was inevitable and imminent.

NOTES

1. In 1975 A.L. Schlebusch resigned as Chairman to become speaker of the House of Assembly. He was replaced by another National Party politician, L. Le Grange. From this point onwards the enquiry was referred to as the Schlebusch-Le Grange Commission.

2. The Commission also decided to investigate the Wilgespruit Ecumenical Centre at Roodepoort on the Witwatersrand. As a church centre for multi-racial contacts and the study of social issues, it was roundly condemned and its director deported.

3. P. Randall (ed.), *A Taste Of Power*, p. 220; *Pro Veritate*, June 1975, p. 8.

4. International Commission of Jurists, *The Trial of Beyers Naudé*, pp. 42–3.

5. In addition to members of SASO and BPC, these included members of the Black Allied Workers Union and the Theatre Council of Natal. *CI Newsletter*, 7 January 1975, p. 5.

6. *Supra.*, p. 96.

7. International Commission of Jurists, *The Trial of Beyers Naudé*, p. 43.

8. Brian Brown, Theo Kotze, Roelf Meyer and J. O. Phakathi, *Divine or Civil Disobedience* (Johannesburg, Ravan Press, *c.* (1974), pp. 1, 9.

9. International Commission of Jurists, *The Trial of Beyers Naudé*, pp. 138–52; *Pro Veritate*, December 1976, p. 10; *CI News*, 13 March 1974, pp. 1–2; *Cape Times*, 13 March 1974; E. Regehr, *Perceptions of Apartheid*, p. 84.

10. *Pro Veritate*, December 1974, p. 4.

11. *Pro Veritate*, December 1976, p. 10.

12. *The Star*, 29 May 1975.

13. In fact Naudé received $350 from the WCC when fighting the libel case against Professor Pont.

14. *CI News*, August 1975, p. 2; E. Regehr, *Perceptions of Apartheid*, pp. 79–91.

15. *Cape Argus*, 5 June 1975.

16. *Pro Veritate*, June 1975, p. 9.

17. One of the more bizarre untruths was the reference to the pacifist

Bishop, Dom Helder Camara of Recife, Brazil (who had some influence on the Institute's thinking), as a priest who had joined the guerrillas armed with a machine-gun.

18. E. Regehr, *Perceptions of Apartheid*, pp. 88–9; 'The Prophetic Task in South Africa Today. The Christian Institute's Response to the Commission of Enquiry into Certain Organisations', *Pro Veritate*, September 1977, pp. 4–6.

19. *Supra.*, pp. 111–13, for the actual position of the WCC.

20. The fact that Vorster threatened to take action against Naudé should the reports prove to be accurate, but had never done so, was conveniently ignored. *Report of the Commission of Enquiry into Certain Organisations*, p. 112; *South African Outlook*, June 1975, p. 1; E. Regehr, *Perceptions of Apartheid*, p. 88; 'The Prophetic Task in South Africa Today', *Pro Veritate*, September 1977, p. 5.

21. *South African Outlook*, June 1975, p. 1.

22. In rejecting the Commissions' findings, the Rev. Manas Buthelezi agreed that, 'as a deliberate and technical model of theologizing, black theology started in the U.S.' However, this did not detract from its integrity, just as 'the fact that Christianity was brought to this country by white European foreigners is no legitimate ground for black people to reject it.' Far from being a 'communistic inspiration' as the Commissioners imagined, black theology was the infusing of a biblically grounded hope which was rooted in the understanding that blacks 'were created in the image of God just like white people.' Blacks had now to take their own initiatives, be creative, liberate themselves and proclaim the Gospel to whites. 'Buthelezi fails Le Grange on Black Theology', *CI News*, October 1975, p. 2.

23. *Ecunews* (Johannesburg, SACC), 4 June, 1975; E. Regehr, *Perceptions of Apartheid*, pp. 212–13; 'The Prophetic Task in South Africa Today,' *Pro Veritate*, September 1977, p. 5.

24. 'The Prophetic Task in South Africa Today: the Christian Institute's Response to the Schlebusch/Le Grange Commission', *Pro Veritate*, September 1977, p. 5.

25. 'C.I. Board of Management Statement', *CI News*, March 1974, p. 2.

26. *Supra.*, pp. 165–6.

27. 'Beyers Naudé Responds', *South African Outlook*, June 1975, p. 84, being an address at the University of the Witwatersrand.

28. B. Naudé, 'A Glimpse into the Future of South Africa', appendix to Christian Institute, 'Director's Report for the Period August 1, 1974 to July 31, 1975', pp. 9–10, being an address to the University of Natal at Pietermaritzburg, 22 August 1975.

29. *Ibid.*, p. 12.

30. *Supra.*, p. 90.

31. *CI News*, March 1974, pp. 2–3; E. Regehr, *Perceptions of Apartheid*, p. 40.

32. Christian Institute, 'What Happens in South African Prisons' (Cape Town, 1974), pp. 1–5, mimeo; Programme for Social Change, *3rd. Report on Arrests, Detentions and Trials*, p. 14.

33. *Supra.*,

34. *United Methodist News* (New York), September 1978, p. 1.

35. *Ecunews*, 17 November 1978; *CI News*, December 1975, p. 4.

36. *Ecunews*, 24 August 1979, p. 2; *Cape Times*, 24 July 1980.

37. *United Methodist News*, September 1978. p. 2.

38. *Supra.*, p. 79.

39. *Pro Veritate*, September 1970. pp. 1–2.

40. *Supra.*, pp. 183–9.

41. See E. Regehr, *Perceptions of Apartheid*, pp. 216–19, and *Pro Veritate*, May 1973, for a full account of the proceedings in Sydney.

42. *Pro Veritate*, May 1973, pp. 22–5.

43. *Ecunews*, 30 October, 1974; *Pro Veritate*, December 1974, pp. 4–5.

44. *Ecunews*, 30 October, 1974; E. Regehr, *Perceptions of Apartheid*, p. 219.

45. *Rand Daily Mail*, 24 April 1973.

46. *Cape Times*, 4 December 1970.

47. *Pro Veritate*, December 1974, p. 6.

48. J. de Gruchy, *The Church Struggle in South Africa*, pp. 70–1.

49. *Human Relations and the South African Scene in the Light of Scripture* (Cape Town, DRC Publishers, 1975). A careful analysis of this statement can be found in J. de Gruchy, *op. cit.*, pp. 70–80.

50. *Human Relations and the South African Scene*, pp. 13, 25–6.

51. *Ibid.*, p. 25.

52. J. de Gruchy, *The Church Struggle in South Africa*, pp. 70–80.

54. *Pro Veritate*, December 1974, p. 4.

55. *Ibid.*, p. 8; *Rand Daily Mail*, 24 October 1974; *Die Transvaler*, 24 October 1974.

56. *Pro Veritate*, December 1974, p. 6; *South African Outlook*, June 1975, p. 83.

57. *Supra.*, p. 79.

58. E. Regehr, *Perceptions of Apartheid*, pp. 220–1. Relations were not helped by the extraordinary intervention of Dr J.S. Gericke, Moderator of the Cape Synod of the NGK, in the internal affairs of the Reformed Churches in Holland. Going over the heads of their synod officials, Gericke placed a letter in twelve Dutch newspapers asking the 800,000 church members to reverse their synod's decision to support the Programme to Combat Racism. *Ecunews*, 13 May, 1974.

59. E. Regehr, *Perceptions of Apartheid*, p. 221; DRC Africa *News* (Cape Town), November–December 1978.

60. Author's interviews with black DRC clergy, February–April 1973.

61. *Pro Veritate*, November 1973, pp. 1–2; E. Regehr, *Perceptions of Apartheid*, pp. 221–4; *Ecunews*, 2 November 1973, 3 December 1973.

62. *Pro Veritate*, November 1973, p. 1.

63. *Pro Veritate*, December 1974, p. 9.

64. A.A. Boesak, *Farewell to Innocence* (Maryknoll, New York, 1976.), pp. 108–10.

65. Meyer had been deprived of his status as a minister of the NGK when he joined the Christian Institute. He subsequently edited *Pro Veritate*.

66. *South African Outlook*, June 1975, p. 95; Christian Institute of Southern Africa, *News/NUUS*, April 1975, p. 1; Ivor Shapiro, 'A Historic Moment in the Synod', *Pro Veritate*, July 1975, p. 11; E. Regehr, *Perceptions*

of Apartheid, pp. 224–6.

67. *Cape Times*, 6 May 1975.

68. Christian Institute of Southern Africa, *Director's Report for the Period August 1 1974 to July 31 1975*, p. 5.

69. White delegates on the Synod strongly opposed this on the grounds, *inter alia*, that the SACC maintained links with the WCC. *Pro Veritate*, July 1975, p. 12.

70. *Ibid.*; *The Washington Post*, 20 June 1975, p. D15; *Ecunews*, 17 June 1975.

71. E. Regehr, *Perceptions of Apartheid*, p. 225.

72. E. Regehr, *Perceptions of Apartheid*, p. 226; *Ecunews*, 17 June 1975.

73. A.A. Boesak, *Farewell to Innocence*, pp. 105–6. Boesak joined the Institute's Board of Management in January 1977.

74. *Infra.*, pp. 200–1.

75. B. Naudé, *The Individual and the State* (London, Christian Institute Fund, 1976), p. 11, being his address to the Royal Institute of International Affairs, 16 December 1975. This address was read for Naudé by Sir Robert Birley (a long-time member of the Christian Institute) as Naudé's passport had been confiscated.

76. Moderator of the General Synod, 'The Netherlands Reformed Church and South Africa' (CCAD, 1977), pp. 3–4, mimeo. While the Church decided to try and maintain its relations with the NGK, it 'made the appeal of the black churches the basis of [its policy'.

77. E. Regehr, *Perceptions of Apartheid*, p. 227; *Ecunews*, 15 October 1976.

78. *Supra.*, pp. 108–9.

79. Christian Institute, *The Christian Principles for which the Christian Institute Stands in Southern Africa* (Johannesburg, 1973), p. 1.

80. B. Naudé, 'A Glimpse into the Future of South Africa', p. 4, an appendix to the Christian Institute, *Director's Report for the Period August 1 1974 to July 31, 1975*.

81. B. Naudé, *The Individual and the State*, p. 11.

82. The Christian Institute of Southern Africa, 'A Summary of the Christian Institute's contribution to and response within the Investment Debate concerning South Africa' (Johannesburg, 1977), p. 1. mimeo. See too Christian Institute, *Management Responsibility and African Employment* (Johannesburg, Ravan Press, 1973).

83. For a brief period the Institute had been prepared to support investment in the Bantustans, but not in the 'central economy' — the white-owned industrial heartland. This was to be an interim stance while black opinion was consulted. In March 1976 Naudé issued a joint statement to this effect with Chief Gatsha Buthelezi, Prime Minister of Kwa Zulu. A call for a national convention with full black representation was an integral part of this statement, the purpose of the convention being to discuss the country's future and such issues as foreign investment. Seven months later, after the trauma of the SOWETO shootings in June 1976, Naudé and the Institute parted company with Buthelezi who continued to support foreign investment in the Bantustans. By this time Naudé had abandoned any hope of a national convention and the Institute accepted the black consciousness movements blanket condemnation of any further foreign investment. In the Institute's judgement,

the condemnation accurately reflected black opinion. The Institute had also come to see that any foreign investment, with its accompanying technology, bolstered the apartheid system whether it took place in the central economy or the Bantustans. See Chief Gatsha Buthelezi and Dr C.F. Beyers Naudé, 'Foreign Investment in South Africa', *Pro Veritate*, February 1976, supplement; 'The Christian Institute of Southern Africa: Investment in South Africa', *Pro Veritate*, December 1976, pp. 6–7; Christian Institute, Summary of the Christian Institute's contribution within the Investment Debate, pp. 9–11.

84. The fact that in the previous year (June 1975) the Netherlands Reformed Church took a stand against all new investment may have nudged the Institute in this direction too. 'The Netherlands Reformed Church and South Africa', CCAD 1977, Session 9, p. 2.

85. Christian Institute, *Summary of the Investment Debate*, p. 5. By the end of 1976, any expression of opinion on the investment issue was heavily muted by provisions in the Terrorism Act. These made it possible for a person advocating an end to investment to be accused of economic sabotage or incitement to subversion. *Ibid.*, p. 4. For a black consciousness view, see R. Nengwekhulu, 'The Role of Foreign Investments in Reinforcing the Exploitative System in South Africa' (London, 1977), pp. 1–7, mimeo. Nengwekhulu was External Representative of SASO and of BPC.

86. Buthelezi and Naudé, 'Foreign Investment in South Africa', *Pro Veritate*, February 1976, supplement. When the Sullivan (USA) and OEEC codes of conduct were published in 1977, the Institute welcomed them, but *not* as alternatives to a moritorium on further investment. While the codes 'could hardly be called far-reaching', the Institute hoped they might improve the conduct of firms already operating . . . within the apartheid system. Christian Institute, 'Summary of the Investment Debate', p. 2. The stand of the SACC was to call for revised and more stringent codes, but it stopped short of calling for an end to all investment. *Ibid.*, p. 10.

87. 'The Christian Institute of Southern Africa: Investment in South Africa', *Pro Veritate*, December 1976.

88. Christian Institute, *Summary of the Investment Debate*, p. 12.

12

THE CRISIS OF 1976–1977 AND THE BANNING OF THE INSTITUTE

While the origins of the black consciousness movement lay in decades of exploitation, the repression of black political organisations and the sense of powerlessness which blacks experienced in the 1960s, the rapid growth of support for the movement in schools and townships during the mid-1970s was the result of a harsh environment in which the fundamentals of apartheid were being applied with increasing ruthlessness. Far from dismantling apartheid, the regime reasserted its control over black labour and black families by tightening up and extending the system of migratory labour. Single-sex hostels were built in the townships at the expense of family housing. Over the decade 1965–75, approximately 2 million Africans were 'endorsed out' of the 'white' areas as 'superfluous Bantu', unwanted dependants or redundant labour.[1] This cruel policy tore families apart and threatened the stability of those families remaining in the urban areas. As a result it contributed to an undercurrent of black anger and to the spread of the black consciousness movement. By 1976 the family life of well over 6 million Africans was directly affected by migratory labour; approximately 1½ million men were migrants and almost ⅓ million African women.[2] The pass laws remained the essential method of enforcing this labour control and of policing the movements of all Africans. Police raids, often in the early hours of the morning with police dogs, were a regular feature of township life. Almost 2,000 persons per day were being hauled before magistrates for pass offences; most lost their jobs, were sent to prison or deported to the dumping-grounds.[3]

Church and even government commissions had condemned the evils of migrant labour for well over fifty years; yet in the mid-1970s the system was being bolstered and extended. The human costs were enormous:

Migrants usually have to live in barrack-like single-sex hostels or compounds. Wives cannot live with their husbands, nor parents with their children. The inevitable results are prostitution (both male and female), adultery, illegitimacy, venereal diseases, juvenile delinquency, drunkenness.[4]

In economic terms migrant labour was ill-trained, turnover was high and wages low — a vicious circle which brought 'misery, violence and crime in its wake'. The reserves or Bantustans deteriorated further as their population densities increased. On the other hand, white-owned and white-controlled industry expanded as a small minority of blacks were trained for skilled or semi-skilled jobs. Apart from this minority, all additional labour needs were met through the migrant labour system as cheap, powerless 'labour units' were delivered to serve white interests.[5]

Conditions in black education also give some indication of the socio-economic reality behind black discontent. With schools remaining free and compulsory for whites, the state spent fifteen times as much on a white as on an African child; nevertheless, Africans paid proportion-ately higher taxes on their meagre incomes.[6] African classes were more than three times the size of white classes and the drop-out rate was staggering: 25 per cent of African children left school after the first year, 50 per cent by the second year and less than 1 per cent of primary school entrants went on to high school.[7] Then, on top of this depriva-tion, teachers, who were struggling in the vernacular and English, were suddenly required to teach several of their large classes in Afrikaans — an exasperating situation for teachers and pupils. English had been the medium of instruction in the higher grades, and this change to a dual Afrikaans/English system was interpreted as an attempt to entrench the language of the hated apartheid regime. As a result the move triggered an intense political reaction among students, teachers and parents.[8] The various organisations making up the black consciousness movement had taken care to avoid direct confrontation with the state, hoping to build up their strength for as long as possible; but this provocation proved to be too much.

In June 1976 the tensions building up within black communities erupted in the SOWETO student demonstrations. These caused what can only be described as a series of police and military riots followed by black violence and widespread arson. The growth of the black con-ciousness movement during the 1970s had provided a focus for the resurgence of African nationalism as well as for Coloured and Indian protests against apartheid. This reassertion of black dignity, with respect for communal and egalitarian values, in turn inspired a vision of a new South Africa liberated from apartheid and restructured under the predominant influence of black-controlled political organisations. As the movement spread from the black campuses into a wide range of cultural and political organisations which coalesced in 1971 to form the Black People's Convention,[9] it also gathered strength among high school and even primary school children. When the children finally turned to demonstrate against the government's crass insis-tence on Afrikaans as a medium of instruction, many parents were drawn into political activity — at first somewhat apprehensively in support of their youngsters, then in outrage as the police and army slaughtered the protesters. On June 16, what started as a peaceful demonstration in SOWETO degenerated under the impact of insensitive police action into stone-throwing and police gunfire. After several days of rioting and shooting, 176 school children were dead and hundreds wounded.[10]

Sharpville (1960) with its sixty-nine deaths[11] had been the symbol of unmasked white power and brutality in repressing black resistence to apartheid. Now it was dwarfed by this new tragedy as outrage and unrest flared up in the major black townships throughout the country. Over the next year the death toll rose dramatically as the army joined the police in imposing curfews and attempting to crush all organised dissent.[12] Thousands of arrests, hundreds of banning orders, systematic torture and further repressive legislation followed as the apartheid regime tightened its hold on the white electorate and tried to contain black demonstrations, strikes and boycotts which continued to disrupt South Africa for the remainder of the 1970s and into the 1980s. What started as a movement of student protest against the use of Afrikaans and against inferior education had been transformed by the shootings into a widespread revolt against the whole system of apartheid, a revolt which, having gestated for decades, now found its most articulate leaders in a new generation of young black activists.

Faced with this explosive internal unrest, civil war in its buffer zones and heightened international criticism, the South African regime set out to modify its policies and improve its public image. It was nevertheless determined to maintain the fundamentals of apartheid and to improve its repressive capacities through the growth of a security state. Adaptation was to mean no more than a removal of the more public insults of 'petty apartheid' and a vague commitment to consult with blacks who were prepared to work through apartheid institutions. Manoeuvering in this way, the government tried once again to divert African political ambitions to the Bantustans and to draw Coloureds and Indians into an alliance with the apartheid state. All this was to be on white terms, the entire operation being designed to avoid the prospect of having to meet genuine black leaders in a 'national convention' on the country's constitutional future. The consequences were to be persisting unrest, a further marked deterioration in race relations and a continued drifting into civil war.

Rather than dismantling migrant labour, the Bantustans and white privilege, the regime began tinkering with the system and in 1976-7 ushered in the first of a series of cosmetic changes. Separate lavatories and separate waiting rooms were maintained in the courts so as to 'eliminate possible racial friction', but the courtrooms themselves were no longer segregated and all lawyers were to share the same facilities. Notices indicating separate entrances to post offices were removed, as were racial partitions in post office lobbies — except where brick partitions made this impossible. The offices of the Department of Revenue were also desegregated. Town councils were encouraged to take initiatives, and Randberg (a white suburb in Johannesburg) applied for and received permission to open a restaurant for blacks in the 'white' town centre. The Johannesburg Parks and Recreation Department reconsidered an earlier decision to prevent African soccer teams playing in parks adjacent to white suburbs. Some municipalities applied for government permits to integrate their bus services. The Johannesburg Chamber of Commerce, arguing that the city centre would not remain economically viable without a degree of integration, proposed an end to discrimination in downtown public facilities.[13]

As the Afrikaner National Party and white opposition parties were restive, so too were business interests. Prime Minister Vorster's talk of a new deal for blacks therefore took on added importance. It was time, he declared, for South Africa to get its house in order — and this would be done within the year, if only outside interference would cease. What he had in mind was the tinkering outlined above, the destruction of black organisations opposed to the fundamentals of apartheid and a new constitution designed to maintain white power. At every level, this new deal for blacks was in sharp conflict with the commitments of the Christian Institute.

In the immediate aftermath of the SOWETO tragedy, the Institute renewed its call for a national convention, one that would include among its leading personalities Nelson Mandela, Oliver Tambo, Steve Biko, Gatsha Buthelezi, Manas Buthelezi, Beyers Naudé and John Vorster. This was 'the difficult road to peace' which might open up a new politics of justice and reconciliation. The country was 'singing with Black Consciousness' and the white government had to negotiate with this reality. The alternative was: 'the hard line of apartheid at any cost, leading to increased police terror, civil disobedience, urban and industrial strikes, power cuts, water shortages, transport hold-ups, petrol rationing, food queues, arson, looting and killing as the anarchy inherent in apartheid [worked] its way out'.[14]

Having turned its back on any thought of a national convention, the government chose the alternative. On 19 October 1977, it banned the Christian Institute and eighteen black consciousness organisations. Black leaders were detained; Naudé and key members of his staff were banned. Shortly thereafter Steve Biko was killed while in police custody, and Vorster, amid continuing unrest and black outrage, called a general election for 30 November. Just as a previous snap election called by Vorster in 1974 after the coup in Lisbon transformed the politics of Mozambique, Angola and the whole of Southern Africa, this manoeuvre was designed to consolidate white opinion behind the apartheid regime. The vote was also taken as a measure of support for the proposed draft constitution which was to abolish the existing Westminster-type parliament in Cape Town, and replace it with a two-tier system of ethnic representation under a powerful executive presidency.

There were to be three separate parliaments for whites, Coloureds and Indians, each concerned with such ethnic affairs as housing, hospitals and education. Common matters such as state security and the country's economic policies were to be the responsibility of a Council of Cabinets[15] presided over by the State President. The President was to be appointed by an electoral college made up of representatives from the majority party in each of the parliaments, their numbers reflecting the population ratios of whites (4.3 million), Coloureds (2.4 million) and Indians (0.7 million), namely 4:2:1. In reality all this meant was that whites, led by the Afrikaner National Party, would remain in control, outnumbering the other two groups at every level of government. The 18 million Africans were to be entirely excluded. Under the continuing system of apartheid, they were supposed to be satisfied with representation in their rural backwaters, the Bantustans, which were all to become politically independent.[16]

Those black leaders who were not yet in prison — African, Coloured and Indian spokesmen throughout the country — rejected these proposals, quite rightly seeing them as a bid to consolidate white power, to maintain the essentials of apartheid and to divide the black consciousness movement. However, the white electorate, English-speaking as well as Afrikaans, moved resolutely behind the regime.[17]

Having rejected the challenge of the Christian Institute to build a new and just South Africa, Afrikaner nationalism set about extending the authoritarian powers of its national security state. A majority of English-speaking whites supported this process of entrenching Afrikaner hegemony over the country's powerful capitalist economy, and did so in spite of a sharp increase in the number of political prisoners, systematic torture and the 1978 Internal Security (Amendment) Act. This Act extended still further the State President's powers to detain without trial, restrict public assembly, control the movement of people, shift entire communities and censor publications. Afrikaner civil religion, bolstered by the fear and greed of whites, had triumphed over the poor, black consciousness and the voices of radical Christian dissent — at least for the moment.

Before 16 June 1976, there had been several prophetic warnings of an impending, violent confrontation, warnings about black anger which was directed at the arrogance and insensitivity of the white power structure. The Rev. Desmond Tutu, who was soon to be consecrated Bishop and to take over as General Secretary of the SACC, wrote as Dean of St Mary's Anglican Cathedral in Johannesburg to the

Prime Minister John Vorster. His appeal was intensely personal: one Christian calling out to another, one grandfather inviting another to work for a future of justice and peace for their grandchildren. Therefore, it was an appeal for fundamental not superficial change: an appeal to end migrant labour and the havoc it wrought in black families, an appeal for the acceptance of 'the urban black as a permanent inhabitant of what is wrongly called White South Africa'. This required the repeal of the pass laws and a national convention 'made up of genuine leaders . . . to try to work out an orderly evolution of South Africa into a non-racial, open and just society.' Writing a month before SOWETO erupted, Tutu described the sufferings of his 'people made desperate by despair and injustice'. He was 'frightened, dreadfully frightened, that we may soon reach a point of no return, when events will generate a momentum of their own, when nothing will stop them reaching a bloody dénouement'. Blacks had been 'exceedingly patient', reiterating time and again that they had no wish to drive whites into the sea. Yet such assurances had been 'flung back in their faces with contempt'. As the worm would eventually turn, Tutu felt impelled to offer a 'grave warning' to the 'highest political figure in the land' so that blacks and whites would know 'that from our side we have done all that it seems humanly possible to do'. Unless something drastic was done, and very soon, 'bloodshed and violence' were inevitable.[18]

Unfortunately, like his predecessors, Vorster was not prepared to pay attention to black leaders who challenged the fundamentals of apartheid. In his reply he simply accused Tutu of making propaganda. Just two weeks before the police opened fire in SOWETO, Tutu had to tell the biennial synod of the Johannesburg diocese that 'the reply of the Prime Minister to my letter leaves me with less hope than ever.'[19]

Three days after Tutu spoke to his synod, on 3 June 1976, Naudé offered a comparably grim warning to a white society 'becoming blind to reality': the future under apartheid would be one of violence under an increasingly arrogant and authoritarian government. Like Tutu, he too called for an end to migrant labour and the repeal of the pass laws; free, equal and compulsory education; and a national convention or forum where black and white leaders might enter into 'open confrontation and frank discussion'. There would also have to be a reappraisal of the country's economic structures. The capitalist system had failed to produce economic justice, and a new, more equitable, economic order would have to evolve — rapidly — if the country was 'to face victoriously the onslaught of communist ideology'. Unless dramatic initiatives were taken to dismantle apartheid, any remaining chance for peaceful change would be lost and the new South Africa would eventually have 'to be built from the ashes of a society which had destroyed itself through its own blindness, its avarice and its fear'.[20]

It was during these last few weeks before the SOWETO shootings that Naudé's colleague, the Rev. Cedric Mason, editor of *Pro Veritate*, made a comparable appeal, this time to the churches as they prepared for their annual conferences and assemblies — 'a last attempt to win support for the Christian influence in the struggle for Africa'. The churches could no longer 'creep along under white leadership'; black gifts, graces and leadership were urgently needed in what had already become a violent and revolutionary situation. Having 'banned the African National Congress and its fellow Congress Movements a decade and a half ago', the government had 'prevented a solution by political negotiation'. As a result, the churches carried major responsibilities to assist in the reordering of society and were being called upon from every quarter of the black community, 'from IDAMASA through SASO and the ANC', to exercise leadership 'in the new society that is coming'. To respond effectively, Mason continued, the churches would have to put their own houses in order, end all racial discrimination, champion the poor, place themselves alongside the victims of apartheid, expound liberation and black theology, and so 'make a non-violent liberation program possible'. But this meant the churches would have to risk all — money, buildings, organisations, the support of the rich — and face repression by the state. It also meant an end to pious religiosity and the illusion of political security which this seemed to offer. In the context of civil war on South Africa's borders and unrest in its cities, the churches had to

become involved with the real issues and the real battle for Christ: with oppressed and oppressors, with prisoners and jailers, politicians and strikers, revolutionaries and propagandists, soldiers and conscientious objectors, trade unionists and students, people blown up by landmines and the victims of indoctrination. That is to become part of the Christian revolution.[21]

Neither the white-dominated church hierarchies nor white parish organisations had become part of such a non-violent 'Christian revolution'. Moreover, there was no time left for them to do so. Tutu, Naudé, Mason, the Christian Institute and *Pro Veritate* remained lonely voices, apparently alarmist and shrill — until 16 June 1976.

Tension had been building up in the junior schools of SOWETO and adjacent townships during the first half of 1976 over the Bantu Education Department's insistence that Afrikaans be used on an equal basis with English as a medium of instruction.[22] School boards opposed the policy and clashed with school inspectors. Board members resigned. Parents' meetings were unanimous in rejecting Afrikaans, and students clashed with principals who attempted to enforce the Department's ruling. In early May, students at a junior secondary school in Orlando West began boycotting Afrikaans-medium lessons and the recently formed South African Students Movement (SASM) encouraged these tactics in other schools. Students also refused to write their examinations in Afrikaans. Teachers who would not teach during student strikes were dismissed, and police cars were despatched to arrest student leaders. These cars were regularly stoned and one was burnt. By early June, SASM had established a network of leaders in every school and a SOWETO Students' Representation Council which quickly set about planning a major demonstration of primary and secondary school students for 16 June.[23] Events were moving towards a crisis, but the repeated warnings from black citizens and journalists as well as the SAIRR were ignored. Thoroughly frustrated, the SOWETO Residents Association (representing parents) passed a resolution rejecting Afrikaans as a medium of instruction 'because it is the language of the oppressor.'[24]

On the morning of 16 June, 20,000 children converged on Orlando West Junior Secondary School where a month earlier the first boycotts occurred. From there, the plan was to march to Johannesburg in a peaceful demonstration. Observers described the youngsters as 'good-humoured, high spirited and excited'. Their slogan was *asingeni* (we shall not enter); some gave the clenched fist salute of black consciousness and many carried placards such as 'Down with Afrikaans', 'To Hell with Afrikaans', 'We are not Boers', 'Viva Azania', and 'If we must do Afrikaans, Vorster must do Zulu!' The first shooting occurred in Orlando West as the students were confronted by 300 police. Scuffles took place as attempts were made to confiscate the placards. Students began to taunt the police and tear-gas was fired into the crowd. It was not clear whether the students started throwing stones before or after the police opened fire; but there were no clear warnings to the students to disperse and no warning shots. Hector Petersen, a thirteen-year-old school boy, was the first to die, shot from behind in a hail of gunfire. Five other students were shot dead, seventeen were wounded and the demonstration exploded into anger and violence.[25]

Anything that could be thrown was hurled at the police. Police cars were overturned and burnt, police dogs knifed, police stations, government offices and beerhalls burnt. Two white officials of the SOWETO Bantu Affairs Administration Board were killed and by the end of the day the death toll stood at twenty-five. As the rioting and shooting spread to all twenty-eight townships of the Johannesburg/SOWETO complex, the government closed the schools and sent in its anti-riot squads with their 'hippo' armoured cars. Within forty-eight hours, the official death toll had risen to ninety and by the end of the week to 176. In fact the actual number of deaths may well have been closer to 300. Funerals became the focal point of the black community's agony, but they too were disrupted and desecrated by police brutality. On several occasions relatives were humiliated at the graveside. Twice police gunfire in the cemetery added fresh corpses before the old ones were interred. When 800 students gathered at the funeral of seventeen-year-old Annah Mkhwanzi, the police diagnosed an 'illegal gathering' on the grounds that leaflets other than the funeral programme were being distributed. In breaking up the crowd, one person was killed and ten wounded. At the funeral of twenty-two-year-old Jacob Mashabane, who was supposed to have hung himself while in detention, the police fired on a peaceful if large gathering of 1,000 parents of students and 15,000 students. This time seven were killed and fifty-one wounded.[26]

Demonstrations, stone-throwing and arson spread along the Witwatersrand, to major cities and to country towns. In August the Bophuthatswana legislative assembly was burnt down and over sixty instances of arson were reported in the Bantustans — in most cases school buildings. School boycotts spread too, a major example being the demonstrations which erupted on 11 August in the African townships of Cape Town when thirty persons were killed. The Cape upheavals continued into September when thirty more individuals died as African and Coloured students, armed with their placards, marched against Bantu Education and called for the release of detainees.[27] Within two months of the first SOWETO shootings, eighty black communities erupted, and by the end of October a further eighty. What the government found even more alarming was the prospect that student protests might mesh with a general strike of black workers in Johannesburg, including migrant labourers housed in SOWETO's single-sex hostels. Approximately 60 per cent of the African labour force stayed home from work for two days in early August, an impressive if short-lived show of solidarity the like of which had not been seen since the Defiance Campaign of the 1950s. A few weeks later, a comparable two-day stay-at-home occurred in Cape Town.[28]

By the end of October 1977, continuing disturbances had claimed at least 700 officially recorded deaths[29] — a total which in reality probably exceeded 1,000. An additional unknown total of several thousands had been wounded or injured in an atmosphere made worse by many ugly incidents of police violence and vindictiveness.[30] In fact the situation had become so rancid, so embittered that J.T. Kruger, the hated Minister of Police and Justice, found it necessary to introduce an Indemnity Act retroactively to protect the police and army — 'the servants of the State' — from civil or criminal proceedings against anything they had done 'in good faith on or after 16 June, 1976'.[31]

The high school student organisations which sparked this resurgence of black activism regularly lost their leaders as they escaped police cordons and fled into exile (like Tsietse Mashinini) or were shot or detained by the police (like Sechaba Motsitsi). Time and again, however, new charismatic personalities emerged, struggled to keep low profiles but were inevitably drawn into organising days of mourning, demonstrations for the release of detainees and continuing school boycotts. Students and black parents' associations extended their demands to include the scrapping of Bantu Education and called for equal, compulsory education for all South Africans. There were also demonstrations against the visits to South Africa of the United States Secretary of State, Henry Kissinger, and that country's Ambassador to the United Nations, Andrew Young. Kissinger was seen as essentially committed to Western capitalist interests in Southern Africa. In the judgement of the student leaders, he was intent on establishing a black client-state in Rhodesia, and damping the fires of black revolt rather than scrapping apartheid in South Africa. Young too was viewed with considerable suspicion as he entered into discussions with personalities the students distrusted, for example Gatsha Buthelezi. Students also saw Young as a representative of capitalist interests and a country that had not itself established justice for blacks. In the opinion of these young activists, President Carter's stance towards South Africa had not changed United States policies in any fundamental way.[32] There was added resentment when Young was accompanied in the black townships by white security guards from the new Bureau of State Security (BOSS).[33]

In January 1977, six months after the initial shootings, attendance in SOWETO's high schools was still only 25 per cent and holding steady at about 50 per cent in primary schools.[34] Attendance then slowly edged upwards until July 1977 when SOWETO's school children again launched a massive boycott. This time a teachers' Action Committee formed and co-operated with the Students' Representative Council to plan an alternative to Bantu Education. As a result, approximately 500 secondary school teachers went so far as to resign their posts.[35] A new generation had been politicised and in the process the dreams of their elders — teachers, parents and grandparents — were reawakened. Far from being the result of a few agitators with foreign ideas, as the government claimed, the sustained character of student unrest reflected deep-seated anger in black communities, resentments which bridged the generations and were being transformed into a positive vision of the future through the growth of black consciousness. These protests of the mid- and late 1970s also revived the hopes which had become an integral part of the political culture of black South Africans in the long years of struggle following the formation of the ANC in 1912.

The size of demonstrations gives some sense of the resurgence of political life that was taking place. Protesters gathered in their thousands: several turnouts of 20,000 occurred in Johannesburg and Cape Town; commiseration meetings and funerals drew crowds of 5–15,000 in the cities, while political gatherings of 2–5,000 were commonplace in smaller towns. Black power salutes were a feature of these mass meetings.[36] A further indication of the sharp rise in political consciousness was the jump in newspaper circulations, the sale of the country's major black newspaper, *The World* (Johannesburg), increasing from 130,000 in early June 1976 to 180,000 in the immediate aftermath of the shootings.[37]

Whites were largely protected from the shockwaves of SOWETO by their segregated residential areas and segregated political culture. From the point of view of most whites, black unrest or black politics were worrying but remote affairs, matters for specialists to deal with — the Department of Bantu Administration, the police and in the last resort the army. Essentially ignorant of or indifferent to the long history of black protests, steeped in a culture of racism and instinctively clinging to the established order, whites were easily manipulated into giving Vorster and his National Party a renewal mandate for apartheid. In stark contrast, the staff of the Christian Institute and of the SACC were horrified by and fully aware of what had occurred in the townships. Their immediate response was to co-operate in launching the Asingani Relief Fund to assist victims and their families: those shot, wounded or detained. Although the Fund was overburdened by requests, it helped to sustain destitute families whose breadwinners had been removed; it paid out bail money, contributed to funeral expenses and supported relief centres which were often operated by black students working out of church buildings.[38] In addition, the staff of the Institute, particularly its black members, maintained close contact with students and with older black leaders who in the traumatic circumstances of 1976 established *ad hoc* organisations which quickly gathered widespread support. The most influential of these groups were the Black Parents' Association, chaired by Bishop Manas Buthelezi, and the Soweto Local Authority Interim Committee — popularly known as the Committee of Ten — under the chairmanship of Dr Ntatho Motlana.[39]

While the Christian Institute and the SACC were profoundly affected by the SOWETO tragedy, something of the determination behind black protests, something of the agony of mourning communities and the full horror of police brutality also got through to the leadership of the multi-racial churches. Although some denominations remained aloof from the Institute's efforts (Methodists, Presbyterians and Baptists might fall into this category), others moved closer and increased their moral support (Anglicans, Roman Catholics, United Lutherans and Congregationalists).[40] Within the latter group, this entailed following up on the Institute's warnings and trying once again to alert white congregations to the persisting injustices of apartheid and the resulting threat of an escalating civil war.

The Roman Catholic hierarchy provided an example of this response. In the aftermath of Vatican II as well as of SOWETO, the bishops were particularly exercised and returned to their attack on apartheid with strong statements on justice, reconciliation and the right to conscientious objection. The Bishops' Conference also had the good sense to show a little humility and admit publicly that the Roman Catholic Church had so far failed to respond with courage to the Gospel's call for social justice. This was a matter of the greatest importance as it was increasingly clear that the pursuit of justice was 'central to evangelisation', central to the church's mission which 'includes work for complete human liberation . . . [and] transforming the concrete structures that oppress people'. In practice this meant placing the church 'in solidarity with all those who work for the promotion of human dignity . . . on the side, therefore, of black consciousness.' In a situation where the majority clearly rejected the existing economic and political order, the bishops wished to add their voice 'to the cry for a radical revision of the system'. Blacks had 'passed the point of no return, and no temporary suppression of violence, only a just sharing of citizenship [could] give hope . . . and prevent the horrors of civil war.'[41]

In making this commitment to place the Church 'on the side of the oppressed . . . the poor and deprived',[42] the bishops were influenced by the Christian Institute and particularly by Archbishop Denis Hurley of Durban, a vigorous supporter of the Institute. They were also shocked and moved by their black colleague Bishop Mandlenkosi Zwane of Manzini, Swaziland. Zwane remained in touch with the black consciousness movement, and, of all the bishops, he alone was able to speak for blacks from a direct and intimate association with their sufferings and political hopes. In the aftermath of SOWETO, he did not spare his white fellow-bishops. 'I am afraid', he told them, 'after June 1976 the possibility of reconciliation in the normal way is gone; the possibility of building bridges between black and white in the normal way no longer belongs to us.' A painful struggle for justice would have to precede any hoped-for reconciliation, a struggle which 'bourgeois affluent' elements in the church would find difficult to understand. The old liberal call for integration, Zwane continued, simply would not do, as 'integration which by-passes the demands of black power means a resurrection without the cross.' Black consciousness was a positive statement about human dignity; it was, he argued, essentially a call to dialogue, to sharing and equality. But in place of dialogue, blacks and Africans in particular 'feel that the white people have declared war', turning the police and army on school children and killing detainees. As repeated statements against apartheid had been futile, the church had only one way to travel, 'the way of irreconciliation with the government; the way of the cross, of action against apartheid and, if necessary, the 'expulsion or imprisonment of every bishop, priest, brother and sister.' Only then would the church have followed Christ 'in the way of Truth, Justice and Suffering'. The resurrection could then 'safely be left to Him'.[42]

In the end, the call to action from Bishop Zwane and his colleagues in the hierarchy produced little change. Race relations continued to deteriorate among Roman Catholics as within other denominations and society at large. As Archbishop Denis Hurley put it, he was pessimistic about the capacity of 'the white section of the church' to respond. His best hope was that 'please God, at least some [whites] will join with men like Beyers Naudé in giving a credible witness to their faith . . . in renouncing the White South African way of life and adjusting themselves to a minority role in a Black society.' Without such a conversion, the white elements in the church would simply have provided a 'negative witness' — a warning to Christians everywhere of the illusions and dangers of theologising and preaching while avoiding the call to action.[43]

Given the inadequate response of the churches, the Christian Institute was left to pursue its prophetic ministry in some loneliness. As we have seen, its immediate reaction to SOWETO was to keep in closer contact with black leaders and to help set up the Asingeni Fund. In the longer run the Institute's response was to reaffirm its support for black political organisations and call out again and again for radical change. South Africa was polarising rapidly, Naudé told what was to be the last annual general meeting in September 1977, and 'would never be the same again after Soweto.' Whites were clinging to their economic, police and military power; but blacks were convinced that the rising power of their liberation movement would 'eventually enforce fundamental change.' In this context, the Christian Institute would continue its attempt to convert whites from their system of 'institutionalised brutality' — ultimately their path of destruction — but its nonviolent political efforts would be directed mainly to the support of black initiatives.[44] Speaking to the Federal Theological Seminary, Naudé warned that the transition would be turbulent, painful and at times violent, 'like that of the birth of a child long delayed'. The existing political order had lost its last residual elements of legitimacy, and the upheavals of the past months were simply the 'outward sign of a movement of deep stirrings towards freedom' which could no longer be suppressed by force. While he offered no time schedule, Naudé concluded that the outcome would be 'the appearance of a new independent and liberated state called Azania'.[45]

Given this analysis, the Institute's Board of Management called on the government 'to give way to a National Convention representative of all peoples of South Africa, including those detained or in exile'. In the interim, until this process of reconstituting the political order was initiated, the Board called for increased mass participation in the liberation struggle and renewed its backing for conscientious objectors who refused 'to use arms in the repugnant and ungodly task of suppressing the Government's opponents'. It also condemned the 'Homelands policy' and the 'independence' of the Transkei as a 'sham and a farce designed to perpetuate white domination' — a pretext for 'arbitrarily depriving millions of black South Africans of their natural birthright of citizenship in a country whose wealth they have played a major part in creating.'[46]

These commitments were already quite enough to invite destruction. Nevertheless the Institute pushed forward in its confrontation with the state, well past the point of no return. In its judgement, the last peaceful means to radical change were 'work stayaways', economic sanctions and the discouragement of white immigration. Moreover the Institute backed all three approaches and did so in support of the 'goals of the Black political movements (eg. the African National Congress, the Pan Africanist Congress, the South African Students' Organisation, the Black People's Convention and the South African Students' Movement)'; that is, those goals consonant with the 'Biblical values of justice, freedom and human responsibilities.' Finally the Institute called on those involved in the struggle to be of good cheer. For no matter what evil lay ahead, 'we shall overcome, we shall overcome in Him who said ''Do not be afraid: I have overcome the world.'' '[47]

There were still other voices, black Christian voices, that were closely aligned with the Institute's stance at this time. In the case of the Ministers Fraternal (a local association of black clerics) of Langa, Guguletu and Nyanga — the African townships of Cape Town — they offered both a warning and an alternative to apartheid. Time had run out, they told the government and 'white South Africans generally'. Unless blacks were allowed 'a full and equal say in the running of the country', an appalling race war would follow. The alternative was a united country under a non-racial system of government. This in turn entailed the scrapping of all differential education, an end to the system of migrant labour, full civil rights for blacks in the urban areas, abolition of the pass laws, municipal self-government in the townships, the right to family life and secure home ownership in the vicinity of one's work, free trade unions and, overall, a humble recognition by whites that the 'primary cause of unrest and of all the violence in our land is the sin of racial discrimination.' Instead of hearing 'the cry for justice — a cry which God has spoken since his Prophets of old — [the government had] responded with Pharoah-like hardness of heart.'[48]

The increasingly influential voices of the Rev. Alan Boesak and Bishop Desmond Tutu were also heard at this time, both taking up the themes of prophetic judgement, a liberating God and the positive role in history of discontent among the poor and oppressed. When Boesak spoke he did so out of the Calvinist tradition, as a young DRC theologian and as chaplain to the (Coloured) University College of the Western Cape. He was by this time also a member of the Institute's National Council. Speaking to the Labour Party, a 'Coloured' organisation which retained the support of the majority of that community and which constantly thwarted the regime's attempts to run segregated political institutions for Coloureds, Boesak took black consciousness as his theme. Like the Ministers Fraternal, he too drew on the Prophets. Times were no different from when Amos spoke: 'They hate the man dispensing justice at the city gate and detest those who speak with honesty. They trample on the poor man . . . turning away the needy.' In Boesak's analysis, the struggle was for power — either power for ethnic and economic privilege or for service in the interests of the common good. The latter was the 'sublime task of Black Power' which was called to liberate all South Africans from the 'unending spiral of violence inherent in the apartheid system'. Apartheid was forcing a pattern of 'retaliatory violence' on the poor and oppressed, an instinct for violence which could only be restrained in the struggle for liberation if blacks remained united. Coloureds should reject all offers of a separate ethnic 'solution'. Black solidarity and black humanity were the 'creative preconditions' for radical change, the minimising of violence and a future of non-racial justice in a united country.[49]

Recently appointed Anglican Bishop of Maseru but still intimately part of the black consciousness movement, Tutu spoke out on many occasions. He offered measured, tough-minded but loving words, as when he gathered with the students of SOWETO on 16 June 1977. Addressing the vast crowd in and around Regina Mundi Cathedral, Tutu spoke of 'the courageous children who died on 16 June 1976'. The God of righteousness was also God of the Exodus, the liberator of slaves and, potentially, also of oppressors. God, he continued,

was always on the side of the oppressed and exploited, not because they are morally better than their oppressors. No, He is on their side simply and solely because they are oppressed. He wants them to be fully human. And when He liberates the oppressed he also liberates the oppressor, because whites in South Africa will never be truely free until all of us are free.

Black and white were inescapably bound to each other; if they could not move to freedom together they would perish together — an 'alternative too ghastly to contemplate'.[50]

With Naudé and his colleagues speaking out so plainly, and with a wider range of black voices calling in comparable terms for liberation, it was not long before a new round of intimidation hit the Institute. Diakonia House was raided in November 1976 by approximately forty members of the Security Police who confiscated a vast quantity of documents. Several publications of the Institute and five issues of *Pro Veritate* were banned. Staff members who possessed passports had them confiscated and once again the Institute was bitterly denounced in parliament.[51] In November 1976 an attempt was made to intimidate Cedric Mason, editor of *Pro Veritate*, by detaining him for fifteen days under the section of the Terrorism Act dealing with 'offences against the state'. Longer detentions were handed out to Oshadi Phakathi and the Rev. Mashwabada Mayatula, both members of the Institute's Transvaal Regional Staff, the latter also serving on Dr Motlana's 'Committee of Ten'. A few months later, on 16 March 1977, Phakathi, now Transvaal Regional Director, was handed her banning order on the very day that Naudé addressed the Federal Theological Seminary on the new Azania. Simultaneously the government was banning or breaking up innumerable political meetings and demonstrations designed to lead up to the first annual commemoration of 16 June 1976.[52]

The banning of Oshadi Phakathi was a microcosm of the impending banning of the Institute itself, an attempt to destroy the effectiveness of a staff member whose influence spread out in a dozen different ways. Phakathi exemplified the Institute's capacity, in spite of all its short-comings, to influence a range of organisations and to sow the seeds of liberation theology in a way that was quite disproportionate to its small-scale organisation, limited membership and meagre financial resources. While Phakathi had retained her ability for dialogue with whites, her most effective work was done in liaison with black organisations. In addition to being the Institute's Transvaal Regional Director, she was President of the Young Women's Christian Association and an executive member of the Black Parents' Association. Her banning order prohibited all contact with these organisations, the Christian Institute, SASO, SASM or the BPC. She was also banned from entering any factory, any Coloured or Indian area, or any 'Bantu township' other than Mamelodi in the magisterial district of Pretoria to which she was confined. Like other banned persons, she had to report regularly to the police, could receive only one visitor at a time, was not allowed to contact any other banned person, could not attend any gathering or assist in the preparation of any publication, could not be quoted in the South Africa press and was forbidden to give educational instruction to anyone other than her children.[53]

Phakathi's public life as a concerned Christian had been wiped out. As we have seen, her influence had extended to a range of black organisations. These in turn radiated their insights and hopes back through Phakathi to the Institute itself. Such a matrix, repeated many times over in the lives of Naudé, Kotze, Manas Buthelezi and other staff members, was intolerable to the custodians of the apartheid state. Consequently it was now simply a matter of their choosing the right moment to destroy the Institute.

As the Christian Institute struggled on amid this turmoil of state violence, black protests and repression, it began to re-assess its organisational structures. To persist in its prophetic stance, to witness in its own fellowship to reconciliation while simultaneously supporting the conflictual processes of black liberation, the Institute's organisation had to be slimmed-down and decentralised. At the same time the Institute's membership needed to understand more clearly their vital but highly vulnerable role as a remnant Christian community: they had to live in hope while preparing for Calvary.

In the course of 1976, Cape members took the initiative and with Naudé's approval set up a committee to revise the Institute's constitution. The intention was to play down the activities of the Johannesburg headquarters and regional offices so as to nurture decentralised small-scale Christian fellowships or basic communities. Belatedly, the Institute was attempting to form a closer bonding of its members, trying to establish confessing communities which could take the strain of political confrontation in a police state. This was not simply the result of being declared an 'Affected Organisation' and so having to trim the budget; more fundamentally, it was the outcome of a prolonged period of radicalisation and the associated search for a simpler life-style. It was also an effort to move away from the provision of capital-intensive office facilities to a more communal approach, an effort to relate more closely to black organisations and to live in a way that would not be an obstacle to meeting with and serving the poor.

There was some discussion at this time as to whether the aims of the Institute should be adapted so that its membership could be broadened to include non-Christians: Jews, Muslims and secular humanists who shared a comparable vision of social justice. However, it was decided to maintain the essential Christian commitment established in 1963. The aims of the Institute were 'to witness to Jesus Christ as Saviour and Lord, to seek the coming of His Kingdom on earth, to serve the Church in its vocation as the Body of Christ'. The revised constitution, which was accepted in September 1977, went on to summarise the new decentralised approach as a commitment 'to develop working groups, however small, of people who are trying to anticipate what a new South Africa conformed to the will of God would be like'; groups which would seek 'to express through their own life styles, relationships and situations, the ethical demands of the Gospel.' Such groups, as 'working models of Christian community', were to grow in confession, penitence, joy and thanksgiving, sharing and simplicity of life, 'solidarity with the poor, the suffering and the oppressed' as well as 'care of the earth'. All this was to involve an 'active listening to the Word and Spirit.' It would also require continued and vigorous public debate plus 'non-violent action for social change'.[54]

As the constitution was being revised, so the number of full-time executive staff was cut.[55] Salaries were equalised and for some this meant a 50 per cent reduction in income.[56] The one exception to this contraction of the administrative network was the establishment of an information office in the Netherlands. Horst Kleinschmidt had slipped out of the country in April 1976[57] to set up the office in Utrecht. There he was joined in March 1977 by Oshadi Phakathi who had chosen to escape from her confinement as a banned person and work from a base in exile. Funded by overseas churches, the information centre was independent of the Institute in South Africa and administered as a separate unit for which an overseas committee drawn from Dutch and British churchmen was legally and financially responsible.[58] Having at first the blessing of Naudé and the Christian Institute in South Africa, the centre was to function for a short while before it was traumatised by a series of internal conflicts which surfaced after the Institute was banned in October 1977.[59]

Having set out to revise its constitution, the Institute struggled on into 1977, trying to effect its internal process of renewal. Early in the year Brian Brown was called back from his Methodist parish to take up his old position as Administrative Director. With his considerable skills he helped to keep the Institute afloat in this period of increasing austerity.[60] In an effort to foster local fellowship groups, a number of courses were held throughout the country, the most important being organised by Theo Kotze, the Cape Director, around the theme 'Facing the Future with Hope'. Drawing on his own experience in Cape Town and travelling widely in the Transvaal, Natal, the Cape and Namibia (where the Institute was co-operating with the Christian Centre of the Anglican Diocese of Damaraland), Kotze was able to nurture old groups and form the nucleus of new ones. Fellowship meetings were also organised as part of the study project on capitalism, socialism and Christianity.[61] In the Cape the Institute was particularly successful in attracting a growing number of blacks to these courses and workshops. The Cape Town office was also involved in assisting those who were made homeless by the township riots over Christmas

1976 and the New Year. In addition support was given to the squatter communities on the Cape Flats in their confrontation with the police and bureaucrats who came in with bulldozers to demolish their fragile homes.[62] In offering this support, four members of the Institute were detained in August 1977. Dr Margaret Nash was arrested when she entered a squatter camp, from which she had been banned, carrying a cross and her Bible. The Rev. David Russell had to be lifted from the path of a demolition bulldozer before he too was arrested. In addition, the Rev. Wesley Mabuza and the Rev. Chris Wessels, both Cape representatives on the Institute's National Council, were detained on account of their activities in the camps, the former under the Riotous Assemblies Act and the latter under the Terrorism Act.[63] For a while the Institute's office in Natal was involved in similar activities, in this instance arranging temporary accommodation for a group of eighty-five squatter families uprooted in the Claremont area.[64]

While the Institute was battling to survive and to renew its commitments in the aftermath of SOWETO, the state was unleashing a campaign of intimidation and terror. Relying heavily on Section 6 of the Terrorism Act (which empowered senior police officers to arrest, interrogate and detain without a warrant), and using the Internal Security Act (which permitted the preventive detention of individuals whose activities the police judged might endanger public order), hundreds of black leaders were rounded up. These victims had no right to a trial or legal representation. They were subjected to solitary confinement for months at a time, systematically humiliated and in many cases tortured by the security police who were creating a sub-culture of brutality and sadism. There were seventy-seven persons detained as political prisoners under these conditions before the June 1976 disturbances. In the following fifteen months, 2,430 blacks were to be detained. Of the 443 held in December 1976, fifty-two were key figures in black consciousness organisations and approximately 200 were university and high school students. There were also thirty-five teachers, sixteen ministers of religion, sixteen journalists, thirteen former political prisoners and six trade unionists. By March 1977 the number of detainees had risen to 471 of whom thirty-three had been held for over a year and 144 for six to twelve months. When the October 1977 crackdown occurred against the black consciousness movement and the Christian Institute, this number rose sharply to 778.[65]

The component of torture in this repression was revealed by the sharp increase in prison deaths (officially suicides) among political prisoners. Between August 1976 and September 1977 twenty-four such persons died in highly suspicious circumstances, the state taking every possible means to cover up the criminal activities of its police thugs. The pervasive nature of police brutality was also revealed by the publication in April 1977 of *Torture in South Africa?*, a booklet produced by Theo Kotze as Cape Regional Director of the Institute. In calling for an independent inquiry, Kotze and his staff simply gathered the scattered evidence of deaths, trial records, sworn affidavits, judges' comments and allegations of torture by political prisoners. The result was a startling exposé of systematic psychological and physical torture: endless interrogation, solitary confinement, sleep deprivation, beatings, whippings, death threats, electric shock treatment and humiliating cell conditions.[66]

Torture in South Africa? was immediately banned. However, the controlled rampage of the security police was quickly brought back into focus by the death in detention of Steve Biko — the very personification of the black consciousness movement. Biko also represented the quality of black leadership the Institute had come to support, leadership which Naudé and his colleagues knew would have to be drawn into a national convention if an escalating civil war was to be avoided. Biko's death and the studied indifference of the state's response, the mounting number of political detainees, the continued incarceration of Nelson Mandela and the wholesale banning of black organisations that was about to take place, all indicated only too clearly that the apartheid regime had opted for war and the resolute defence of white privilege.

Steve Biko was first banned in February 1973 at the age of twenty-six. Having formed SASO and played a major role in launching the Black People's Convention (of which he was made Honorary President in 1977), Biko worked for the Black Community Programmes. At the time of his banning to the magisterial district of Kingwilliamstown, David Russell, who was both his friend and his parish priest, wrote of Biko as a passionate man of peace whose stand was 'at rock-bottom a fundamentally Biblical one'. Russell recognised that Biko articulated more effectively than anyone else that resurgence of African resistance, that rebirth of hope which 'like some great groundswell of history' sought justice for the deprived and destitute.[67] In Biko's view, this black consciousness, this commitment to the poor, could lead to the liberation of all South Africans, eventually offering whites the chance to be freed from their fears and their desperate clinging to power. It was this view of liberation that Naudé and the Institute came to share with Biko and the black consciousness movement.

Biko grew up in the Anglican church. But, like so many of his generation, he began to question the brand of Christianity which was still a captive of the colonial process — a church with its white establishment, white theology and Western mores, liturgy and dress. The question he put was 'Does the necessary decolonisation of Africa also require the de-Christianisation of Africa?' His answer was 'No'; for this questioning had given rise to the quest for a black theology which did 'not challenge Christianity itself but its Western package.' The purpose was 'to discover what the Christian faith means for our continent'.[68] In political terms Biko was committed to a unified black protest movement, a drawing together of the ANC, PAC and the BPC. Although it functioned openly within South Africa, the BPC was 'not a third way among blacks, next to the ANC and PAC'. It was committed to non-violence and to operating within the law, but it was part of that broader historical struggle and, in Biko's judgement, set on a path of rapprochement with the older exiled organisations.[69]

In a typically frank interview given on the eve of his final detention, Biko offered a glimpse of his hopes for the future. Internationally he saw South Africa as a 'pawn in the politics of pragmatism, in the game of power between the USSR and the USA'. The alternative was for a free South Africa to establish its own internal structuring and its own political economy, and to conduct its own foreign policy. This meant checking the spread of the American-dominated capitalist system, but simultaneously blocking the imperialist designs of Russia. The black consciousness movement did 'not want to accept the dilemma of capitalism versus Communism'. Rather it would opt for 'a socialist solution that [was] an authentic expression of black communalism'. Biko admitted that the details of this alternative were not yet clear. Nevertheless he recognised, with the experience of independent tropical Africa in mind, 'that the change in the colour of the occupier does not necessarily change the system.' Blacks in the liberation movement were searching for new collective and less individualistic models of development — but that did not mean taking over the Russian model.[70]

Like the Christian Institute, Biko had no illusions about the prolonged and tragically violent transition that lay ahead. In refusing to countenance fundamental change, Afrikaners had made violent conflict inevitable. The alternative round-table or national convention presupposed an acceptance of black equality, and that was exactly what the apartheid state refused to accept. Biko therefore expected the regime to become even more intransigent and to rely increasingly on its police and military power. This in turn would force blacks to reassess their strategy. Such reliance on repression, he thought, might well go hand in hand with a 'last-ditch attempt' to distribute some of the benefits of capitalism to black capitalists and to a small black middle class. However, he was convinced this would not work as the racism of apartheid and economic exploitation of capitalism would continue to generate support for the liberation movement. Unlike the American civil rights campaigns, the liberation movement was not struggling to dismantle racism within an acceptable constitutional framework; black South Africans were demanding a new constitution which could not be imposed by whites. Whites would remain 'as part of the solution' after the transition. Their participation in political and economic life was 'imperative'. But they would have to accept radical change: 'substantial economic sacrifices', probably a freezing of white salaries and wages for a number of years, and perhaps proportional representation.[71]

In the years following his banning in 1973, Biko was arrested and detained on several occasions for allegedly breaking his banning order, and again in August 1976 following the SOWETO massacres. During this latter imprisonment he was held in solitary confinement for 101 days and then released. Given his liaison with black students and continuing unrest throughout the country, he was arrested once more in March 1977, released and temporarily detained in July. Finally he was taken into custody by the security police on 18 August, placed in leg irons, manacled and held in solitary confinement in Port Elizabeth. Twenty six days later he died of extensive head injuries and acute renal failure. His body showed a wide range of other injuries and he had not received adequate medical attention. Indeed, he was driven 740 miles from Port Elizabeth to Pretoria, naked and unconscious in the back of a Land Rover. He died on 12 September 1977 in custody on a mat on a stone floor, the twenty-fourth political prisoner to die in a South African gaol since March 1976.[72]

Blacks were outraged. The authorities took it more lightly. Calm voices from the South Africa Broadcasting Corporation assured their audiences that the police were innocent and went on to speculate about the possibility that Biko committed suicide, 'a pattern which has become common among detainees in South Africa'. Numerous detainees, broadcasters told the country, had testified to receiving Communist training and indoctrination which included 'specific instructions to commit suicide rather than divulge information to the police'.[73] When the Minister of Police, James Kruger, addressed a National Party Congress two days after Biko's death he was in a jocular mood. Biko's death, he told his audience, 'leaves me cold . . . I shall also be sorry if I die [laughter]. [. . .] Incidentally I can just tell Congress, the day before yesterday one of my own lieutenants in the prison service also committed suicide and we have not yet accused a single person [laughter].'[74]

The last editorial of *Pro Veritate* saw things differently: Biko's martyrdom cut through the fog of confused thinking to reveal government policy as 'white domination' through 'power and violence'. His death revealed the position of those who supported the *status quo* by 'their votes, their acquiescence, their investments, their excuses, or the nauseating fascist-type enthusiasm of their political rallies'. They shared responsibility for prison torture, prison deaths and the escalating violence of the regime. Biko's death also revealed the 'weak folly of those who think in terms of trying to reform the Government. A false Gospel, an evil binding ideology, cannot be reformed.' It had to be rejected and replaced by a 'total and fundamental change'. Biko's life showed that black consciousness was neither racist nor Communist, but a vital quest 'for that fullness of humanity and liberation which Christ proclaimed'. Biko's death was 'a portentous event. From the ghettos of Ginsberg to the chancelleries of the West' it had created a new awareness 'that this ungodly and revolting society will be destroyed'; Scripture warned that judgement and the destruction of evil were an inescapable part of history.[75]

In the short run it was not the apartheid state and its politicians who were destroyed; but black organisations, black leaders, the Christian Institute and *Pro Veritate*. With the black consciousness movement gathering further strength in the aftermath of Biko's death, and with a general election due to be held in November 1977, Prime Minister Vorster decided to tighten his repressive hold with a round of further detentions and bannings. The white electorate always appreciated a show of *kragdadigheid* (might). In addition black leaders with mass followings had to be neutralised if apartheid was to have any chance of nurturing an alternative client-group of black functionaries.

The Christian Institute too had to be silenced. Not only had it gravely embarrassed the white DRCs, destroying their capacity to legitimise apartheid and ending their relationship with the international community of Reformed Churches. The Institute had co-operated with the WCC, supported conscientious objection and played a significant part in generating the anti-apartheid turmoil developing within the black DRCs. While gathering increasing support from the Christian churches of North America and Europe, the Institute had identified with the hopes of the black consciousness movement, called for a national convention, exposed the systematic use of torture and begun to offer a critical analysis of the capitalist system. Therefore, within a few weeks of Biko's death, on 19 October 1977, the security police were out in force with their dogs, pounding and kicking down front doors in pre-dawn raids across the country.

Seventeen black consciousness organisations were banned as well as the Christian Institute. Seventy key black leaders were detained — a veritable 'Who's Who' of black activists who were not already in prison.[76] In addition the Institute's journal *Pro Veritate* and *The World*, a relatively outspoken black newspaper, were banned. Percy Qoboza, *The World*'s editor, was among those detained, and the attack on the press was extended to include Donald Woods of the East London *Daily*

Despatch — an editor prepared to report the views of the black consciousness movement and a friend of Steve Biko. BPC, SASO, SASM, BCP, the Black Parents' Association and the Union of Black Journalists were among the banned organisations.[77] In the case of the Christian Institute, its leading members were banned as it was destroyed: the Rev. Beyers Naudé (National Director), the Rev. Theo Kotze (National Deputy Director and Cape Regional Director), the Rev. Brian Brown (Administrative Director), the Rev. Cedric Mason (Editor, *Pro Veritate*), Peter Randall (former Director of SPROCAS and lecturer at the University of the Witwatersrand) and the Rev. David Russell (Anglican passive resister and member of the Christian Institute).[78]

There was of course, an outcry from the editorial pages of the English-speaking press, and telegrams and messages of protest from within South Africa and abroad. Cardinal Owen McCann of Cape Town was 'shocked and amazed'. A spokesman for the SACC called it 'a terrible day for South Africa' and Fred van Wyk, Director of the South African Institute of Race Relations, spoke of 'an act of ruthless tyranny . . . insensate in its stupidity, tragic' in its consequences. In Gatsha Buthelezi's view, persons like Beyers Naudé have been 'the only reason most black Christians thought that there was any hope of reconciliation', a hope now destroyed by the detentions and bannings, by this 'callous and politically ruthless action'.[79]

The annihilation of black political organisations in 1960 had been repeated seventeen years later. From the viewpoint of the regime, this was calculated repression, a way of dividing and controlling the black majority. For blacks it meant once again that any prospect of constitutional politics had been destroyed; the state had lost any shred of legitimacy it ever possessed and for many the arguments for a just revolution were strengthened beyond any shadow of doubt.

Black unrest was to persist, including school boycotts; many more protesters were to be shot down in the streets of South Africa; young refugees and recruits continued to cross the border for education or guerrilla training; and the white electorate went to the polls to give the Afrikaner National Party a resounding victory (135 of the 165 seats in the House of Assembly) for what had become a system of 'total security' with strong overtones of fascism. When Professor Gerrit Viljoen, Rector of the new Rand Afrikaans University and head of the *Broederbond*, addressed a crowd gathered to celebrate the Day of Covenant on 16 December 1977, he told the *volk* that the battle of Blood River was a 'victory for the timeless cultural values' of Afrikaner-ruled South Africa. On the other side of Johannesburg, at an interdenominational prayer meeting in SOWETO's Regina Mundi Catholic Church, a black minister of the DRC was offering a different view to a young and crowded congregation:

Today the Afrikaner nation is rejoicing in its shame. To kill is shameful . . . To be a robber is shameful . . . To be a racist is shameful and to want to reap from nothing and live on the sweat of others is shameful.[80]

The Christian Institute and black consciousness organisations had been banned and their leaders silenced, but the voice of a prophetic Christianity had not been stilled. The prayers, speeches, songs and skits in Regina Mundi went on for three hours, preaching black consciousness and the liberation of South Africa.[81]

NOTES

1. *Financial Mail* (Johannesburg), 27 January, 17 February, 1978; International Defence and Aid, *Focus* (Cambridge, Massachusetts), March 1978, p. 9; M. Nash, *Black Uprooting from 'White' South Africa*, p. 1. There were plans to move at least an additional one million Africans.

2. P. Randall (ed.), *A Taste of Power*, p. 24; South African Institute of Race Relations, *Annual Survey of Race Relations, 1977* (Johannesburg, 1978), p. 223; J. Kane-Berman, 'The Crisis over the Land', *South African Outlook*, March 1979, pp. 41–3.

3. J. Kane-Berman, *Migratory Labour — the Canker in South African Society* (SPROCAS Background Paper no. 3, 1972), p. 2ff.

4. *Ibid.*

5. *Ibid.*

6. All Africans, irrespective of dependents, paid income tax when their annual wages reached R360. Other racial groups began paying at R676 if single, R1151 if married, R1601 with one child and R2601 with two. In addition, all African men paid a poll tax of R2.50 a year irrespective of income. P. Randall, *A Taste of Power*, p. 23.

7. *Ibid.*, p. 19.

8. The intensity of African feelings on this issue can be seen in the fact that when the Bantustans gained control of their education systems, they turned from Afrikaans and adopted English as the sole medium of instruction from upper primary school onwards.

9. *Supra.*, p. 150.

10. J. Kane-Berman, *South Africa: the Method in the Madness* (London, 1979), pp. 26–3. See too B. Hirson, *Year of Fire, Year of Ash: the Soweto Revolt: Roots of a Revolution?* (London, 1979).

11. *Supra.*, pp. 8–12.

12. J. Kane-Berman, *op. cit.* pp. 26–33.

13. South African Institute of Race Relations, *Survey of Race Relations 1977*, pp. 425–6; E. Regehr, *Perceptions of Apartheid*, pp. 30–1.

14. *Pro Veritate*, September 1976, p. 3.

15. This Council was to comprise the Prime Minister of each parliament plus one Indian, three Coloured and five White representatives.

16. South African Institute of Race Relations, *Survey of Race Relations 1977*, pp. 7–9; *Sunday Times* (Johannesburg), 15 June 1978; International Defence and Aid, *Focus*, March 1978, p. 1.

17. Vorster and his Afrikaner National Party entered the election with 123 seats in the House of Assembly. The opposition United Party had splintered into the New Republic Party (24 seats), the Progressive Federal Party (18 seats) and the South Africa Party (6 seats). After the election the National Party held 135 seats.

18. 'Desmond M.B. Tutu, Dean of St Mary's Cathedral, Johannesburg, to the Hon. Prime Minister Mr John B. Vorster, 8 May 1976', *South African Outlook*, July 1976, pp. 102–4.

19. *South African Outlook*, June 1976, p. 104.

20. *Pro Veritate*, June 1976, pp. 3–4, being an address delivered at the University of Cape Town, on 3 June 1976, at the invitation of the Students Representative Council.

21. C. Mason, 'A lot said but not done', *Pro Veritate*, June, 1976, pp. 11–13.

22. The issue of Afrikaans in African schools was a longstanding one, dating back in its apartheid form to the early 1950s. By 1968 only a quarter of African schools were even approximating to the official guideline that Afrikaans be used as a medium of instruction on a 50–50 basis with English. What is more, that proportion was falling. Then in 1975, the Department of Education insisted on the 50–50 rule being applied to standards 5 and upwards. English was to be used for general science and 'practical subjects', Afrikaans for social studies and mathematics. J. Kane-Berman, *South Africa: the Method in the Madness*, pp. 11–14.

23. 'Soweto and After', *South African Outlook*, February 1977, pp. 20–1; 'Soweto and the events thereafter' (1977), mimeo, pp. 1–8; 'Events of 1976 which culminated in the riots of June 1976' (Johannesburg, SAIRR, 1976), mimeo, pp. 1–2.

24. 'Events of 1976 which culminated in the riots of June 1976', pp. 7, 9.

25. J. Kane-Berman, *South Africa*, pp. 1–10; 'Events of 1976', p. 8; 'Soweto and the events thereafter', p. 2; *South African Outlook*, February 1977, p. 20.

26. J. Kane-Berman, *South Africa*, pp. 32–3.

27. *Ibid.*, pp. 5–7.

28. *Ibid.*, p. 5; *South African Outlook*, February 1977, p. 21. African workers had not been fully drawn into the black consciousness movement. They remained suspicious of student leaders and were victims of *agent provocateurs* who encouraged violent clashes between migrant workers and township residents, including students.

29. J. Kane-Berman, *South Africa*, p. 33.

30. *Ibid.*, pp. 30–2; General Secretary of the Catholic Bishops Conference, 'Press Release: Statement on the Current Situation' (Pretoria, 1977), pp. 1–2, mimeo.

31. J. Kane-Berman, *South Africa*, p. 36.

32. The student and black consciousness leaders refused to meet Young during his visit in May 1977 as they felt he should have insisted on meeting the 'real leaders of the black people in South Africa such a Sobukwe, Mandela,

Biko and others'. Instead he met white industrialists and the 'political chameleon' Chief Gatsha Buthelezi. No matter how sincere Young might be, he could not change U.S. policy which was determined by 'the American system as a whole', not least the 'board rooms of IBM, Ford Motors and other major companies'. Young's 'outright support for the continued existence of capitalism in South Africa' indicated that he did 'not have a full grasp of the real problem facing Blacks in South Africa'. That he lacked understanding was confirmed by 'his likening of our struggle with the 1960 Civil Rights Movement in the United States'. The crux of the matter was 'the economic exploitation of our people by the white regime working as agents of the major imperialist powers whose interests are to maximise their profit at our expense.' A fundamental change in U.S. policy would require 'the withdrawal of American investments,' and 'end to vetoing U.N. Security Council resolutions against South Africa . . . active support [for] the liberation struggle' and an end to 'undercover support for the Bantustans by investing there.' Unless these changes occurred there was nothing to be gained from 'meeting people like Mr Young', 'The "New" Policy of the U.S.A. towards South Africa: the Black Consciousness Movement's View' (1977), pp. 1–6, typescript.

33. 'Soweto and the events thereafter', pp. 4–5.

34. *South African Outlook*, February 1977, p. 31.

35. J. Kane-Berman, *South Africa*, p. 5; 'Soweto and the events thereafter', p. 7.

36. J. Kane-Berman, *South Africa*, pp. 5–6.

37. *Ibid.*, pp. 9–10.

38. *Ibid.*, pp. 16–17.

39. *Pro Veritate*, April 1977, pp. 7–8. Prior to his consecration as Bishop, Manas Buthelezi had been the Institute's Regional Director in Natal. Dr. Motlana, who in his younger days attended Fort Hare and joined the ANC Youth League, operated a mobile clinic in SOWETO which was supported by the Black Community Programmes. In a situation where the despised and purely advisory Soweto Bantu Council lacked all credibility and had disintegrated, Motlana's Committee of Ten quickly gathered unprecedented support, including student support. Rather than negotiate with such a body, the regime banned all public meetings in Soweto. See C. Smith, 'Soweto and the Committee of Ten', *South African Outlook*, November 1977, pp. 167–8.

40. Christian Institute, *Director's Report 1977*, p. 4.

41. General Secretariate of the South African Catholic Bishops Conference, *Press Releases*, (Pretoria, February 1977), 'Statement on the Current Situation', pp. 1–2; 'Declaration of Commitment by the Church', pp. 1–3; 'Statement on Conscientious Objection', pp. 1–2. See too 'South African Bishops. A stand Against Apartheid', *Origins* (Washington D.C., National Catholic News Service), 3 March 1977, pp. 583–5.

42. Bishop Mandlenkosi Zwane, 'Human Relations', being his address to the South African Bishops Conference, February 1977, reprinted in *The Catholic Worker* (New York), October–November 1977, pp. 3,6. Bishop Zwane died in a car accident in 1980 — a tragic loss for Roman Catholics and Christianity throughout Southern Africa.

43. Denis E. Hurley, O.M.I., Archbishop of Durban, *The South African Situation and the Attitude of the Church* (Durban, 1977), p. 10.

44. Christian Institute, *Director's Report 1976*, pp. 2–3.

45. C.F. Beyers Naudé, 'Christian Ministry in a Time of Crisis', *Pro Veritate*, April 1977, p. 4, being an address to the black graduates of the Federal Theological Seminary at Edendale, Pietermaritzburg.

46. *Pro Veritate*, October 1976, p. 14, being a statement by the Christian Institute's Board of Management.

47. *Ibid.*

48. 'Time has run out: a Message for 1977 from the Ministers Fraternal of Langa, Guguletu and Nyanga, January 1977', *Pro Veritate*, February 1977, pp. 12–13.

49. A. Boesak, 'Black Consciousness, Black Power and "Coloured Politics" ', *Pro Veritate*, February 1977, pp. 9–12, being an address to the Labour Party.

50. 'Greetings from Bishop Tutu to the Soweto Students, June 16, 1977', *Pro Veritate*, June 1977, p. 6.

51. According to the Nationalist MP for Algoa, J. J. Engelbrecht, Naudé came from a staunch Afrikaner home and bore the name of General Beyers, one of the nation's bravest heroes. But he had 'done more harm to South Africa than any other living person that I know of', *Cape Times*, 5 June 1975.

52. *Pro Veritate*, December 1976, p. 5; April 1977, pp. 7–8; Christian Institute, *Director's Report 1977*, pp. 4, 7; International Defence and Aid, *Focus*, summer 1977, p. 7.

53. 'To Maphefo Jane Phakathi (I.N. 2438634 V/F)Q5957, Mamelodi, Pretoria. Notice in Terms of Section 10(1)(a) of the Internal Security Act, 1950 (Act 44 of 1950),' *Pro Veritate*, April 1977, pp. 7–8.

54. *Pro Veritate*, June 1976, p. 20; October 1976, p. 13.

55. *Supra.*, p. 165.

56. Christian Institute, *Good News/Action Program* (Johannesburg, 1976), p. 3.

57. *Pro Veritate*, June 1976, p. 20.

58. Christian Institute, *Director's Report 1977*, p. 6.

59. Realising that the Institute was likely to be banned in the near future, the intention was to maintain a Christian voice of protest in exile. The Utrecht office was expected to lobby and to function as an information centre. However, tensions quickly developed over issues of violence/non-violence and relations with the ANC. The situation was further complicated by differences between Kleinschmidt and Phakathi. These came to a head after the banning of the Institute. Whereas Kleinschmidt had come to see the ANC as leading the liberation struggle and spoke at the United Nations in support of that organisation, Phakathi was committed to working for a separate black consciousness movement in exile. She was also increasingly outspoken on the need to use force in the liberation struggle. These disputes were a grave embarrassment to the remnant members of the Christian Institute in South Africa. They no longer existed as a formal organisation and certainly had no control over the independent Utrecht office. Yet they were vulnerable to charges of being associated in some loose way with a group that appeared to be espousing the

use of force and was given to supporting banned organisations. When Theo Kotze escaped from South Africa in August 1978 — breaking out of his confinement as a banned person in Rondebosch — he tried to heal the rift and bring the situation under control. This proved difficult, and with the South African security police giving the exile group their close attention, Kotze reluctantly decided, after consultation with the Institute's supporters in Britain and the Netherlands, to close the Utrecht Office in 1979.

60. *Pro Veritate*, February 1977, p. 8.

61. Christian Institute, *Director's Report 1977*, pp. 2, 8; Christian Institute of Southern Africa, 'National Council Meeting, Johannesburg, 9 September 1977', Regional Reports.

62. Christian Institute, *Director's Report 1977*, pp. 2–3; *Pro Veritate*, October 1976, p. 15.

63. Christian Institute, 'National Council Meeting, 9 September 1977', 'Report of the Cape Office', p. 1.

64. *Ibid.*, 'Report of the Natal Office', p. 4.

65. J. Kane-Berman, *South Africa*, pp. 38–42. See too Christian Institute of Southern Africa, *Detention and Detente in Southern Africa* (Johannesburg, 1976); South African Institute of Race Relations, *Detention Without Trial in South Africa, 1976–1977* (Johannesburg, 1977). These reports were banned.

66. Christian Institute of Southern Africa, *Torture in South Africa* (Cape Town, 1977), pp. 1–75.

67. D. Russell, 'Living in the Land of a Banned Man', *Agape*, September 1973, pp. 6–8.

68. 'An Interview with Steve Biko', *The Reformed Journal* (Grand Rapids, Michigan), December 1977, p. 13. This interview took place in July 1977 with B. Zylstra of the Institute for Christian Studies, Toronto.

69. *Ibid.*, pp. 12–13.

70. *Ibid.*, pp. 14–15.

71. *Ibid.*, pp. 16–18.

72. For further details on the life and death of Biko see M. Arnold (ed.), *Steve Biko: Black Consciousness in South Africa* (New York, 1979); H. Bernstein, *No. 46 — Steve Biko* (London, 1978); D. Woods, *Biko* (New York, 1978).

73. 'Police have never been responsible for killing or torturing a single detainee.' South African Broadcasting Corporation, 16 September, 1977, reprinted in H. Bernstein, *No. 46 — Steve Biko*, pp. 22–3.

74. *Ibid.*, pp. 20–21.

75. 'Steve Biko', *Pro Veritate*, September 1977, pp. 2–3.

76. These included Dr Nthato Motlana, Chairman of the Soweto Committee of Ten, and six other members of the Committee; Kenneth Rachidi, President of the Black People's Convention, his General Secretary Thandisizwe Mazibuko, and virtually the whole executive; Aubrey Mokoena, Director of the Black Community Programmes; Mongezi Stofile and Diliza Mji, past Presidents of SASO; Bishop Manas Buthelezi, Chairman of the Black Parents' Association as well as Winnie Mandela and Fr Smangaliso Mkhatshwa of the executive, the latter also being Secretary-General of the South African Catholic Bishops' Conference.

77. The full list also included the Black Women's Federation, the Border

Youth Organisation, the Eastern Province Youth Organisation, the Medupe Writers Association, the Natal Youth Organisation, the Soweto Students Representative Council, the Transvaal Youth Organisation, the Western Cape Youth Organisation and the Zimele Trust Fund. *Cape Times*, 20 October 1977; *Rand Daily Mail*, 20 October 1977; *Cape Argus*, 21 October 1977.

78. *Ibid..* After his banning Naudé turned to the *Kerk van Africa* as his immediate church community.

79. *Cape Times*, 20 October 1977.

80. *Rand Daily Mail*, 17 December 1977; *Washington Post*, 17 December 1977.

81. On 16 June 1981, the police fired tear gas into a crowd of 5,000 gathered in and around Regina Mundi for a memorial service commemorating the fifth anniversary of the Soweto massacres. A one day 'stay at home' was more than 50 per cent successful in Soweto. *New York Times*, 17 June 1981.

INDEX